DAVE BING

ATTACKING THE RIM

MY JOURNEY FROM
NBA LEGEND TO BUSINESS LEADER
TO BIG-CITY MAYOR TO MENTOR

DAVE BING with **T.V. LoCICERO**

TRIUMPH
BOOKS

Library of Congress Cataloging in Publication Data

Names: Bing, Dave, 1943- author. | LoCicero, T.V., author.

Title: Dave Bing: attacking the rim : my journey from NBA legend to business leader to big-city mayor to mentor / Dave Bing with T.V. LoCicero.

Description: Chicago, Illinois : Triumph Books, [2020] | Summary: "Reflecting on his playing days with the Detroit Pistons, Washington Bullets, and Boston Celtics, Bing takes readers inside the exciting world of pro basketball. From inside the Detroit mayor's office, he offers a first-hand look at the city's plight."—Provided by publisher.

Identifiers: LCCN 2020029884 (print) | LCCN 2020029885 (ebook) | ISBN 9781629378473 (hardcover) | ISBN 9781641254847 (epub) | ISBN 9781641254854 (kindle edition) | ISBN 9781641254861 (pdf)

Subjects: LCSH: Bing, Dave, 1943- | African American basketball players—Biography. | Basketball players—United States—Biography. | African American businesspeople —Michigan—Detroit—Biography. | Mayors—Michigan—Detroit—Biography. | Mentoring—Michigan—Detroit—Biography.

Classification: LCC GV884.B56 A3 2020 (print) | LCC GV884.B56 (ebook) | DDC 796.323092 [B]—dc23

LC record available at https://lccn.loc.gov/2020029884

LC ebook record available at https://lccn.loc.gov/2020029885

This book is available in quantity at special discounts for your group or organization. For further information, contact:

Triumph Books LLC
814 North Franklin Street
Chicago, Illinois 60610
(312) 337-0747
www.triumphbooks.com

Printed in U.S.A.
ISBN: 978-1-62937-847-3

Design by Preston Pisellini
All photos courtesy of the author unless otherwise indicated.

I dedicate this book to the memory of my parents, Juanita and Hasker Bing, who provided me the foundation to realize my potential and my dreams. All of my achievements are the fruits of their labor and the seeds planted for my children and grandchildren: my daughters, Cassaundra, Bridgett, and Aleisha; my grandchildren, Kenneth, Caris, Denzel, and Alexander; and my great-grandchild Delilah, and those yet to be born.

—DAVE BING

CONTENTS

FOREWORD

AS DAVE BING PUTS IT IN THIS WONDERFUL BOOK, he knew me "from the beginning." At the time I was "conceived and born," my biological father, Jimmy Walker, was Dave's backcourt mate with the Detroit Pistons. I never knew my father, but for me, Dave was the very model of responsible fatherhood. He really was a godfather to me.

While at Southwestern High School, my basketball coach, and Dave's friend, Perry Watson, put us together as mentor and mentee. The NBA legend Dave Bing was rapidly becoming one of the country's top Black businessmen, and one of the many things he gave me was a summer job at Bing Steel. Yes, he gave me the job, but he also made it clear that I would need to work my ass off to keep it. I worked as a press operator, which was hard and demanding work, but I never complained. I'd heard the stories about how Dave had hired friends and fellow NBA alums, like Campy Russell, Curtis Rowe, and George Trapp, and then fired them when they apparently thought they'd be getting a free ride. Point well taken.

While at Bing Steel, I got to see Dave every day and witnessed how under a great deal of pressure running multiple businesses with several hundred employees, he never appeared to be upset or to lose his cool. I marveled at that, and his leadership, his focus, his attention to detail, and how he was extremely hands-on and knowledgeable about each facet of the business. Dave challenged me as a young would-be entrepreneur and shared all the tools and tricks of the trade he'd learned in order to be successful, and I'm forever grateful for that.

Away from the job we naturally talked hoops, and one of the 50 greatest players of all time schooled me in the finer points of body-positioning, getting that crucial first step on an opponent, and the challenges and advantages of being a 6'8" point guard. Dave's expectations of me were high. Even when my name would appear in the paper or I'd score 25 points or win a state championship, Dave's quiet advice was, "Don't forget to take care of business in class and make the honor roll. Make sure you're ready to go on to college."

When I chose University of Michigan over his beloved Syracuse he was, as always, supportive and happy for me. And in the midst of all the "Fab Five" pressure and wild excitement, I appreciated even more the calm, steady, even-keeled friendship Dave offered. As usual, he encouraged me to look ahead. "No matter what happens, make sure you finish your degree," he would say. It took me a while, but that's what I did. Although I left school early for the NBA, Dave's voice stayed in my head, until I returned to complete my degree. His wisdom was a model for me, and having him as an influence gave me the courage to do it, and so much more.

In July of 2007, when I got word that Jimmy was dying of lung cancer, Dave and I made plans to go see him. Unfortunately, by the time we arrived, he had already passed. He was 63. I never got to meet my father, but fortunately I could share that sad moment with the man who was a deeply important father figure to me.

Looking back, Dave has been present for some of the most significant moments in my life. In 2011, when I started the Jalen Rose Leadership Academy, an open-enrollment, tuition-free, public charter high school in the Detroit neighborhood where I grew up, Dave Bing—Hall of Famer, business leader, mayor of the City of Detroit—was right by my side at the ribbon-cutting ceremony. With all the many busy demands on him, he took the time to be there for me. He later joined our board of directors, where he continues to make significant contributions.

Dave's level of commitment and dedication to his work and to others is truly inspiring.

His extraordinary and unique accomplishments, his great heart and great discipline, his proud self-belief and genuine humility are all part of the rare and admirable combination that is Dave Bing. In this fraught time of cutthroat business and financial dealing, racial animosity, and heartless political leaders, Dave's remarkable story has lessons for us all.

—Jalen Rose

FOREWORD

THERE ARE EVENTS AS A SPORTS FAN THAT YOU WILL NEVER FORGET. For me, one of those moments was March 18, 2018.

As a proud alum of Syracuse University and a nearly two-decade resident of Metro Detroit, it was the perfect intersection of things I love. Syracuse's basketball team was playing a second-round NCAA Tournament game in downtown Detroit against Michigan State. Nothing in sports turns me back into a passionate fan like my alma mater and March Madness. The day pitted two Hall of Fame coaches and personal friends, Jim Boeheim and Tom Izzo, against each other in one of those made-for-March moments.

The day was made even better by the company surrounding me. To one side in our row of the Syracuse rooting section was my wife, who grew up in Michigan, and our two children, who grew up rooting for the Orange. Seated to the other side were arguably the two greatest basketball players in Syracuse history, both of whom call Detroit home: Derrick Coleman, the No. 1 pick of the 1990 NBA draft, who I had the pleasure of covering during my days in Syracuse, and Dave Bing, the No. 2 pick of the 1966 draft by the Detroit Pistons.

Public figures are often introduced by the title that indicates their most significant life accomplishment. If Dave Bing walked into a room, he could be introduced by a different title of acclaim every day of the week.

College All-American, NBA All-Star, Naismith Memorial Basketball Hall of Famer, member of the Top 50 NBA all-time team, founder and CEO of the largest steel company in Michigan, mayor of Detroit, or founder of a groundbreaking youth mentoring program for African American middle and high school boys.

What a résumé. What a man. What a story.

Over the years, I have been fortunate to have many opportunities to cross paths with Mayor Bing (which is what I always call him). Any time there is a big event involving Syracuse basketball, he is there to support his college roommate and fellow Hall of Famer coach Jim Boeheim. When Detroit reaches back to its basketball history or calls on the leaders of the community, Dave Bing is always there.

The arc of Dave's life story is familiar to me. I knew he was raised in Washington, D.C., had a legendary basketball career, and, after excelling in business, took on the challenges of repairing the reputation of beleaguered Detroit. But in *Attacking the Rim,* I have learned that there is much more to the man. His incredibly humble nature has not only been at the core of his many successes, but also has benefited so many around him.

Every step of the way, Dave has displayed a selflessness mixed with self-belief that has allowed him to assess situations and shine a positive light in even the most difficult of times. Syracuse basketball was not the perennial national power it is now until Dave Bing arrived on campus. "Dee-troit Basketball" was not representative of the city's great legacy with the game, until a rookie turned Pistons games into an event attended by Motown stars. The 1980s decline of Detroit-based industries did not deter the growth of the Bing Group from four employees to 1,400, evolving into one of the nation's major auto industry suppliers.

Those of us living in the area saw firsthand the stability and respect that Mayor Bing restored to a city that was in financial ruin after years of corrupt leadership. This was not a job Dave needed to take but one he felt a calling to accept to help those around him. That trademark has constantly been a hallmark of everything he has touched.

The most recent chapter in Mayor Bing's career of sharing his gifts has become extremely meaningful in 2020. In his post-political career, Dave has established a foundation providing one-on-one mentoring for African American boys. The program provides a male presence in the lives of young men who are missing that leadership at home. The impact of this initiative serves as another illustration of someone who has already given so much still finding ways to share his wisdom.

Dave's story is one of overcoming hardship, maximizing opportunities, and constantly giving to those who are in need. It's a story I am sure you, like me, will find inspiring. In covering sports, we come across greatness often, but we rarely see those stars become Hall of Famers long after the game has ended. In Dave Bing, we have found one.

Or, as the PA announcer at Cobo Arena used to say after one of Dave's highlight plays.

"BINGO."

—Mike Tirico

INTRODUCTION

MY MOST TELLING BASKETBALL TACTIC, my signature move, was attacking the rim. It was always a key to my success, from those long boyhood hours on the asphalt courts of Washington, D.C., to my days as a high school star and an All-American at Syracuse, to a long NBA career that put me in the Hall of Fame. The rim, and sending the ball through it, was, after all, the goal, object, and purpose of the game. So with a darting move past defenders, I would lift to the basket for a layup, a twisting up-and-under, or a slam dunk, or, if it occurred to me as I headed to the hoop, a shifty handoff or a slick pass to an open teammate for a better shot.

Of course, between me and the rim there was usually someone, often bigger and stronger, trying to stop me, and things could get nasty in the paint. A smaller guy like me can get swatted away like a fly. That legendary defenders like Bill Russell and Kareem Abdul-Jabbar called me fearless in attacking the rim, pleased and flattered me, but I was never sure if it was calculation, instinct, recklessness, courage, or maybe a little of each, that ultimately moved me.

Certainly, it helped that among the many wonderful things the good Lord blessed me with was the bounce in my step. In basketball parlance, that commonplace phrase means you have "hops," "ups," or "springs," a fortunate melding of structural leverage and muscular strength that produces the kind of leg power to keep you heading up while others are already coming down. There's certainly much more to the game than the ability to elevate, to get off the floor and above the rim, but there's no question that those who can leap high and hang have an advantage.

To me, beyond basketball, attacking the rim came to mean driving to achieve and pursuing success in a variety of endeavors. And having a bounce in your step also meant having confidence, energy, optimism, and a bright way of meeting obstacles and challenges. It suggests the ability to pick yourself up after life knocks you down, to keep your eye on the rim and continue attacking and moving forward.

In each of the four major phases of my professional life, in basketball, business, the mayoral years, and my mentoring foundation, I've experienced the highs and lows, the wins and losses that life hands out to all of us.

I was lucky to play basketball well enough and long enough to be named to the 50 Greatest Players in NBA History. But despite all that success, there was also an injury that might have ended everything. There were key moments in pivotal games when my teammates and I failed to play up to our potential and get the job done. Those failures and losses were always tough to take.

In my nearly three decades in the business world, my companies and I enjoyed many lucrative and rewarding years. We were able to employ many Detroiters and help to improve their lives. All those well-earned profits made it possible to give to worthy groups and causes. But there were also those down times, recessions and reverses that made razor-thin profit margins disappear completely and risk-heightened ventures turn cruel.

In the mayor's office of a proud city in bitterly tough times, we started with high hopes for a new day in Detroit. In fact, we were able to restore integrity to a place swamped with corruption, and our determined hard work would eventually contribute to a heralded turnaround in the city some years later. But in the meantime, all the crucial economic decisions we faced were between crushingly bad choices, and a massive and heart-rending bankruptcy proved inevitable.

The mentoring program we installed in Detroit over the last few years has been enormously rewarding both for all those African American boys and the generous Black men they've paired up with, but also for all of us who help make it happen. Yet the need is so great, with the numbers of boys falling through society's cracks, that we still find ourselves worried about the ones we haven't reached.

Ultimately, I am deeply grateful for what I think has helped carry me through both those marvelous moments of triumph and the low times that occasionally brought me down—my penchant for always attacking the rim and that God-given bounce in my step.

1

THE COIN FLIP

I WOKE ON MAY 11, 1966, a Wednesday morning, knowing full well it was a special day, one that would reveal where I'd be playing NBA basketball for the foreseeable future. But I had no idea that the events of this day would continue to impact in no small measure the rest of my life.

The National Basketball Association's draft was scheduled for later in the day, and as I pored over the morning paper, I noted once again that the so-called experts were speculating on which players the two teams with the top picks might select. The general consensus was that the two most coveted college players eligible for the draft were the University of Michigan's Cazzie Russell and yours truly. Which of us would go to which of the two teams with the worst NBA records—the Detroit Pistons and the New York Knicks—was still up in the air.

Cazzie, a 6'5½", 215 pound forward, had been on everybody's radar for quite a while. Coming out of Chicago, he'd been widely considered the nation's top high school player. At U of M, he had led the Wolverines to three Big Ten titles and two Final Four appearances.

In his senior year he'd averaged 30.8 points per game and was named the College Basketball Player of the Year.

At age 22, I was 6'3" and 180 pounds. I had led Syracuse in scoring all three of my varsity years, averaged 28.4 points per game as a senior, and made consensus All-American. Pundits called me a kind of hybrid or combo guard, both a scorer and a playmaker. They said I was lean, fast, explosive off the dribble, and with great hops to finish at the rim. Some of them also said I might be the better choice.

But I'd seen Cazzie perform several times on TV and thought he was a great player. He was athletic, a good ball-handler and rebounder, and while I thought I was probably a better shooter, I certainly felt he deserved all his accolades. We'd met briefly once at a hotel in New York where our teams were both playing in a holiday tournament. We both said we'd really like to play against each other, but that had never happened.

Now if all this buzz about Cazzie's NBA fate and mine were happening under the rules in place one year earlier, the matter would have already been settled. For 16 years the league had been giving teams the option of forfeiting their draft order selection to instead make a territorial pick, choosing a star player at a college within a 50-mile radius, the kind of local hero who would be a good bet to fill the too-often empty seats of their NBA arena.

But a few months back the league owners had voted to end the territorial rule for this year's draft. And the Pistons were now ruing their luck. The team had made it crystal clear that, with that territorial pick in hand, they would have selected Cazzie, the Michigan star, in a heartbeat.

And what's more, if that first draft pick had simply been handed to the team with the worst won-loss record, the Pistons—with only 22 wins against 58 losses, compared to the Knicks at 30 and 50— would have chosen first and, again, grabbed Cazzie. But the league didn't want its teams to tank, or more or less lose on purpose to get themselves the top pick. So for the first time in league history, the issue would be settled between the two bottom teams by chance... with the flip of a coin.

What about my preference? There was no question, I wanted to play for the Knicks in New York. I was an East Coast guy, after all, and so were all my friends. In Detroit, I knew no one. New York's Madison Square Garden, where the Knicks played, was basketball Mecca, the center of our sport's universe. With Syracuse I had played at the Garden many times and had enjoyed some of my finest collegiate moments there. The New York fans knew and appreciated my game, and I was pretty sure that nobody in Detroit had ever even heard of me.

If you wanted your game featured on national TV in those days, you had to play in New York, Boston, Philadelphia, or Los Angeles. Fame and fortune were much more likely to come your way if you played in one of the big four. With my wife, Aaris, and our two daughters to care for, I was already trying to think carefully about life after basketball. In my view, New York was hands down the place to be. There would be lots of Syracuse alums in the city ready to help out, and success would bring contacts with more of those important folks who could open doors to the worlds of business and finance. That's where I knew I wanted to be after my playing days were over.

Yes, with a young family, a smaller, more manageable city like Detroit might be easier to live in. But millions of those who worked in New York lived with their families in bedroom communities outside the city. That's what we would do. So, New York was my obvious choice, and with the Knicks' pick not yet officially on the board, I could still hope against hope.

How much did Detroit want Cazzie? As I would learn later, the Pistons were so desperate to get him they had actually acquired a twenty-dollar gold piece like the one the league would officially flip, and they were tossing it and tabulating the results on the chance that some anomaly in the forging of the piece might favor either heads or tails. The team finally gave up the experiment as hopeless.

Then, a few days before this morning here, the Pistons' 26-year-old player-coach, Dave DeBusschere, arrived at a room in New York's Plaza Hotel for the official flip. There he met with a league official and a representative of the Knicks and was asked to make the call.

"Tails," said DeBusschere.

The gold piece landed heads.

So New York would get the first pick in the draft, and while the team was trying to play it close to the vest, rumors had them going for Cazzie. Still, the matter would not be settled until the Knicks made their choice official later today.

• • •

There was, of course, other news in the paper that morning, including a story I had been following avidly for some time.

A week before, a gubernatorial primary had been held in Alabama. The state's segregationist governor, George Wallace, had served his four years and was not allowed to run again. So he had put his wife, Lurleen, on the ballot. This was in the wake of the civil rights explosion in the state in 1964, with the vicious police violence against the Selma-to-Montgomery Freedom Marchers and then the passage of the Voting Rights Act a year later.

The Alabama primary was billed as a major test of whether Blacks in the South would, in spite of many efforts to discourage them, actually turn out to vote. The news that morning, much to my relief and satisfaction, was that four out of five registered Black voters had in fact exercised their precious right to cast their ballot.

Yes, I thought, as I turned back to the sports pages, there was plenty going on around me that was really more important than basketball. But I also needed to check out the practical reality of where I'd be playing—and making a living—for the next year.

I kissed Aaris; our two-year-old, Cassaundra; and our baby, Bridgett, left our married–student housing apartment just off the Syracuse campus, and headed for the dorm room where my old roommate Jim Boeheim and a half dozen other teammates and friends were waiting. The plan was to listen to a radio broadcast of the draft being held at the Plaza.

With only league officials, the press, and reps from each of the nine (soon to be 10, with the addition of Chicago) teams in attendance, the low-key, two-hour session was a far cry from today's spectacular event that involves all the top college players waiting in sartorial splendor for their million-dollar paydays, thousands in a live audience offering their cheers, boos, and hisses, and millions more around the world watching on TV as 30 NBA teams make their much-calculated moves.

Boeheim, now the legendary Hall of Fame coach at Syracuse, was one of the smartest guys I knew, and he and the others greeted me with upbeat takes on what was about to happen. They were still trying to convince me there was a good chance the Knicks would do the "smart" thing and take me. And when that happened, they said, they would all come to the Garden or watch on TV as I matched myself against NBA greats like Oscar Robertson and Jerry West.

They were all, of course, good East Coast friends, and I loved their support and enthusiasm, but deep down I didn't think what they were hoping for was likely to happen. Sure, in my mind I was the best choice, and given the chance, I would prove it. But we all know, I told them, what the vaunted New York press is like, and the fan base as well. They'll give the Knicks holy hell if the team fails to take the consensus number one player in the draft.

Finally, it was time for the teams to announce their selections, and with all of us gathered around, the radio in that small room was blasting away. First up: the Knicks' general manager, Eddie Donovan. "New York," he announced, "drafts Cazzie Russell of Michigan."

Short and not so sweet. There were moans and groans from my friends, but I hardly heard them, lost in the disappointment of the moment. Not because I had not gone number one. That was not the most important thing to me. It was just that I had wanted so much to play in New York.

Then the guys were all telling me how unfair this was, what a mistake the Knicks had made, and how bad they felt for me. I was grateful for their words and support and assured them I was all right, not bitter or angry, just realistic about how this had all gone down. You just had to accept something like this and move on. And, hey, there was more to hear on the radio.

Now Donovan was saying, "We've talked to him and we're satisfied he wants to play here." There had been rumors that the Harlem Globetrotters were ready to pay big bucks to have Cazzie tour with them, but Donovan added that he did not foresee any serious problem in signing Russell. And then on the radio the Detroit Pistons announced they were taking Dave Bing of Syracuse.

There were cheers and congratulations now. They said going number two out of all the eligible college players in the country was pretty damn great, and soon I was going to show the Knicks what a big mistake they had made.

Back home with Aaris, I found her excited that I had gone so high in the draft and looking forward to whatever happened next. Later I took a call from the Pistons' GM, Ed Coil, who said the team was very pleased and happy with the prospect of my playing in Detroit. He sounded friendly, cordial, and genuine, and said they would arrange for me to fly to the city in a day or so.

So what did I know about Detroit? Not much. I'd never been there, but, of course, I knew it was a top 10 U.S. city, a major population center, and home to two industries with world-wide reach, heft, and importance. Historically, Motown was legendary in the music and entertainment business, and the automotive industry was a behemoth, which, during World War II, had made the city the Arsenal of Democracy. Beyond a vague sense that it would be an acceptable place to live and raise a family, that's what I knew about Detroit.

When I arrived in the city a couple of days later, I learned that my downtown hotel, the Book Cadillac, also housed the Pistons' business offices, so I could walk to my first meeting with GM Ed Coil. In person he seemed every inch the accountant he in fact was and just as pleasant as he had been on the phone. Knowing little or nothing about basketball, he'd been on the job for about a year, and it was his task to basically balance the books and keep things running smoothly for team owner, Fred Zollner, who had moved the franchise from northern Indiana a decade earlier. Back then they'd been known as the Fort Wayne Zollner Pistons, named after the auto engine part that had made Zollner a wealthy man.

Also in the office to greet me was Dave DeBusschere, who, in addition to being one of the team's star players, was the youngest coach I would ever have. He was friendly and said all the right things about being happy to add my talents to the team, but underneath I sensed the lingering disappointment he had over losing that coin flip and thus losing their local hero, Cazzie Russell.

When it was just Ed Coil and myself in the office, we got down to business. Ed seemed pleased, maybe relieved, that I would not be using an agent to handle contract negotiations. With my college major being economics and marketing, I felt confident that I could represent my own interests. And I simply didn't want to give up 10 percent of my salary to an agent who would probably not do much better for me than I would. Was I overconfident? Probably a little, but I also figured that negotiating for myself could be a valuable learning experience as well.

Coil was also okay with my suggestion that we think in terms of only a one-year contract. Since I couldn't be sure how things would turn out, I wanted to have options. I might not get the maximum, dollar-wise, from that first contract, but I had enough confidence in my ability to think I would play well, maybe even at a star level. And then after a good rookie year, I wanted the chance to sit down and negotiate from a stronger position.

As the number two guy, I knew I wasn't going to get as much as Cazzie, the number one. And you're going to get paid more in New York than in Detroit. But I also knew that the cost of living in New York was higher than in Detroit. And with my family to think about, I wanted a home, not an apartment. I had grown up in a nice home in a decent neighborhood in Washington, D.C., so that's what I wanted in Detroit. I was intent on getting a salary that would give us a good home and a new car as well.

I also knew for a fact there was a pay scale in the NBA, with the minimum salary at that time being $7,500, and the average for the veteran players somewhere in the low $20,000s. Was I going to get that as a rookie coming in? I didn't think so, but I told myself, "I'm going to be okay. I'm going to let them see that they made the right choice and position myself to have a lot more leverage the next time around."

Coil and I talked numbers, but only in a preliminary way, and then he suggested we both think about it a bit and then settle on a salary on my next visit. That was fine with me. I liked Ed and felt we had already developed a level of mutual respect that would lead to a contract I could feel was competitive.

Before I left, the only guy I already knew quite well with the Pistons came in to say hello. Back in the '50s, Earl Lloyd had been the first Black player in the NBA, and now he was a Pistons' scout. He was from D.C. and had played for a while with the NBA's Syracuse franchise, so we had become friends. The first time he ever saw me play live was in a Christmas tournament in New York, back in December. I had dropped 45 on Vanderbilt, and now he told me he'd been trying for quite a while to convince the Pistons that I was actually a better choice than Cazzie. He said, "Don't worry about not being selected number one." And with a glance at Coil: "We've got the best player."

Later I got a look at where I'd be playing in Detroit. Unlike Madison Square Garden, Cobo Arena, with only 10,000 seats and lots of fans right up close to the action, was one of those venues that announcers liked to call "intimate." I knew that Detroiters had little or no idea what they were getting in me, but I imagined I'd soon be getting an earful of what they thought of my game.

That evening, three of my new teammates picked me up at the hotel and took me out to dinner. Eddie Miles would be my running mate at guard. He and forward Ray Scott were two of the team's stars, along with DeBusschere, and John Tresvant was a back-up forward, originally from D.C., where I knew his family. We went to a nightclub on 12th Street, and it was a good time. I'm sure they were thinking, "This is the number one draft choice. We'll take him out and see what kind of a guy he is." They had all seen me play, at least on tape, and when they introduced me around at the restaurant, everyone made me feel welcomed.

When I told the guys I wanted find a home to buy in the city, they said they'd show me their neighborhoods and help me find a good fit for my family. I left town in the morning feeling good about the visit.

A couple of weeks later I was back. At school, I'd talked with my wife and friends, my coach, and some others, and I had a top end of $18,000 in mind. Again, it was just Ed Coil and myself in the office, and we went back and forth. He started at $12,000 and I said I'd like $18,000. We traded numbers for a time but soon arrived at $15,000, twice the NBA minimum. Could I have gotten a few more thousand dollars playing hard to get? Maybe, but I wanted to leave that office on good terms, knowing it would help me the next time around when I hoped to have more clout. In any case, I had a solid idea of what I'd need to get that home and car, and I felt comfortable enough with $15,000.

Later, the Pistons held a press conference at a popular downtown restaurant called Carl's Chop House. I was sitting there with Coil, DeBusschere, Ray Scott, and Earl Lloyd, and they had a jersey with my name on it and the number 21. I had always worn 22, but that was DeBusschere's, so I had asked for something close.

Of course, all the media guys were there, from the newspapers and TV, and they pitched the usual questions on how I felt about the coin flip, was I happy to be there, and what did I know about my teammates and about the city. I sensed they knew little about my game beyond the fact that I'd gone number two. But they also knew and respected Earl Lloyd as a straight up kind of guy whose knowledge and opinion they could trust. And the word from Earl was, "We got the best player."

Over the next couple of days, I visited several different neighborhoods to look at homes. Eddie Miles took me to the area he lived in. Tresvant and Earl did the same thing. They were all neighborhoods on the northwest side of Detroit, where most of the Piston players lived. Eddie lived in the Eight Mile and Schaefer area. Earl and Tresvant both lived off Linwood and Six Mile. And they were all very nice neighborhoods, especially back then.

But Earl showed me a home he had noticed for sale on Prest Street, near Seven Mile and Greenfield. A three-bedroom, two-bath home in good shape, with a finished basement, a garage, and a good backyard for the kids. The neighborhood was really nice, and I pretty quickly decided this was what I wanted.

The next day I went to the National Bank of Detroit with Billy Rodgers, one of the Pistons' front office guys, and he introduced me to a vice president at the bank. The veep listened to me about the house and to Billy about my contract with the team, and then finally said that he was sorry, the bank could not provide me with a mortgage. "You're just coming out of college," he said. "You've got no credit history, and we just can't do this."

Talk about feeling slapped down. Here I was, the team's number one draft choice, the number two player in the country, a family guy with a solid salary and no debt. But they declined.

I lived with that rejection overnight but then told myself, "Be a realist. There's nothing you can do about that banker's response. Try someone else."

And so the next morning I went to Manufacturer's Bank. I told them the same story, with all the same data, and this time the answer was, "Yes, we'll do this."

The irony is that it wasn't long before the National Bank of Detroit would do a complete about-face and play a role in my financial future. But on my way back to Syracuse that bank was the last thing on my mind. The way ahead was now clear. I knew I was going to play in Detroit for the Pistons. I knew where I was going to live. I knew I had a one-year contract that would provide enough money for the down payments on the home and a vehicle. That all those things were lined up and in order made me feel very good about my first two visits to the Motor City.

In August, about a month before the Pistons' training camp opened, Aaris and I loaded all our clothes, furniture, and other belongings in our car and a U-Haul trailer hooked behind it, put the girls in their car seats, and drove to Detroit. Driving through Canada, we crossed the Detroit River on the Ambassador Bridge and, from high on that huge suspension span, got a great view of the sprawling metropolis that would be our new home.

That this city would continue to be the center of my universe for basically the remainder of my life was still just as unthinkable as it had been on that fateful NBA draft day back in May.

2

STARTING IN D.C.

AMONG MY EARLIEST MEMORIES are the long car rides our family would take every summer back to the old homestead in rural South Carolina. My parents, Hasker and Juanita Bing, had met as teenagers when they were itinerant farm workers, and they married young. They had soon moved north to Washington, D.C., a place that seemed to offer more options and better opportunities. My dad had honed his construction skills—carpentry, plumbing, electrical, and his primary trade, bricklaying—and made a decent enough living that my mom could devote all her time to keeping their home and raising their four children.

But once each summer, Dad would take a week or two away from his busiest construction season and pile the four of us kids in the car to head south. Along with my older sister, Dorothy; my younger brother, Hasker Jr.; and our little sister, Brenda, I knew it would be a long day in the car. It would take more than eight hours to cover the 550 miles down to the farmland around little Aiken (population 7,000) in south-central South Carolina, about 20 miles from the Georgia border and the city of Augusta.

Mom would pack enough food for all of us to last the trip, and she and Dad would have the route carefully planned. They'd always start with the gas tank topped off, because once we headed south through Virginia and West Virginia and into North and South Carolina, there were only certain places where we could stop to buy gas or use the facilities, and many places where we could not, since the owners of those gas stations and restaurants did not want the business, or the presence, of African Americans. And even at the places where we'd leave the car and go inside, it was always with stern reminders to be quiet and mindful—don't do this and don't do that.

It was all part of Southern life back in the 1940s and '50s, something with which our parents were only too familiar and that we quickly learned as well.

Dad was one of 13 children, the second oldest boy, and his father was a Baptist preacher, a man I never met because he had passed away before we began making those visits to Aiken. But there were still lots of aunts and uncles working the farmland down there, and this city boy, when I wasn't running barefoot races with my cousins, joined them in picking beans and cotton and chopping tobacco. And in the evening, our elders—our parents, aunts and uncles—would tell stories of how it was when they were growing up and, in many cases, the way it still was. And so we learned for the first time the reality of overt racism.

Back up north in D.C., we lived in the city's northeast quadrant, which was 80 percent Black and perhaps the poorest section of our nation's capital. We knew, of course, that our city housed the nation's government in those monumental buildings we would visit with our school groups or our families, along with the marvelous museums, the beautiful architecture, and those important and meaningful monuments that made Washington an enormously popular destination for hundreds of thousands of visitors every year.

But the everyday reality of our lives was basically circumscribed by the limits of our own neighborhood, and most of what was important to us—our churches, schools, rec centers and playgrounds, our grocery and drug stores—were all within easy walking distance. Racism, including the overt kind we heard about and experienced down South, was not something we commonly encountered in our neighborhood.

We lived in a one-story frame house on a quiet street where all the homes were similar in size and style. Inside it was about 1,200 square feet in a typical layout, with a kitchen, dining and living rooms, one bathroom, and two small bedrooms. In the basement there was a coal furnace, and particularly in those two cold months in D.C., December and January, it was my chore to keep a fire going in that furnace by shoveling coal into it.

My siblings and I were all about a year and a half apart, and as younger kids, all of us shared one bedroom with two sets of bunk beds, one for my brother and me, and the other for our sisters. In the backyard, as you might expect of folks with a background in the rural South, we maintained a good-sized garden, growing a variety of vegetables. Yes, we were poor, but there were no serious financial worries. Always working long, hard hours and with skills well-developed and much in demand, Dad always managed to pay the bills and keep us reasonably comfortable. Generally, ours was a happy home. We kids were all close-knit, and our parents were always good to us and to each other. I never, ever heard them arguing. Now, maybe it did happen, but if so, they were smart enough to never air their disagreements in front of us.

Our street was a friendly one, filled with nicely kept homes and lots of good people who knew what it meant to be good neighbors. My dad was such an easygoing, friendly guy, and a kind of leader in our neighborhood, that people felt free to come to him and ask for help with things they needed. He'd fix or build this or that and often "forget" to charge for his labors, but those neighbors were like one big family with us, and they'd usually find ways to repay. Actually, we also had real family members in the neighborhood. Just one block away was one of my dad's sisters, and she had seven kids, and three blocks from us was another of his sisters, with nine children. So we had lots of cousins close by, most of them older than we were, and thus a good support system, serving as ready-made friends who would always show us the ropes.

The proximity of good neighbors, friends, and family, all looking out for each other, was an early but enduring life-lesson on the value of community, the strength of working together, and the importance of teamwork.

Also within walking distance, only a few blocks away, were the projects—seriously overcrowded, government-subsidized housing with small two-room units often holding more than one family, and with people literally living on top of one another. There the lesson more often concerned the possible consequence of way too much togetherness. In the 1950s, D.C. had not yet suffered the common urban scourge of rampant drug-trafficking, with its attendant addiction, violence, and dysfunction. But there were young, tough groups we'd call gangs today, who indulged in the time-honored underclass activities of robbery, petty theft, shake-downs, and intimidation. And so we quickly learned to tread carefully when in or near the projects, or to skirt them altogether.

. . .

As it did for his father before him, our local Baptist church played a central role in Hasker Bing's life. Dad was a deacon at Mount Olive Baptist Church, just a couple of blocks from our home, and next to the pastor, he was among the most important members of the congregation, a kind of church elder. It was a position of honor and confidence, and Dad treated it as such, which also meant that religion was deeply important in our family life. My dad sang in the choir, and before long my older sister, Dorothy, and I joined the junior choir as part of the service every Sunday. As the time passed, I consistently found singing those hymns both soothing and comforting in some way. I think it was the chance to lose yourself in something spiritual and reaffirming. And, frankly, back then I thought my voice wasn't half bad.

But church on Sunday was more than just the eleven o'clock service. There was Sunday school every week, and occasionally there'd be a three o'clock service or even one at eight in the evening. But always in the mix was Sunday dinner at home, a ritual that took on an almost religious dimension. Mom would always spend long hours cooking something special, usually for the six of us, but sometimes the meals included some of our close-by cousins, aunts, and uncles.

So Sunday, both in the church and in our home, was the Lord's day, a sacred time for devotion, reflection, and moving closer to God.

Religion, I think, gave us a center and a foundation, a way of looking at our world and dreaming of something better. It's no surprise that the pulpit is where the Civil Rights Movement was born, because Sunday was always a time to imagine a place of equity, fairness, and genuine community.

• • •

When I was five, my favorite programs on the small-screen television set in our living room featured cowboy heroes like Roy Rogers, Gene Autry, and Lash LaRue. They rode their beautiful, well-trained horses in one adventure after another and filled my young fantasy life with dreams of doing the same. The problem was there were no horses at all in our D.C. neighborhood, and while I had seen a few on our summer visits to South Carolina, I'd never had a chance to ride one.

There were, I knew, toy versions, with a small hobbyhorse head on a stick that you could hold between your legs and go galloping off into your fantasyland, but it was out of the question that our limited household budget would hold enough to spend on frivolous playthings. So feeling creative, I found two sticks of appropriate size, along with a rusty old nail, got my father's hammer and nailed them together. Feeling proud of myself and working my young boy's imagination overtime, I slipped the longer stick between my thighs and went running and skipping around the neighborhood in search of horse thieves and other adventurous missions.

I had been at it for quite a while, and maybe I got just a bit careless, when I stumbled across a sidewalk crack and went tumbling. As I fell to the concrete, the point of that nail I had used to make my horse came up at just the right angle to strike my left eyeball. There was an initial stab of pain, and when my hand went to that eye, I felt a trickle of blood. With my dad away at work, I ran home, showed the eye to my mother and told her what had happened. The eye was very bloodshot, she said, and seemed a bit swollen, so she wrapped some ice in a cloth and told me to keep my eye closed and hold the ice on it to bring down the swelling. We'd wait until Dad came home and then see if he thought anything else needed to be done.

Of course, at age five, I had no awareness of things like a regular family doctor, emergency care, or insurance, none of which we had access to at the time. And later, when Dad had a look and told me to cover my right eye and tell him what I could see with the injured left, I said it was blurry, which was what you'd expect with an eye so bloodshot. Dad said we should let it heal for now and then reassess. But by the time the eye was no longer bloodshot, I had naturally begun to adjust to the condition and, without consciously thinking about it, to compensate. I was a five-year-old, and I just learned to live with that damaged left eye, squinting or closing it at times to get a better look.

The injury had not been something like a broken arm or leg that would have obviously demanded emergency medical care. And none of us knew anything about the finer details of vision loss, things like peripheral vision and depth perception. My damaged left eye was simply a condition I would grow up with and gradually become accustomed to, and my lack of complaints meant to my parents that their earnest prayers for my full recovery had been heard and answered by a benevolent God. It is not clear to me even today what, if any, difference an emergency visit to an ophthalmologist might have made at the time. The one thing perfectly obvious is that specialist care would have been costly indeed for our family, while prayer was free of charge.

Soon after my eye injury I started kindergarten at Burrville Primary. I was there from K through third grade. Then it was on to Meritt Elementary from fourth through sixth, and for junior high—seventh grade through the ninth—I went to Kelly Miller. They were all close to our home, all within easy walking distance, and I liked the school experience at all three.

D.C. schools had a good reputation among large urban systems, but for a while, like most kids, I didn't understand or appreciate the importance of education. I always enjoyed school, never had a problem with it and never wanted to miss it—that was where all your friends were, after all. But there was another factor that grabbed my interest as well. School was often and in many ways competitive, and I was always up for any opportunity to prove I was better than the next kid.

Back then, it was a common observation that boys showed less interest in school and were perhaps developmentally slower than were girls. Certainly there were teachers who thought girls were smarter in those early school years, or at least better able to negotiate class-room hurdles. But I so enjoyed competing at everything, I not only wanted to be the top boy in class, I wanted to best the girls as well. Consistently through those school years my favorite subjects were math and English, and my penchant for reading books started early.

As for parental attitudes in our home toward school and educa-tion, both my dad and my mother had come from large families in which all the children were expected to contribute fully to the family's support. Each worked—in the fields or with trade skills—as soon as possible, so going further in school than the eighth grade was rare. But they both emphasized how vital it was to get a good education in the changing world we were facing. They always closely checked our report cards, and later in school, while they weren't always able to help us with our homework, they made very sure that time was set aside for it.

My dad would always say, "I don't want you to do what I do. I make a good living, but my work is hard." Ten months out of the year it was all strenuous outdoor construction, and in the other two winter months he'd do plumbing and electrical inside—still hard work. His message was always, "Go to school and get a good education. You can always fall back on a trade, but you don't want that to be your primary way of making a living."

Working—both chores and regular jobs—was mandatory as kids in our household. If we weren't in school or involved in church activities, we were working. My first real job was delivering papers in the neighborhood. I was eight or nine years old, and, in a sense, I learned how to function as an entrepreneur on the job as a paperboy. When you do your collection, you have to know what to charge your customers, how much the papers cost, and what days you missed. At age 10 or 11, in the summertime, I worked with Mr. Evans when he'd cut grass, and I'd serve as his helper. I also had a job at a neighborhood grocery store, helping to clean up the store and making deliveries. Dad let me keep what I made from those jobs as pocket change, but when he began taking me at age 12 to construction sites every day, what I made went straight to support the household.

My first construction job was as a water boy. I'd take water around to all the men on the site, so they wouldn't have to leave their posts. It meant carrying a five-gallon bucket around, which wasn't easy, and those guys expected the water to be clean and cold. So I was the water boy, and I was good at it, for two summers, and then I became an apprentice. I was laying brick, which, of course, I learned how to do from my dad, and I did that for the next few summers on various construction sites.

Now by this time, though nobody from my family had made it past high school, going to college was clearly in my sights. But as Dad had pointed out, it was smart to have a trade as a fallback just in case. So even as a 14-year-old, I took that summer construction work seriously. One day I took on a project without my dad knowing about it—building a concrete block wall that I thought was pretty decent. When I finally showed Dad the wall, he gave it one of his keen-eyed once-overs and then leaned against it. To my surprise and chagrin, that wall I'd spent so much time on came crumbling down. My anger flashed, and I said, "Dad, why did you do that?" Because, he said, he never accepted a "half-ass" piece of work, and neither should I.

"Don't ever equate being done with something with actually doing a job well," he said. And I realized it was the same with school. He never wanted me to be happy getting a B. Yes, a B was good, but it could always be better. The lesson was simple but vital: life was about constantly striving, always testing yourself to be, not just good enough, but the very best you can be.

That experience was all about the importance of expectations, and it's telling that the one teacher who still sticks out in my memory from back then was my ninth-grade math teacher at Kelly Miller. His name was Mr. Ellis, and he was the very definition of a taskmaster. We all thought he was mean, because he simply took no trash from anybody and had such high expectations for all of us. And I remember him so well as my math teacher, because I tried so hard to live up to those elevated expectations of his.

It was around this time that some of my pals started calling me "Duke." That happened because Kelly Miller, my junior high, was on the other side of the projects, and coming home after school meant making a decision about which route to take. You could either take the long way and walk around the projects and, thus, avoid a confrontation with the so-called tough guys who lived there and didn't like anyone who didn't live there coming through. Or you could take the shortcut—straight through the projects. For me, it was the shortcut. Yeah, for the guys in the projects, that was their territory. But to me it made no sense to go the long way home. So I had a few fights. I remember this one kid who was the bad—meaning tough—guy in the projects in our age group, about 14. He was the self-appointed enforcer. And so I got into a fight with him on more than one occasion, and finally one time I beat him up pretty badly. And, of course, if you beat their guy, you're not an easy target anymore and walking home through the projects was no longer an issue.

When my parents learned about the fights, they wanted to make sure I was not being a bully. I explained the situation, and my dad said I was right to stand up for myself and to not back down from a fight. My mom said, just don't go looking for one. In any case, that's when I became "Duke." Some of my friends still call me that today.

• • •

From the time the Brooklyn Dodgers introduced Jackie Robinson to major league baseball as its first Black player in 1947, Hasker Bing was a big-time Dodgers fan. When the team added more Black stars, like catcher Roy Campanella and pitcher Don Newcombe, Dad's devotion to the Dodgers only grew, and I too became a Brooklyn fan and a baseball fanatic. The kids in our neighborhood, almost all of them Black, were heavily into baseball, and every summer day from ages nine through 13, and when I wasn't working at one of my jobs, I'd join a bunch of my friends to play the game on a diamond at the local rec center.

Early on, these were just pickup games, but intensely competitive all the same. At age 12 or so, we graduated to organized ball. We had coaches, uniforms, and we'd play teams from other rec centers all over the city. I played centerfield, first base, and one season they put me at catcher, but wherever I played I was good, and if you had asked me back then what I wanted to be when I grew up, I'd have told you: a major league baseball player.

But it was around this time that I began to notice that the injury to my left eye was beginning to have more of an impact. When I got to be 13, 14, 15, and the kids I was playing against, particularly the pitchers, were bigger, stronger, and throwing harder, I found it more difficult to pick up and track a pitch with that damaged left eye, the lead eye in my right-handed batting stance. And perhaps for that reason, or maybe also for several others, I began to find myself gravitating toward basketball.

Later, I would still play baseball for all four years on our high school team and was considered one of the better players in the city.

But once I began playing organized basketball in the ninth grade at Kelly Miller, I was hooked.

Why? Well, at 12 or 13, I was 5'7", 5'8". By the time I'd finished with junior high, I was six feet tall. And I quickly found basketball to be a much more intimate, more personal sport, an up-close, *mano a mano* contest, which appealed to my competitive nature. It was by far the most popular sport in D.C., with no contest from baseball or football. In D.C., basketball was king. And the game is also one you can practice all by yourself. You've got a ball and a hoop in your backyard or on a playground? You're good. So it's a game for which you can develop some of your most needed skills—shooting and ball-handling—all on your own.

There was also a major practical consideration. I was already certain I wanted a college education, an expensive proposition for my family. And as much as I loved playing baseball, major league teams signed kids right out of high school, so there were no full-ride baseball scholarships out there that would get me to a university. The clear choice was to concentrate more on basketball because that would probably take me farther.

By the way, if you're wondering about me and football, I was a good enough athlete to do well at that as well. But soon my coaches made it clear that I shouldn't play all three of the major sports. They thought it would probably hamper my academic performance.

Late in the summer of 1958, I was 14 and getting ready to start the ninth grade at my junior high, Kelly Miller. High school classes at Spingarn High were still a year away. Spingarn was a relatively new school, but its first graduating class in 1954 included a guy who was already a legend in D.C. basketball. Everybody called him "Rabbit"

back then because of his great leaping ability. His real name was
Elgin Baylor.

Elgin held all the scoring records in D.C., and, as I would soon learn,
you couldn't do anything as a high school ballplayer without being compared to Baylor. He had gone on to star at Seattle University and would
soon join the Minneapolis Lakers for his rookie NBA season. But first
Elgin was on a mission to burnish the reputation of D.C. basketball.

In a series of games at local outdoor courts, he and some of his
friends, all good D.C. players, were ready to challenge a team from
another basketball hotbed, Philadelphia. The Philly team was led by
a 7'1" phenom who was the best player in college basketball, a guy by
the name of Wilt Chamberlain. Wilt had left Kansas University early
and was about to spend a year touring with the Harlem Globetrotters
until he'd be eligible to join the NBA.

So it was Wilt versus Elgin, Philly versus D.C., and when one of the
games was set for the playground at Kelly Miller, there was nothing
that could keep me away. As it turned out, about 500 other people
felt the same way, so I had to snake my way into a good spot at a
close-by fence to take in all the action of an extraordinary spectacle.
Both players put on a sensational show, and as I looked around at the
excited crowd, I noted again something I'd begun to notice recently:
how much girls liked to watch boys play basketball. And that was
one more good reason to devote myself to the game.

Of course, as a 14-year-old just embarking on a love affair with
basketball, I had no idea what was in store for me.

Yes, I had a good imagination and a healthy estimate of my
own athletic potential, but if you had told me then that within 10

years I would lead the NBA in scoring and the two runners-up would be Elgin and Wilt, I might have suggested you get your sanity checked.

3

A STAR AT SPINGARN

AS BASKETBALL TOOK OVER as the focus of my young life in sports, Sundays became problematic, particularly Sunday afternoons, and especially in the summer I was 15. The 10th grade at Spingarn High School loomed in the fall, and in both academics and athletics, things were about to get serious.

In 1954, Elgin Baylor had been in the school's first graduating class, setting just about every city record in basketball, but whether in the classroom or in sports, expectations for student performance at Spingarn were high. As for my game, I knew that if I wanted to improve, I needed to play against the best, and that meant getting to our neighborhood park and rec center, Watts Branch, by noon on Sunday. That's when many of the best players from across the city, of whatever age, would converge on two well-maintained outdoor courts for highly competitive pick-up games that would last all afternoon. As always with this kind of setup, the more you won, the more you played, and the more you played, the more you could learn from—and test yourself against—the best.

The problem for me was that in our household, Sunday belonged to the Lord. At nine every Sunday morning, Dorothy, Brenda, Hasker, Jr., and I would attend Sunday school to learn the finer points of our faith at the Mt. Olive Baptist Church. Then, at 11:00, we would join our parents for the regular Sunday service, and there were times when that service would seem to go on forever, sometimes until two in the afternoon. For my dad and mom these were the week's most important hours, and I didn't get very far when I tried to explain to them that if you wanted to become competitive in basketball, you had to play against those guys who'd come to Watts Branch at noon. Of course, I didn't have to tell them that most of those guys never bothered to go to church. They just came out and played basketball.

For a while, I tried sneaking away from church in time to get to Watts Branch by noon, hoping Mom and Dad just wouldn't notice me missing from a pew. Or I'd concoct a story about having a job, like cutting someone's lawn, but my folks would remind me that Sunday was a day of rest, and, besides, where was the cash I'd earned?

Eventually, over the next year or two, when news of my doings on the court would occasionally hit the papers or my dad would hear from friends about how I was looking like I might be something special, this problem would smooth out a bit. But for a time, it was a real problem. It was even tougher on those Sundays when Dorothy and I would join our folks in the choir, where they would be sure to notice my absence. Also, my feelings were genuinely mixed, because I really enjoyed singing in the choir, always feeling up-lifted by the experience.

It was about this time that I met a guy at Watts Branch who also loved both playing ball and singing. Like a lot of the guys I was playing

with or against, he about four years older than I was and, and, at 6'3",
a little bit bigger. He looked like he might have some game, but once
on the court it was obvious that he was no better than average. And
at Watts Branch on Sunday, average didn't cut it. He couldn't begin
to stay with me, and after a while he stopped trying. Nonetheless we
became friends, and I learned that he had grown up in the projects,
nurturing some of his own special aspirations. One Sunday, instead
of playing, he just stood on the sidelines, swaying and making his
moves and singing his heart out as if he were on stage.

For years I lost track of him, but when I finally ended up in Detroit
with the Pistons, we reconnected, because he had become one of
Motown's most popular singers.

And some years back, when the powers that be in D.C. decided
to rename Watts Branch Park, they didn't turn to Elgin Baylor or
Dave Bing.

They called it Marvin Gaye Park.

• • •

After Labor Day in September, Spingarn High School opened its doors
for the new term, and for the first time I did not walk to school. All
my previous schools had been only blocks away from our house, but
now Dorothy and I had to walk to a bus stop, wait for a city bus, and
then ride for 15 or 20 minutes to school.

My feelings on my first day at Spingarn? That too was something new—I felt intimidated. All through primary, middle school,
and junior high I had done well, consistently getting mostly A's and
always proud of my ability to compete in the classroom, not only with

the boys but also with the girls. But now my older sister, Dorothy, who was two years ahead of me at Spingarn, was doing a good job of letting me know that all that success was in jeopardy. Just wait, said Dorothy, until I got a look at some of these tough high school teachers. Just wait until I hit freshman algebra and encountered the notorious female math teacher who would waste no time in letting the class know about her impossible grading standards. A, she would tell us, was only for the author of the book we were using. B was only for the teacher herself, and for an ace student, the best of the best? He or she could expect a C.

Did I have any options here? No, Spingarn was the designated high school for our area of the city. There was Phelps Vocational, adjacent to Spingarn, but I had no interest in going to a vocational school. So Spingarn was it, and I told myself to remember that it also had a first-rate basketball program, starting with the great Elgin Baylor. But to play, of course, I'd have to pass all my classes.

Those first few days at my new school were certainly an adjustment, and I soon learned that Dorothy had not been telling tall tales. That algebra teacher turned out to be a strict and scary older woman who described the way she graded just as my sister had outlined. I resolved to do my very best to meet her challenging standards. My other classes included new subjects (Spanish and biology) and old favorites (English and geography). Most of the teachers were young and demanding, with high expectations and high standards.

From our neighborhood I knew a lot of the kids in the school, and, because by now I was a budding athlete, a lot of people already knew me. There were kids, like Tap Williams from the projects and Donald Hicks, who had gone to other schools, but with whom I had played recreation league ball in the summers. They were classmates now, and we cemented friendships that have lasted to this day, some 60 years later. Back then we'd hang out together, go to parties, and watch a lot of sports on TV—baseball with the Washington Senators, football with the Redskins, and once a week on Sundays an NBA game. Very seldom could we see those games at the stadium or arena, because the tickets were way too expensive.

Naturally, there were many other kids who were new to me at Spingarn, from other neighborhoods and some tough places like the projects, but no one tried to pick on or bully me. Of course, by then a lot of my pals called me "Duke." And if you're wondering, everyone at Spingarn, every administrator, teacher, service staffer, and student, was Black.

Organized basketball practice started in late September. All the facilities were nearly new, so the gymnasium and the locker rooms were well-maintained and in good shape. I was anxious to prove myself, but all 10th grade players were assigned to the junior varsity team, and that's where I started. The varsity would practice in the afternoon after school, so the JV team was forced to practice before school opened, at seven in the morning. Every weekday morning I was up at 5:30. I'd throw on my clothes and catch the bus and get to school in time to practice for maybe 45 minutes or an hour before school started. The JV coach would put us through our drills and scrimmages, and this went on for a couple of weeks. But after a while I began to notice that the varsity coach, Dr. William Roundtree, was showing up every morning to watch us go at it. He'd say nothing and let our JV coach run things, but one morning he came up to me to say they had decided to bring me up to the varsity.

Obviously, he had noticed that I could play, and while I knew the JV coach wasn't happy to lose his best player, I thought I deserved it. I had been watching the varsity practice in the afternoons and knew it was a much more competitive game they were playing. Everybody was much bigger, stronger, and quicker. But I had also noted that their best players were the bigger guys, like Ollie Johnson, a 6'6" junior who was becoming one of the city's best. Their guards were nothing special. They needed a guard, I thought, and I immediately fit in really well with the varsity. Not only could I drive to the basket and make things easy for Johnson and the other big guys. I could also score. I was clearly the best guard on the team, and soon I was starting.

I also sensed quickly that Dr. Roundtree was a special coach. He had earned his PhD in physical education, and at Spingarn he would eventually coach the basketball team to 11 city championships. Then he left to become the principal at Calvin Coolidge High in N.W. Washington, and later he would head up the physical education department at Howard University. He would also become a Baptist minister. We always called him Dr. Roundtree.

Before practice he would usually meet with us as a team, always talking about the things we should consider most important. He would often act more as educator or a counselor than as a coach. He'd talk about what he expected of us, and about what we should expect of ourselves. He talked about life skills as much as basketball skills, about living in a way that would keep us away from trouble, about following the rules that would give us a chance to reach our goals.

In terms of basketball savvy and teaching the game, Dr. Roundtree understood as well as anyone I've ever encountered how the sport was always a mix of team play and individual brilliance, and how the key to success in the game was learning how to effectively blend the two.

He would always impress on me how important the concept of team was in the game of basketball. The individual player, his exploits and statistics, was not the most important thing. It was the team and its overall performance. "It's the team that wins or loses," he always told me. "You can play and play brilliantly, you can score, maybe 40 a game. You're always going to be a high scorer. But that doesn't necessarily mean that we'll have a good team. You've got to get the other players involved."

So he wanted to be sure that I was never hung up on stardom. It was all about the team, and that became an important, ingrained concept for me. Frankly, I knew that my hops were better than what most guards had, and I could get my shot almost anytime I wanted. So there were many times, even as a youngster just up from the JV squad, when I had the ball in my hands and thought to myself, "I know I can take this guy right now."

But then I'd think of Dr. Roundtree and know I should do something else. Yes, I didn't always avoid going off and doing my thing, and when that happened, he'd always quietly call me on it and rein me in. And my response was always that he was right. He was the coach and had my total respect. Needless to say, Dr. Roundtree became like a second father to me.

The public high schools in D.C. were divided into the High East and the High West, and our Spingarn basketball program was one of the powers in the East. Unlike the rumors we heard about certain athletes getting academic breaks at some of the other public schools in the city, players at Spingarn always had to toe the mark.

Dr. Roundtree didn't let anyone slide. If you didn't have the grades, you did not play on the team.

Once the fall term really got underway, I began feeling much more comfortable in the classroom. My grades were right up where they had been in the past, close to an A average. I felt more comfortable, and things were no longer intimidating. My success on the court may have given me the confidence I needed to compete across the board, and I enjoyed classroom competition. I was very aware that many people felt that athletes weren't that smart or had little interest in "brainy" activity, and that the expectations were lower for us from an academic standpoint. From early on I had a problem with that. I knew I was as smart as the next person. I worked as hard as the next person. I expected to do well in the classroom, and I did.

On the court, we started out winning and pretty much kept at it. As a 10th grader I played pretty well and averaged in the low teens per game. Out of 25 games we lost only two or three. That made us the city's top public school team and put us into the Inter-High championship game against the top Catholic school team. For the first time ever, the big game was scheduled for the University of Maryland's Cole Fieldhouse. But at that point we were about to run into a buzz saw.

John Carroll High School had won 54 games in a row across two years and was generally considered one of the top teams in the country. At center they had a 6'10" senior named John Thompson, who would play in the NBA and become a legendary coach. Tom Hoover, 6'9", would play also play in the NBA. And their other big was 6'6" Edward "Monk" Malloy, who eventually became the president of the University of Notre Dame. That was their high school front line. Then they had two of the best guards in the city: George Leftwich, who was probably D.C.'s best all-around player, and John Austin, another 10th grader, who I'd be competing against for the next two years. They had an unbelievable team.

Naturally they were the heavy favorite, but we gave them a hell of a game and lost by only a half-dozen or so. I scored 14 or 15 and held my own, and since we were losing only one senior and they were graduating all their starters except Austin, we knew we'd be back the next year with the best team in the city.

John Austin also understood that power shift, and for his 11th grade year he transferred from John Carroll to DeMatha. And that's when DeMatha began their string as one of the most successful high school teams in the country. Catholic schools recruited the best players from all over the city. For them, there were no restrictions in terms of where you lived. Unlike public school players, you could live anywhere in the city and go to the Catholic school of your choice.

Every spring I continued to indulge my first love in sports by playing on the Spingarn baseball team. But by the summer between 10th and 11th grade, basketball had completely taken over my heart. Having played for the city championship, Ollie Johnson, our teammates and I were anxious to keep playing together and improving, so a heavy dose of summer league basketball was on tap. We'd play on our rec center team and criss-cross the city to play other rec center teams. And at this point there were no age-limits, so we were often playing against guys who were in college and beyond. The competition in the summer league was as good or better than high school, and playing together in the summer, we got to know both our teammates and our opponents much better.

My game got stronger and so did my confidence. I played against John Austin more than once, and I ended up knowing I could outplay him. Yes, he was scoring more points, because he was his team's big scorer, and I was trying to get my guys better as a team. But when we went head to head, I knew he couldn't handle me, and I couldn't wait for the school year to start again at Spingarn.

And then one day that summer I came home from playing ball and found my mother deeply worried. She told me that my dad had suffered an accident on the job. He had been laying brick on the ground floor of an apartment building his crew was working on, and somehow a scaffold a couple of floors up had shifted just enough to send a brick hurtling downward. It struck Dad flush on the head.

Because he had been wearing a hardhat, it didn't kill him instantly, but they had rushed him to the hospital where doctors quickly decided there was so much blood on his brain that they needed to operate immediately. At the hospital, my mom and I learned that the operation had relieved some of the pressure from that blood on his brain. The surgeon thought they had probably managed to save his life, but there was no way to know for sure how much brain damage he might have incurred.

At the hospital waiting for him to regain consciousness, I spent some of the worst moments of my young life. I was afraid he was not going to make it, and over the next couple of days we weren't able to say anything to him. So at that point we were filled with troubling questions about whether he would ever come out of it, and if so, whether he was ever going to work again. And even if he did live, I was worried that maybe he wouldn't be back to his normal self.

I was full of fears, but for my mom it was all in God's hands.

And finally, he came out of it, and we tried to exchange a few words. For the next week or so, before he was released from the hospital, we'd go up there every day, and I could see him struggling to come back, struggling to talk, to find the right words and to make himself understood. And so for a while we had eye contact and very little else.

Back at home as he slowly improved and he could begin to express his thoughts, I could see that while he was fighting to come back, he was also trying to keep me from being too concerned about him. Dad never said he was worried—I'm sure his faith in God helped him feel he was going to be okay. But I also think he didn't want me to feel that as the oldest boy, I was going to have to assume the responsibility now of stepping up and taking care of the family. I think he never wanted to put that kind of pressure on me.

For a while after he came home and began to speak and move around a little, it was really tough on him. Because he had been such an active guy, such a doer, to be forced to sit around and do little or nothing was painful for him. But then little by little we saw him getting better. And at that point I was hopeful that he would come back to 100 percent in the healing process. But to be absolutely honest about it, I don't think he was ever really the same again. In the neighborhood, in the church, and with his family, my father had been such a vigorous, energetic guy. But that brain injury had really slowed him down. I could never fully assess or fathom the impact it had on him, but he definitely moved more slowly after that injury.

He could still work and did so for several years after that, but I'm sure he knew that he could have died from that accident, and I think he was afraid for me and for my future. And so he was very careful about what he took on and definitely slowed down. Did it affect his sharpness, his mental acuity? I think the answer has to be yes. But he started doing more interior work, more carpentry, more plumbing, the kind of work he could do at a somewhat less demanding pace and do it all year round.

Dad and I had always been close, and he had always urged me to think beyond construction work. But after the accident he was adamant about not wanting me to go out there and do that kind of risky, physical labor. I knew that paying for a university education was well beyond what my folks could afford, but I was starting to see basketball as a ticket to college, and Dad was beginning to get that as well. I told him not to worry, that I had no intention of ever doing construction work again.

• • •

As the 11th grade started for me at Spingarn, I had high hopes for our basketball team. All of us had played together all summer in the recreation league, and we knew we were good. Ollie Johnson, our star big man, was a senior and the center of recruiting attention from lots of college coaches, and of course when they came out to see him, they also had a look at me. And in fact we had a great season. We dominated most teams and again won the public school championship, which gave us the right to play for the Inter-High championship against the Parochial champs.

Once again the game was at the University of Maryland's Cole Field House. But this time we were up against the Catholic power-house DeMatha. Now, because of all those summer league games we had played against a lot of the DeMatha guys, we pretty much knew who we were up against. They had an outstanding team, and the media had made them the favorites. Again, I was matched up against John Austin (who, like I said, had transferred to DeMatha), and many people said we were the two top guards in the city. Because he had been part of that undefeated John Carroll team the year before, he was still getting most of the ink. But once we hit that fieldhouse floor, that was over. We beat DeMatha pretty handily. I was the high scorer for Spingarn with 24 points, and Ollie Johnson had 18.

And so for us another season was in the books. Even though DeMatha went on to play in other tournaments and against teams in Maryland and Virginia, we were finished, because public school rules dictated that our teams could not play beyond the city championship. But there was still basketball excitement at the Bing house, because lots of college teams had apparently discovered me. A number of different coaches had started getting in touch with me earlier in the season. They'd either send a letter to the house or they'd get to me through Dr. Roundtree at Spingarn. So Jack Kraft from Villanova was the first college coach who talked to me, but all five of the Philadelphia colleges—Villanova, Temple, St. Joe's, Penn, and LaSalle—were basketball powers and recruited heavily in D.C. They all expressed interest in me, and then there was NYU, and actually St. Bonaventure was the first to offer me a scholarship in my junior year.

Now I was aware that St. Bonaventure had a really strong program, but at this point I knew very little about any of the 30 other colleges that got in touch with me in my junior year. I could read in the paper about how their teams were doing and learn about their records and some of their players, but I never lined up or ranked the schools that I might be interested in, and I didn't have a favorite. I thought I'd just let this process play out, knowing I now had a very solid shot at a full college scholarship.

• • •

So what was my social life like at Spingarn? Well, at just about any high school, if you're a star player and a decent-looking guy—given the fact that girls like basketball—with girls you probably have no problem. But as I started my senior year at Spingarn, there was still no one really special for me. And then one day I was in the hall waiting for our Spanish class to begin, and I saw this lady walking down the hall and heading into our classroom, and to say the least (using the vernacular popular back then) she was stacked.

I turned to one of my buddies and said, "Who is *that*?!" And this girl I had not noticed before turned around and said, "That's my sister."

And that's how Aaris and I met. I had gone out with several girls over the past two years, but, as I said, no one special. So I quickly learned that Aaris was a sophomore, just starting in Spanish, and while my eyes told me she was a very nice-looking gal, I soon found out she was also a nice person, good-hearted and smart. So we hit it off.

We started dating before the basketball season started and did the usual—going to parties, movies, or to a couple of eating places where everybody would meet. Eventually I met her mother, and she was okay with us dating. Actually, Aaris had an older sister who was a senior and in one of my classes. So the sister knew who I was and what I was about. And I'm sure she told Aaris, "A lot of girls are after him, so be careful… but he's a pretty nice guy."

So my senior year started off well and got even better. We had another strong team, and what made many of our games special for me was that my dad was able to take off from work to see me play. We again won the public school championship to set up another big face off with the Catholic League champ. This time it was against Mackin High, which had defeated DeMatha and my old nemesis, John Austin. With my buddy Donald Hicks as my backcourt mate, we beat Mackin for our second straight Inter-High championship. But this time my season did not end, because, as a graduating senior, I no longer had to abide by the rules against postseason play.

So late in March, John Austin's coach at DeMatha, Morgan Wootten, who was in the process of becoming a local legend in D.C., was putting together an All-Star team from the metropolitan D.C. area for a tournament in Allentown, Pennsylvania. Of course, he had Austin on the team, but he also wanted me, and so the two of us were about to go up against the best in New York City, Philadelphia, and New Jersey.

Austin and I were quite a backcourt, both named to high school All-American teams. But with a grade point average of just under 4.0, I was just as proud of making an academic All-American team as well. Along with us, Wootten had put together a hell of a team for D.C., with four of the five starters eventually going on to the NBA. Austin had already committed to playing for Celtics great Bob Cousy, who was the new coach at Boston College, and Morgan Wootten told Cousy he might want to take a look at me as well. But while it was a thrill to meet Cousy in Allentown, it made no sense for me to follow Austin to Boston College.

We ended up winning that Allentown tournament, and I was named the MVP, but I had already received offers from some 60 different colleges, so for me those games were just a great opportunity to compete against the best of the best. Yes, there was a whole bunch of college coaches there to watch and be impressed. But by now I knew I was going to college. I knew I had scholarship offers and a lot of choices. It was just up to me to decide where I wanted to go. But even with all that, it was surprisingly out of that Allentown tournament I was recruited.

At Syracuse University there was a new coach named Fred Lewis. This was his first year there, and Wootten had passed along the word that he needed to get to Allentown: "You need to come out and see this kid Bing's game." I had no idea who Lewis was or that he was there, and Syracuse was not on my radar at all. But after our first game, he came up to me and introduced himself and said he'd like to have breakfast with me the next morning. He'd like to get to know me and tell me about Syracuse.

The next morning at breakfast, he said, "I like what I see in your game, and I would love for you to come to Syracuse. I know you've got a lot of offers, but I'd like for you to at least visit the campus."

Now I had visited other colleges at that point—Villanova, NYU, St. Bonaventure—and those were all possibilities. Ollie Johnson had urged me to join him at the University of San Francisco, but I had turned down the West Coast at that point as being too far away from home. The University of Michigan offered as well, but I knew that Cazzie Russell had already committed there, so that was not a good place for me.

By this time, I had offers from pretty much every Black school—Grambling, North Carolina A&T, North Carolina Central, Texas Southern—but I had ruled out a Black college, and I also didn't want to go down South. I had no interest in going to any ACC school, including Maryland and the University of Virginia, because of what I learned about racism on our visits back home to South Carolina. Actually, Maryland wanted me to be the first Black student-athlete to get a scholarship there, and I believe I would have been the first Black player in the whole ACC, but that was not going to happen.

So Coach Lewis and I had breakfast, and I was impressed with him. I liked what I heard about how he wanted to play the game, with a fast-break team and a pressing man-to-man defense. Because he was brand new at Syracuse, he actually didn't know a hell of a lot about the school, beyond the fact that it was sound academically and that it was, of course, a football school. Their great running back Ernie Davis had just been named the Heisman Trophy winner, the first African American to get that award, and he said, "You come to campus and I'll make sure you meet him. I want you to spend some time with Ernie and let him tell you about Syracuse."

Frankly, I felt comfortable with this coach. He had been an outstanding player himself, and he was a little younger than some of the other coaches I'd met. And I liked his honesty. He said, "I'll tell you the truth. We've got a horrible program, and that's why I'm here now. The reason I got this job is because they were so bad." They had lost 27 consecutive games over a two-year period. So they obviously didn't have the players. And he said, "You can be the catalyst to turn this whole program around."

Fred Lewis had grown up in New York City, was an East Coast guy, and knew about a lot of the best high school players on the East Coast. He told me he was recruiting a really outstanding player from Boys High in New York. And he said, "I've got some commitments from guys out of Albany, New York, and New Jersey. So I think we've got the makings of a very good team."

But the big thing that got me thinking about Syracuse was the style of play that he wanted to install. What you often saw in college in those days, especially in the ACC, was a slow-down game, and I didn't like that. I knew teams in the Northeast played a pressing man-to-man defense. And my thought was: "Man to man, I'll beat most guys. I'm too quick for most of them. I can jump better than most backcourt guys. I can score." So that's the kind of game that I wanted to play, and that's what he said he would play.

I knew they'd had only one Black player over the years, and currently there was not a Black player on the team. But the subject never came up with the coach, and I left that breakfast thinking that Syracuse was a real possibility and that I'd definitely be visiting the school. At the tournament, several other coaches got in touch with me, but no one else tempted me the way Syracuse had.

So a couple of weeks later they flew me up there, and it went unbelievably well. I was there for a weekend, and this was late April, early May, and the weather was beautiful. The students were going crazy because the snow was gone, and everybody was outside having a great time. I roomed with another basketball recruit, an Italian guy named Frank Nicoletti from New Jersey, and we hit it off so well that we remain fast friends to this day.

Ernie Davis and the great tight end John Mackey were the two guys assigned to show us around, I guess because nobody on the school's basketball team was good enough to convince us to come there. We were introduced to the president of the university and the athletic director, and, as you would expect, both said all the right things.

But when Frank and I got together with those two football players, we were tremendously impressed. Davis was the number one player in the country and about to be the top pick in the NFL draft. But also impressive was that he was a good student, majoring in economics, and just a really good person. And Mackey, who was heading into his senior year in pre-law, was the same way. They talked to us a lot about how Syracuse was a really good academic institution. And Davis told me, "Look, basketball has been terrible here, but you can turn this whole program around. Yeah, I haven't seen you play, but I've heard all the good things about you, and they tell me that you can be the catalyst. The program could be centered around you."

So Frank and I hung out with Davis and Mackey, socialized, and went to a party. I didn't know the racial makeup of the school at all, but when I looked around, I saw a hell of a lot of White faces. The guys were honest and told me what to expect: "We've got 14,000 undergraduate students in this school. It's private, expensive, and primarily Jewish. And out of those 14,000 undergrads, there are about 100 Black students."

Now Black and White was not a big issue with me. Our part of D.C. was basically all Black, including all the schools I had attended from kindergarten through the 12th grade. But my parents were just good people and never let us get hung up on the whole Black and White issue. You are who you are. And it's important to know the history and reality of your people. But under the skin everybody's the same. And so when Davis and Mackey told me about the ratio at Syracuse, it didn't really faze me, because I'd be there for two reasons: to get an education and be the best basketball player I could be. I wasn't concerned about anything else.

When I returned from that visit, I talked to my parents and to Dr. Roundtree, and when I told my sisters that Davis and Mackey had also said that of those 100 Black students only 20 were females, they both said be very careful. Meaning be very careful of the White girls. In those days dating a White girl was basically out of the question.

Coach Lewis had given me his phone number and said, "Call me when you make the decision… and I hope it's here." But maybe a week had passed when he called our house. I was out, and he tried to get my parents to tell him if I had made a decision. They said, "Well, you have to talk to him."

When I called him back and let him know that I was coming to Syracuse, he was pretty excited. He said, "This is the beginning of a great opportunity for you and for the school. We're going to grow this thing together."

Syracuse had a brand-new basketball facility, a fieldhouse that was also used for football practice when there was a lot of snow. On my visit I had found it very impressive. But the single most important factor in my choosing to go to Syracuse was my experience with those football players, Ernie Davis and John Mackey. When I got in touch with them, they were really happy to hear I was coming. Ernie was graduating, so I wouldn't be there with him. But Mackey was coming back, and he said, "You're going to be with me. I'll be your big brother."

Now there was one other difference-making experience in that summer before college. Coach Lewis knew a lot of NBA guys and told me about a camp that Dolph Schayes, a 12-time NBA All-Star, was putting on in July in Lake George, New York. The coach said some of my incoming freshman teammates would be attending, and it would also be a chance to go up against a bunch of NBA players who'd be working out and playing at that camp.

When I got there, I found myself squaring off with guys like Hal Greer and Larry Costello, both All-Star guards. I had never played against a professional NBA player, but here I was, just finished with my senior year in high school, and I seemed to be holding my own. When both Greer and Costello took me aside later and said, "Hey, you're gonna be okay," I figured I could play.

What suddenly seemed like a realistic dream of someday playing at the pinnacle of the game in the NBA was born for me at that camp. The next big step would be proving myself at that football powerhouse in Syracuse.

4

THE SYRACUSE YEARS

A S A COUPLE WHO HAD become something of an item over the course of my senior year at Spingarn, Aaris and I were busy with the usual round of graduation activities, including the senior prom and parties with classmates and friends. I had met her stepfather and had a good relationship with her mother, and our families got along well. So she was my girlfriend, but to infer anything more than that, or to say that we were doing anything like long-term planning for a life together, would be going way too far.

I was occupied with getting ready to leave home for the first time and go off to college (the first in my family, with sister Dorothy now in the service as a WAC in Germany), while Aaris still had two more years of high school to finish. With so few Black female students at Syracuse, my expectation was that my social life there would definitely be limited, so I reassured Aaris that I'd be writing her letters and calling on a regular basis to keep her posted and let her know what college life was like. When we parted at the end of the summer, we did not expect to see each other again until the Christmas break.

In August I moved to Syracuse for the first time. My dad and my Uncle John drove me and all my belongings from D.C. to the campus in Syracuse, not far from the center of New York State. Leaving home and not knowing what to expect, I was just a bit apprehensive. But then we got to the dorm and hauled everything from the car up seven floors to the room I was assigned to share with Frank Nicoletti. All the clothes came out of the suitcases, including some new items because I was always a good dresser, and in high school all the guys had been competitive about wanting to look good.

The dorm room was simple—two closets, two desks and chairs, two beds, no bathroom, but a communal bath down the hall. We were in a large new building, no more than two or three years old, so it was very comfortable. Along with lots of other students, Nicoletti and I and all the other basketball players were in this dorm, while John Mackey and all the football players were in another dorm some distance away, on the edge of campus.

Only the freshman class was on campus that first week, so our time was occupied with the typical round of orientation meetings, mixers, and hanging out in b.s. sessions in somebody's room. What was it like living among mostly White folks for the first time? I got along fine with everyone, I think partly since I was a pretty easygoing guy, but also because everybody seemed to be open and welcoming. So it wasn't at all a big deal for me to quickly and easily make friends in the dorm who were both White and Black.

Those mixers and b.s. sessions were a great chance to learn about other people, where they were from, their backgrounds, and what they were like. Beyond my teammates, in the dorm there were kids from all over, though mostly they were East Coast people, largely from New York City, New Jersey, and Connecticut. There were lots of Jewish kids, maybe 70 to 80 percent, and they were clearly the dominant group in terms of numbers. To me they were all pretty decent people. Syracuse had the reputation of being a very wealthy school, so a lot of those kids came from well-to-do families, and for whatever reason I detected very little racism.

Syracuse was also known as a good academic institution, and Coach Lewis had emphasized that to stay eligible we would need to work hard to keep our grades up. He provided each of us with an academic adviser who helped put our schedules together. For some that meant easy, so-called "jock" classes. But I made it clear that wasn't the kind of schedule I was looking for. So I took English, Spanish, zoology, world history, and math—all the basic courses—and in my freshman year I took either 15 or 16 hours each semester.

Once the semester actually got under way, my biggest academic surprise was how large the classes were. I was used to classes in high school of 25 or 30, and here you had large lecture halls full of hundreds of students. You just sat there and listened and took notes with little or no chance to interact. I didn't much care for it.

Of course, autumn in Syracuse meant football, and we had another good team. Each fall there was a schedule filled with games with big time teams featuring outstanding players. So we saw Gale Sayers with Kansas, UCLA's Mel Farr, and Pitt's Mike Ditka. And I saw our own All-American, John Mackey, all the time, both on the field and on campus, where he was indeed like a big brother to me.

As for our freshman basketball team, I had met some of my teammates at Dolph Schayes' summer camp. Besides Nicoletti, there was Sam Penceal, the other Black recruit, from Boys High in New York.

He was 6'3", maybe 205, and played both guard and forward with Connie Hawkins when they won the city public school championship in New York. Norm Goldsmith was an all-stater from Long Island, and Chuck Richards, a 6'8" center who could shoot, came to us from West Point, but, as a transfer, would have to sit out for a year. And in the dorm that first week I met two other guys with some size: Dick Ableman, 6'6", and Rex Trowbridge, 6'8". So when we all hit the court for the first time, I was thinking, "Okay, we have a pretty decent team."

There was also a guy named Jim Boeheim. There were no scholarships left, so he was a walk-on, and his parents were paying his way freshman year. As for his game, it was nothing exciting. He was about 6'4", less than 170 pounds, wore glasses, wasn't particularly quick and couldn't jump much. But he was a good shooter and, as I'd soon learn once our practices got underway, a genius at getting open, and so he managed to play his way into our seven-man rotation.

When we had our first scrimmage against the varsity, they had no one who could stop me, and we thoroughly whipped them. And at that point word began filtering around campus that if you wanted to see good basketball, go see the freshman team. With the season underway, lots of students would come to the freshmen game and leave before the varsity game got started. It was embarrassing for the varsity, but this was the team that had lost 27 in a row over the previous two years, and those were still the days when NCAA rules dictated that no freshman could play on the varsity. The real excitement would have to wait until we became sophomores.

We went 17 and 3 against the freshmen teams of all the schools the varsity played. With our coach, Morris Osburn, who was Fred Lewis' assistant, we would make those same trips with the varsity, always traveling by bus, because most of the teams were from East Coast schools—West Virginia, Pittsburgh, upstate at Niagara, at Seton Hall, at Georgetown in D.C., and teams in New York like Manhattan and NYU. We played well against all of them, but we already knew we were good, because we continued to beat our varsity.

So at Christmas I was halfway through my first year, and I was pleased with my choice of Syracuse. Everything had pretty much gone as I had hoped. I was doing well in my classes. We had a good team. My teammates were all good guys, we all went out together on weekends, and in the process we became a very close-knit group.

That first fall term had been mostly all studies and basketball. I'd spent Thanksgiving week on a very quiet campus, and, as expected, I had no social life with the opposite sex. But, as I had promised, I stayed in close touch with Aaris, with lots of letters and phone calls on the weekends. When I finally came home for Christmas and New Year's, let's just say I was starved for female companionship, and we did what came naturally. And Aaris became pregnant.

Of course, we wouldn't know that for a while, and back at school I was busy again. I learned that things were different when our travels with the team headed south. At West Virginia it was tough—people calling you the N word and more—but surprisingly playing at Penn State was rough as well, maybe because we were up in the mountains there. Penceal and I were the only two Black players on the team, and we heard them all too well.

As I've mentioned, in our scrimmages against the varsity there was nobody who could stay with me. But in our games with a wide variety of opponents I also did well. I averaged over 25 a game as a freshman and usually led the team in assists and rebounds. I don't think I had ever lacked confidence, but playing with that freshman team confirmed that I was not just a top guy in D.C. Now I was going up against players from all over the country, and they couldn't match up with me either. D.C. had prepared me well.

When we finally learned that Aaris was pregnant, there was no time for angst or difficult decision-making. Our parents got together, and the matter was settled quickly. Basically, my good, old-fashioned mom and dad said, "You don't have a choice in this." Abortion was out of the question, and Aaris' folks said the same thing. And so when I came home for spring break in April, we got married very quietly in a small, simple service. I went back to school and finished my freshman year, and Aaris stayed in D.C., remained in school, and completed the 11th grade.

In May when we were finished with final exams, I invited Frank Nicoletti to come home with me to D.C. for a few days. As roommates, Frank and I had become very close and remain best friends today. He's an attorney in New York, and we talk monthly. Back then in D.C. we were, of course, up for some playground basketball. So we showed up at Watts Park, and here I was bringing the only White guy within miles with me. And I could see all my old playground pals looking at us and thinking, "What the hell's happened to Bing?" I'm sure they all assumed he couldn't play. But Frank was about 6'2" and 210, a big, strong guy, and tough, and he wasn't afraid of going up against anybody. And so we all hit it off.

• • •

For the rest of that summer, I worked in the D.C. Recreation Department as a youth counselor. And I spent a lot of time with Aaris, who by then was very pregnant. When I was getting ready to return to school at the end of August, her delivery date was less than a month away, and I knew I'd be returning soon for the birth of our baby.

Back at Syracuse, as a sophomore I had decided I was interested in business, and the counselor had urged me to take a couple of economics courses to see whether I liked them. So I did, along with all of my core courses, and liked econ enough to think I would make it my major. I was already pretty sure that someday I'd be in business for myself.

Yes, I was married and about to become a father, but I told no one at that point. And I had a new roommate. Coach Lewis wanted me to room with Jim Boeheim, who had just received a scholarship because one of our players had lost his by getting into enough trouble to be kicked out of school.

Boeheim and I respected each and got along well. He'd talk about what it was like in his small town about an hour from Syracuse, and I'd talk about what it was like in D.C. I had known he was smart, but when we took a couple of classes together, I was really impressed, because he never studied. Now I was a good student, but I had to be diligent about doing my work. Jim had a hell of a memory, and he seldom did any studying until there was going to be a test. And then he'd take NoDoz, stay up the whole damn night cramming, and then ace the test. He did extremely well academically.

Of course, we talked basketball. A lot. We talked about plays and options, about Coach Lewis and our teammates. Jim was obviously not a gifted athlete, but he was constantly in the gym and usually I was right there with him. That he would later assemble one of the greatest college coaching records of all time at Syracuse over more than four decades never surprised me.

Later in September, I went home to D.C. in time for Aaris to give birth to our daughter Cassaundra. I looked at that brand-new baby girl and knew my responsibilities had just doubled. When they left the hospital they came to stay at my folks' home, where my mother could help with the baby. And Aaris would start back to school for her senior year at Spingarn the following September.

Back on campus, my plan was to remain quiet about my status, but some of the guys on the team wanted to know why I wasn't dating. As a budding star on the basketball team with the season soon to start, I was now a fellow of interest for some of the girls on campus. So a few of my teammates kept asking why I wasn't going out, and I finally decided to tell them, while asking that they keep it to themselves. There was also one girl, a freshman with whom I was just friends and who was like a little sister to me. I ended up also telling her that I was married and now had a child.

My own personal issues seemed almost petty on November 22, 1963, when someone came into our room and told Boeheim and me that President Kennedy had been shot and killed in Texas. For African Americans and for Jews as well, John Kennedy had been a very popular political figure, so we were all hurting, and the whole campus was in shock and mourning. We were all glued to TV sets, none of us knew what to think, and lots of conversations went deep into the night.

It was probably inevitable that Coach Lewis would hear sooner than later the rumor about me being a husband and father. Basketball season was about to start when he called me in, spelled out that rumor, and asked if it was true. I told him it was.

Actually, he was understanding about it. He said, "Well, it is what it is, and it's going to be tough for you because academically and athletically you've already got a lot of stuff to be thinking about. And now you've got a whole different kind of responsibility. So this coming summer we've got to get you a job. We've got to try to help find you a decent-paying job because you've got a family to take care of now."

So he was supportive, but he also told me that when we had our next team meeting, he would need to let all the other guys know. And when that meeting happened, he told them that it was going to be a tough situation for me and that nobody should follow my lead, or they would surely regret it.

As for the season itself, we were sure we'd be pretty good. Chuck Richards, the 6'8" transfer, was now able to play. He was a legitimate big man, a good scorer, and would average about 20 points a game. He and I started, along with Sam Penceal, and Boeheim played some, so the team was dominated by sophomores.

We had high expectations for turning the program around when we started with blowout wins at home against Toronto and Buffalo. But then at Penn State we were manhandled 95–76. Back at home we squeaked past Cornell 86–84, but lost to Eastern Kentucky 90–72. So we weren't sure about ourselves when we traveled down to Miami for the Hurricane Classic tournament late in December. There we'd be facing two of the best players in the country, Princeton's Bill Bradley and Miami's Rick Barry.

In Miami, the day before our first game, our trainer, Jules Reichel, asked Penceal and me if we'd like to meet Cassius Clay. "Of course," we said.

We then learned that Jules had worked at the 1960 Olympics in Rome, and while there he got to know Clay. Now it turned out that the boxing sensation was in Miami, training at the Fifth Street Gym for his first heavyweight championship fight against Sonny Liston. So Jules took us to meet Clay.

When he introduced us at the gym, we were just immediately taken with the personality of the guy, that charismatic aura and the incredible mouth, but also, of course, with those amazing physical skills. He was so brash, funny, and full of outlandish things to say. He was such a braggart, but he actually knew what he was doing, because he was one hell of a fighter.

Cassius said he wanted to drive us around in his big red convertible, but we had to say no, because we needed to get back for practice. When we were on the floor the next night getting ready for Princeton, though, in walks Cassius Clay and his entourage to sit in the first row. He was chirping his encouragement at us the whole game.

Maybe that distracted Bill Bradley, because Mr. Everything in college basketball at the time fouled out of that game. With Penceal on him and looking like a defensive ace, Bill scored 17, the least points he'd ever have in college, and fouled out with 13 minutes left in the game. Chuck Richards led us in scoring with 26, and we beat Princeton 76–71.

The next night we played Miami for the championship. Rick Barry, their All-American and one of the nation's leading scorers, had missed their first game with the flu, but they still beat a good Army team.

He was ready to play against us, and now Chuck Richards had come down with something similar and was out for us. In any case, Barry scored 25, but we beat them in overtime, 86–85. I scored 29 and won a 12-inch trophy that said I was the tournament MVP.

One night later, at Cassius Clay's invitation, Sam and I joined him and some others at a Miami club where the singer Dee Dee Sharp was performing. He didn't drink that night, but we were all up pretty late and had a great time.

Two months later, almost nobody would expect him to beat Sonny Liston, and when he knocked the man out, the whole world blew up for him. After that he converted to Islam and became Muhammad Ali. That angered a lot of people, but he didn't care. He would always do things his way, and that included saying he was a conscientious objector and refusing the draft. As he put it, "I ain't got no quarrel with them Viet Cong."

It was not uncommon in those days for Black athletes to take a stand on important public issues and voice their opinions in outspoken ways. Some of the guys I most admired were Jim Brown, Bill Russell, Kareem Abdul-Jabbar, and Arthur Ashe, but the most famous and outspoken of them all was, of course, my friend Muhammad Ali.

After Miami we thought we were now on our way to a good season, whereupon we lost our next three in a row. Finally, with a revenge win at home against Penn State, we really got it going. We won 11 of our last 13, ended with a record of 17–7, and got ourselves invited to the National Invitational Tournament in New York. In those days, the NIT was right up there with NCAA tournament, and lots of teams preferred it. We drew a really good NYU team with three guys who would play in the NBA: Barry Kramer, an All-American;

Happy Hairston, who I played with on the Pistons; and Stan McKenzie. We gave them a good game but lost 77–68. The *New York Times* writer who covered the game wrote: "Dave Bing of Syracuse was the game's top scorer with 31 points, the 6-foot 3-inch guard showing some fantastic moves."

So personally I had a good first year, averaging 22.2 points per game and 8.2 rebounds, and if they had kept good stats on assists back then, I might have averaged close to a triple-double. Our turnaround season had generated a lot of excitement on campus about this basketball team. Students flocked to our games in unprecedented numbers, stopped to talk with us between classes and in the dorm, and even professors were getting into it. They knew who we were—not that they gave players a break or went easy on us—but they were happy to see the change as well.

At the end of the term, Frank Nicoletti invited me to his home in Weehawken, New Jersey, right across the river from New York City. Frank's folks were Sicilian, warm and friendly, and it was the first time I had stayed in a White person's home. We had a great time for a few days, and in that summer of 1964 the World's Fair was happening in New York. So Frank and I hit the Fair along with a couple of our buddies who were varsity football players. And with all the great attractions at that World's Fair, these four young college guys, three White and one Black, ended up drinking beer all day at the Heineken exhibit, because Frank, who was good-looking and a real player, was trying to make time with this beautiful blond German woman who was working there.

• • •

Between my sophomore and junior years I again worked in the D.C. Recreation Department. And that was the summer Bill Bradley came to D.C. to be a congressional intern. He was heading into his senior year at Princeton when he would be named consensus Player of the Year. And, in addition to learning the congressional ropes, he naturally wanted to play ball. We had met in Miami back at the Hurricane Classic, and Red Auerbach, who always spent his summers in the Washington/Maryland area, gave Bill my number. So we ended up playing on the outdoor courts in Bethesda, close to where he staying.

As always, D.C. had an unbelievable number of good players on its courts, including John Thompson, who was then an All-American at Providence; Tom Hoover, who also went to the NBA; and so many others I grew up with. That's what Bradley wanted—some really good competition—and that's how we got to know each other a little better that summer. Over the years, through the NBA and after, we always remained friendly and respected each other so much. Later, when he made his presidential run, I would host a fundraiser for him at my home in suburban Detroit.

Going into my junior year, my level of confidence was high, both for our team and for my personal performance. As a sophomore, when I played against guys at schools across the country, it was clear to me that I was better than most of them. So my confidence had soared, but when I'd come back to D.C.—often with the likes of Nicoletti, Boeheim, or Bill Bradley—I was always just one of the regular guys. And I'd always give credit to the people I grew up with on those outdoor courts. Some of those older guys were proud they had given me the fundamentals, the basics to be outstanding player, and they still considered me one of them.

As a junior I was now majoring in economics and doing well in the classroom. I had been enrolled in ROTC in my first two years at Syracuse, but something told me not to do that again in my junior year, even though it would start to provide some much-needed pay at that point. It wouldn't be too long before we'd begin hearing about a war on the other side of the world in a place called Vietnam, and I'd be thanking my lucky stars that I had not signed up again, because I would have been headed for service in the Army.

Boeheim and I were rooming together again but in a different dorm. And as we picked up our basketball talk again, our expectations for the team were very high. Building on our solid sophomore year, there were two really promising players joining us from last year's freshman squad, two more heralded Black players that Fred Lewis had recruited from New York City. One was Penceal's former teammate, Vaughn Harper, who was considered maybe the top player coming out of high school. He was 6′5″, and they called him the Kangaroo Kid, for obvious reasons. And the other was Val Reid, 6′9″, who had played well against Lew Alcindor in high school. Adding those two—plus a couple other White players with size and skills, Rick Dean and Marty Goldstein—to what we already had, we thought we might well be ranked as a Top 10 team. And when the AP preseason rankings came out, there we were at No. 7.

Fred Lewis had proven something I already knew: he was a hell of a recruiter. And we continued to get along very well. He saw me as a leader, as the guy who was turning around our program. And I think he was pleasantly surprised that, even though I was the team's best player, I worked as hard as anybody. I always practiced as hard as I played, was a good teammate, didn't have a big head, and helped pull people together. On my side, I loved the way our team played, the kind of up-tempo game he had promised to install. And now we really seemed to have the kind of good athletes you need for that kind of game.

The first thing that went wrong was Vaughn Harper's grade-point average. He flunked out in that first term and had to sit out the season, while concentrating on getting his grades up. Still our season opener against American University was a runaway 127–67 win, in which I recorded my first triple-double: 20 points, 15 rebounds, and 11 assists. Assists weren't officially recorded in the college game until the following year, but we had a young team statistician named Bernie Fine, who was meticulous. So we started with a laugher... and then we stopped laughing.

We lost our next six games in a row, including blowouts at Penn State and the University of Kentucky, and a 10-point loss to Princeton and Bill Bradley in the Holiday Festival at Madison Square Garden. I had a good game and scored 28, but I guess Bill was kind of upset because the media had made a big deal out of his getting only 17 points against us in last year's Miami tournament. So it didn't matter what Sam Penceal, or anybody else, did in trying to guard him. Bill had an unbelievable game, scoring 36 before fouling out again, this time with only three minutes left. We had been hoping to go on and meet Michigan and its star Cazzie Russell, but losing to Princeton meant we had to settle for Manhattan. We beat them to finally break that six-game losing streak, but then we started the new year with two more losses to LaSalle and Cornell.

Yes, the loss of Vaughn Harper had hurt us, and Coach Lewis had put a pretty tough schedule together. But by then a lot of our guys had good reason to question if we were really ready for prime time. And yet we somehow pulled ourselves together and started to play up to our potential, winning 11 of our last 13 games. Nonetheless, our dream of being ranked had quickly gone out the window and never returned. And when we were invited back to the NIT tournament in March, Fred Lewis said no, we're not going. He let us know he was very disappointed in our play overall and wanted to send a message for next year.

So we went 15–10. Personally, I had averaged more than 23 points and 12 rebounds per game and made a number of All-American teams. But not going to a tournament was depressing for all of us. So our seniors had to focus on how to turn things back around.

• • •

Not long after that frustrating basketball season, Aaris and I learned she was pregnant with our second child. She was soon to finish her senior year and graduate from Spingarn, and now as we made plans to move our family to married student housing just off the Syracuse campus, we knew there would another mouth to feed come November. As with Cassaundra, the new child had not been planned, but of course I needed to step up to this additional responsibility.

More than ever now I needed that decent-paying job Coach Lewis had talked about, and so he arranged to get me into highway construction work on the I-81, running north-south past Syracuse. I spent the summer, along with a few Syracuse football players, doing heavy physical labor. It paid good money, but we earned it, and I was able to get us a car. Married student housing turned out to be a nice place to live for $72 a month, and it was good to have our little family finally together, comfortable in a two-bedroom apartment.

We definitely had to watch our pennies, but with that construction job and my scholarship transferred from the dorm to student housing, we were okay financially. Bridgett was born just before the basketball season started. I hadn't been in the room when Cassaundra arrived, but I was there to greet Bridgett, and it was a pretty awesome experience.

Our senior-year expectations for the team were once again very high. Vaughn Harper had raised his grades and was back with us. He, Val Reid, Rick Dean, Sam Penceal, Boeheim, and myself all started or got heavy-duty minutes. In the Coaches preseason poll we were ranked 20, and we moved up to 13 as we won our first seven games, including solid wins over Kent State, Bowling Green, Penn State, and Cornell.

We had finally managed to get off to a good start, and now after Christmas we were headed out to California for the L.A. Classic tournament that included a number of good teams. The luck of the draw pitted us against Vanderbilt, who the Coaches poll had at No. 2 in the country. Their star was Clyde Lee, a slim 6'10" forward with a great shooting touch, who would later go right after me in the NBA draft. In a hell-bent, up-and-down, racetrack of a game, we and Vandy put on quite the show. I had 46 points and 13 rebounds, and Lee put up 39, but we came out on the short end, 113–98.

We stayed in L.A. for two more games. Against Northwestern I had a triple-double, then hit up St. John's for 38, and we beat them both handily, scoring in triple digits each time. So I played well in all three games, and the California fans seemed impressed. On the way home we played at Creighton and lost, so after our West Coast trip, the first ever for Syracuse basketball, we stood at 9–2 and felt pretty good about ourselves.

As he had in previous seasons, my dad was able to see me play a few times that year. He came up to Syracuse with my uncle to catch a game or two, and when we played Georgetown and American University—both in D.C.—they came to those games as well. He enjoyed the fact that I was having a good collegiate career, but with his work schedule, he couldn't be at most of the games. For me it was always special when he was there. I always wanted to impress him.

We lost only three more the rest of the way and ended up with a regular season record of 21–5. The Coaches Poll never dropped us out of the Top 15, and we were the highest scoring team in the country, averaging nearly a 100 a game.

In fact, going into our final regular season game at home against Colgate, if we could manage to score 124 points, we'd average 100 on the nose, something a major college team had never done before. The game was on a Saturday, and a record crowd of 7,100 jammed Manley Field House. When my name was announced, I got a standing ovation, a loud thank you, I thought, for the past three years and for helping to make Syracuse basketball exciting again. And then the P.A. announcer surprised and pleased me by introducing my parents to the crowd.

Now Colgate was not a very good team, but they certainly didn't want us to set the record against them. So they played hard, and near the end we were even letting them score to get the ball back. With 12 seconds left I sailed in for a slam dunk that made it 122–91, but we never got our hands on the ball again and so missed out by a few slim percentage points.

In the postseason, the NCAA tournament beckoned, but back then it was not the March Madness we know today. There were 22 teams selected to play in the four regionals, and the two top seeds in each regional caught a bye. We got one, so if we could win two games in the Raleigh, North Carolina regional, we make it to the Final Four.

First up for us was Davidson, and we handled them pretty easily, 94–78. Now Duke was in our way. They were ranked No. 2 in the nation and had three guys who would end up going to the ABA or NBA: Jack Marin, Bob Verga, and Steve Vacendak. Also, their coach, Vic Bubas, had an assistant named Chuck Daly, who much later would guide the Detroit Pistons on their championship runs. Apparently, Chuck had been studying our high-powered offense and decided that the best way to beat us was to stop me.

So he devised a defense that put double and triple teams on me the whole game. He wanted to make sure that I just didn't have any space to shoot the ball. Some people call it the box-and-one, and it was some version of that, with one guy playing a tight man-to-man on me and the rest of the team going with a zone. So everywhere I went and whichever way I turned, I ran into somebody or had somebody's hand in my face.

It was an approach we hadn't seen before, and to say that it messed with the rhythm of our attack would be an understatement. After the first 10 minutes we were 16 points down. During a timeout I looked at everybody and said, "You work hard to get open, and I'll find you." By halftime I had a pile of assists, and we were only seven down, 44–37.

In the second half I continued to find the open man, but my path to the basket was almost always clogged, and my shot was off. With 11 minutes left, I did get to the rim for a layup, and we actually took the lead, 60–59. But at that point Duke really turned up the defensive pressure and also got hot from the outside. We ended up scoring 18 under our average and lost 91–81.

In the biggest game of our lives I had scored only 10 points, the lowest of my college career. I looked over at Jim Boeheim in the locker room and thought of all the times we had talked and fantasized about winning it all in the Final Four. Feeling that I had let down Jim and all my teammates was very hard to take.

Fred Lewis talked about how proud he was of all of us and said that we had done something powerful and lasting in turning Syracuse basketball around. And my dad and mom were there outside the locker room to pick up my spirits. But it was a tough, tough loss that had ended my college career.

So it was time for postmortems on the season. Was I the best combo guard in college basketball that year? There were some experts who thought so. How about the best all-around player in the country? There were some who said that also. But from the beginning of season, the question of who would be named Player of the Year had come down to Michigan's Cazzie Russell and me. We were both preseason All-Americans, and both ended up consensus first-team All-Americans. I had followed Michigan's fortunes closely all year and of course followed Cazzie. So I knew how great he had been playing, but I too had played well. I had averaged 28.4 points, 6.6 assists, and 10.3 rebounds per game. Cazzie had averaged a couple of points more and a couple of rebounds less.

Could I have tried to score more, to top Cazzie? To me that was not the right question. From the beginning, with my Spingarn coach, Dr. Roundtree, I had always been taught that you simply played the best you can play—for your team. We had averaged almost 100 points a game, and that was in great part due to our up-tempo style. Yes, I probably could have averaged a few points more. But as a team player, it was important for me to make sure I played the total game and not let things like scoring records ever cross my mind. "Get your teammates involved" was always my mantra, "and help them be the best they can be."

Cazzie ended up being named the consensus Player of the Year, and I was somewhere down the ballot. Neither of us at that point ever imagined that a stroke of sheer dumb luck would send him to play in my preferred NBA city, New York, and then drop me in Detroit.

5

ROOKIE OF THE YEAR

A S I WAS SURE SHE WOULD, Aaris loved the house and neighbor-hood I'd picked out in Detroit. She knew immediately that 19711 Prest Street would be comfortable for us and a great place to raise our daughters. We wouldn't need the nearby Bowe Elementary School for a few years, but by reputation it was one of the best in the city. And the neighbors, when they learned that the Pistons' top draft pick was moving in, were all warm and welcoming. Actually, it was a mostly White neighborhood at that time. There was only one other Black family on our block.

Once we settled into the house, I had some time to find my way around. I bought that new car I had my eye on, a '66 Oldsmobile Cutlass, and found out that most of my teammates were tuning up for training camp with pickup games in Detroit at the Considine Rec Center on Woodward.

On most days, DeBusschere and most of the guys were there, and as soon as we started going at each other, it was obvious to me that I would play a lot for the Pistons. My teammates knew it as well. They accepted me quickly, saw I could play, and knew that I was going to make them a better team.

Training camp started in September. We were lodged outside the city at the St. Clair Inn, a very pleasant, comfortable place right on the river, but our practices in the gym at St. Mary's High School were really grueling. For the first week it was just the rookies and free agents trying to make the team, and then the veterans joined us for two more weeks of two-a-days. In the morning we'd go from 10:00 to 12:00, then have lunch and rest a bit before coming back to go at it again from 4:00 to 6:00 or 6:00 to 8:00.

It was extremely demanding physically, and when the vets came in, many of the rookies and free agents were cut. Frankly, two-a-days were a bitch on your body. At night there were lots of sore muscles and lots of sleep.

My roommate for those tough training camp weeks was Reggie Harding, now a sad and infamous name in Piston and NBA history, but back then a young 7-foot center with great potential and a history of off-the-court problems. Normally a team would pair a vet with a rookie like me. Instead they put me together with Reggie, who at 24 was only a year older than I was, because they apparently saw an unusual maturity in me and were hoping some of it might rub off.

Reggie had size and lots of talent, but he had grown up on the tough streets of Detroit's east side with some shady friends and detrimental habits. The Pistons saw a great upside but knew there was a downside to match. Their idea was that maybe with my level head and being close to the same age, I might influence Reggie for the better.

Actually, I found him to be a very engaging personality and a likable guy, and I wanted to help. I had known others like him back in my old D.C. neighborhood, players with real potential, but perhaps because of a lack of structure and foundation in their lives, they had a hard time shaking a rough past. I considered myself lucky to have had a number of positive male figures in my life, starting most of all with my dad, and I knew they had made a huge difference for me.

But as a teenager Reggie was already getting into trouble and spending time in jail. Still there were those who thought he was the best player ever produced by the Detroit public schools, and his perceived ability on the court kept bailing him out of tough spots. He graduated from Detroit's Eastern High, but college was not an option. He attended a Tennessee prep school, then played for semi-pro teams for a couple of years and, when drafted by the Pistons, tried to become the first player in NBA history to make it in the league without any collegiate experience.

For a while the young guy did well, averaging a double-double in points and rebounds in 1964–65. But the NBA then suspended him for all of the '65–66 season for reasons it had kept under wraps. Word was that Reggie had gone to one of his favorite nightspots, Detroit's 20 Grand Club, found a long line to get in, and decided he didn't want to wait. At the door, a security guard told him to go back in the line, so Reggie pulled a pistol and slapped it across the guard's face. One of the city's top defense attorneys had managed to keep Reggie out of jail, and now he was coming off the league's one-year suspension.

Did I really think I could make a difference with Reggie? No, but if solid guys like Ray Scott and Eddie Miles and some of the other Pistons joined with me to offer consistent advice and support, maybe there'd be a chance.

And for a time that season, the effort looked like it might be working. Reggie was behaving himself and working as hard as the rest of us in training camp. Later when the season started, he played well for a while. And then the old negative habits began to show themselves again. He was bringing a gun in his gym bag into the locker room, and early the following season that gun came out of the bag to threaten another player, and Reggie was traded to the Chicago Bulls. He wouldn't make it to the end of the season with the Bulls, and he was soon back in Detroit and haunting some of its meanest streets.

As one legendary story has it, Reggie, with a mask and a gun, was in the process of robbing the same gas station for the third time when the exasperated owner said, "C'mon, Reggie, we know it's you."

"No, man," said Reggie, "it ain't me."

As Ray Scott put it, "Reggie just left you shaking your head. He'll always be one of the biggest 'What ifs' that ever happened."

Drug addicted and often homeless, he lasted five more years before someone put an end to one of the saddest sports stories I know with a bullet to Reggie's head. Because there seemed to be no one else to do it, I paid for his funeral.

• • •

By the end of those three demanding weeks in training camp, we were all in great shape, because we had just run our tails off. That camp was, of course, a reflection of our player-coach, DeBusschere. Dave was a tough, smart player who had earned a reputation of leaving it all on the floor in every game. He was driven and relentless, and what he demanded of us was nothing less than what he asked of himself. He was also a hell of a player, aggressive, a good shooter, and a strong rebounder and defender. As I said, tough and smart, but he was also a very down-to-earth, everyday kind of guy. The title of coach had not gone to his head, and he treated himself as a player just like everybody else on the team.

Being a smart player was something I had always prided myself on. I was always looking for an opponent's strengths and weaknesses, trying to pick up tendencies in their game. That way I could play to my own strengths and minimize my disadvantages. For example, throughout high school and college I had never told anyone, friend or foe, about the accident I had at age five, in which a nail had penetrated my left eye and left it with little more than the ability to see light. And I was not about to start talking about it now as a pro.

With no peripheral vision on my left, I was more prone to take someone off the dribble to the right, but that was something I kept to myself, and somehow my quickness made up for that tendency. And I had long ago learned to turn my head on a swivel to check with my coach on the sideline or find my teammates as I crossed mid-court or settled into a play sequence. And overall, the lack of that lateral vision did not seem to seriously limit what I could do.

Over the course of my NBA career, I would be one of only three players who, at that time, averaged over 20 points and more than six assists. The others were two of the greatest of all time, Oscar Robertson and Jerry West.

But at the moment in training camp, I was trying to win a starting guard position. The holdovers from last year were Eddie Miles from Seattle and Tommy Van Arsdale from Indiana. Eddie was a scorer, the best shooter on the team, and both of them were big, strong guys,

6'4", 6'5", 220–225 pounds. But it was clear from the beginning that I was way too quick for either one of them. Yes, when we played half-court, they were so damn big, they tended to beat me up. But when we went to full court, in game conditions, I was too quick, too fast, and neither one could stay with me. Honestly, I thought it was pretty obvious that I was going to be one of the team's top guys.

Our exhibition season included a couple of games against the Celtics, who had Sam Jones, one of the league's top guards. Yes, the veterans didn't play a lot until the last couple of games, but I played very well against everybody and was our leading scorer. And I heard that the word was out to the teams we'd be playing soon: You better get ready for this new young Piston guard. He can really play.

So to say I was disappointed when I learned I would not be starting in our first regular season game would be a gross understatement. I was totally shocked and hurt. Certain I had outplayed everybody in the exhibition season, I just couldn't believe DeBusschere had decided on Eddie and Tom, the guys who were the starters before I got here.

I said nothing to anyone, but Eddie and Ray Scott must have sensed what I was feeling. Eddie was the player I was closest to. We had become friends during that August transition period and our families had gotten to know each other. We had talked about playing the backcourt together and just figured we'd be starting. And so both Eddie and Ray said something to me about not getting down, that things would turn around. Ultimately all it did was make me fan the fire. Yeah, okay, if you think I'm not good enough to start, whenever I do get the chance, I'll show you how mistaken you are.

Our opening game of the season, on October 15th, was in Cincinnati against the Royals and the great Oscar Robertson. Oscar was one of my all-time heroes, and I was just in awe. Whenever I'd seen him play I had marveled at his skills and that quiet but intense demeanor on the court. So when I finally got the call to come off the bench and get on the floor, I was so amped up and, honestly, so taken with Oscar's presence on the floor, that I was pressing. In fact I pressed so hard that it would turn out to be one of the only games in my career in which I didn't score. I went 0 for 6 from the field and missed the only free throw I had.

For the most part, Oscar and I were not matched up head to head. Because of Oscar's size, 6'6", 230, Eddie Miles guarded him. But Oscar was such a smart player that he'd always use picks to create situations where I had to switch and take him, and then he'd clear the floor. You could just see him thinking, "Okay, I got this rookie, and he's a mouse." If you were a smaller guy, they used to call you a mouse. Some of the guys would call out, "Got a mouse in the house." But Oscar said nothing. He'd just back you down, and he was so big and strong, there was nothing you could do. Plus, he had that big-time reputation, so who was going to get all the questionable calls? The rookie? No, it was Oscar every time.

So I suffered through a terrible night on both ends of the floor, but no one was calling me out or rubbing it in. Yeah, there were guys who would run their mouth back then—Dick Barnett with the Knicks comes to mind—barking things like "You can't guard me" and trying to get into your head by saying they were going to do this or that to you. But trash talk wasn't as prevalent as it is today. And for the most part, guys in the league respected each other and didn't try to embarrass other players.

As I said, in the heat of the game, Oscar had said nothing to me. Actually, he saved all his venom and curses for the officials. He always let them know when he was unhappy. He was really hard on the refs, and maybe that was another reason he got all the calls.

But after the game, when Cinci had beaten us, and we were walking off the floor, Oscar came over to me. He shook my hand and said, "Look, you just had a bad day. Your shot was off. I know you can play, and you'll do well. So don't worry about it."

I said thanks but could hardly find another word. For Oscar, an idol of mine and one of the greatest of all time, to say that to me meant a lot. That was the beginning of our long and deeply valued friendship, and many years later Oscar would induct me into the NBA Hall of Fame.

In the locker room my teammates told me not to worry. "It's over, it's done, so be ready for the next one. We know you can play." And back at the hotel, I knew they were right. Despite the bad night, my confidence was not really shaken. Yes, I had missed my shots, but somehow I knew I was going to be okay, and I vowed to never again be so awed by a superstar's rep and presence on the court that I'd let it affect my play.

And now I was looking forward to the next game, two days off and once again against Cincinnati. But this time we'd be at home, for our opening night at Cobo Arena, and I couldn't wait, because I had something to prove. Not so much to myself but to all the fans in Detroit who had never seen me play. All that disappointment had welled up again about not being New York's choice and the Pistons feeling they had to settle for second best, and that too fueled my resolve. Oscar's running mate was Adrian Smith, and from what I'd seen in that first game, I felt he couldn't guard me. I made my mind up that this time I'd be ready.

Now the Pistons were not a great franchise. They had some good steady players, but no big star or marquee types. Even DeBusschere, though solid, well-rounded and respected, was not the kind of guy that created a lot of excitement. Neither was Ray, and while Eddie's shooting could produce a hot streak, he was not the consummate guard.

No, at Cobo, halftime was when all the stars came out. Of course, I'm talking Motown. The company was still dominant then, and a lot of its star performers were big-time basketball fans. They'd all come down—Aretha Franklin, the Supremes, the Four Tops, the Temptations, the Dramatics, Smokey Robinson and my old playground pal from D.C., Marvin Gaye—and they were all big fans. When they came, they'd put on such an incredible fashion show that you thought you were at some kind of Hollywood ball. The players wanted to get out of the locker room at half-time just to see who was strutting their stuff. I had never seen anything like it.

And with so many people so close to the court, Cobo was a different place to play. Hearing those fans respond to your game and picking up everything they were saying, practically every word, was something new. They were certainly not afraid to tell you what was on their mind, if you didn't play well, or just made some dumb move. They were all over it. Everybody there was a coach and on your case.

Fortunately, that first night, again coming off the bench, I had a decent game, scored 12, and we won. That was my introduction to Detroit, and I began to connect with those fans. I hit a couple of shots early on, and they got behind me. They saw I could drive to the basket, I could jump, and I could hang. Being both quick and fast, I could go baseline to baseline, and I was good one-on-one. So those Detroit fans began seeing things they had not seen from our players before, and I could hear people saying things like, "Oh, my God, look what he did!" And, in turn, hearing that convinced me again that sooner or later I'd be starting and everything between me and the Pistons was going to be okay.

There was energy in that building, and I was feeding off it. Frankly I think players who say they pay no attention to the fans are skirting the truth. I didn't know those people close to the floor, but they made me feel comfortable, energized, and at home. And then the Motown folks were all over the place at halftime and made things even more festive. I'm sure a lot of people also came down to see *them*. Especially on an opening night like that one, it was one big happy family.

But after the game we just stuck together as a team. We were always ready to go out as a group, at least four or five players together, and have fun and celebrate at one of our favorite clubs or restaurants downtown. Aaris had been at the game, and she and the other wives, with whom she had quickly become friends, went out with us. My scoreless game a few nights earlier now seemed like a distant memory.

Over the next 15 contests I continued to come off the bench. I averaged more than 15 points a game, and that included several highlight performances: 25 at San Francisco, 21 against Philly, 23 in another home game against Cincinnati, 28 at Los Angeles, and 20 against the Knicks. Finally, for Game 18 on November 18, a month into the season, I got the call to start for the first time against the L.A. Lakers, who brought another of my idols, the great Jerry West, to Cobo Arena.

If there was anyone I had modeled my game after, it was West, since we were similar in size and his skills were remarkable. A great outside shooter, he also drove to the rim, played tough defense, and was just a marvelous all-around player. In that game we weren't matched up, because UCLA's Gail Goodrich and I were guarding each other, and I pretty much ran him ragged. My first step was explosive, I scored 35, with seven assists and eight rebounds, and we beat the Lakers 121–118.

On nights like that I felt so quick, I thought there was no one who could keep up with me. And afterward, West praised my game, saying I had a great future in the league. He thought it was impressive that I could play so fast, yet always seem under control, especially for a rookie.

As a team, the Pistons were doing a little better than last year and playing close to .500. Over the next few weeks we would beat the vaunted Boston Celtics three out of four times, and their legendary player-coach Bill Russell also had kind things to say. The most intimidating defensive center of all time called me fearless in driving to the basket.

• • •

So approaching Christmas I felt like I was beginning to hit my stride in this first NBA season. My play was getting noticed, the P.A. announcer at Cobo would call out "Bingo" with every basket I hit and there was some talk of my being in the mix for Rookie of the Year. But we had already played close to 30 games, about as many as I had played in any of my collegiate seasons, and there were still 50 or so ahead.

Negotiating the rigors and demands of an 81-game regular season was for most rookies a stiff learning process. But I already knew the importance of eating well and getting enough sleep, and for both I considered being married a major plus. Most of the young guys coming into the league were not married. For them fast food and running around were commonplace, but I had a wife and two kids to care for, and I'd never been a fast-food guy. Like my mother, Aaris was a good cook, so I had full, well-balanced meals all the time.

Sure, in Detroit we'd go out to a restaurant to eat and come down after a game, but on off-days after practice I'd head straight home. I had a regular pattern to my life, and unhealthy meals and carousing at night were not part of it.

On the road, of course, it was a little different. Players were all in the same hotel, often doing things together, and stronger friendships were forged. Today it seems like a lot of the players are not really close friends, and that may have to do with the big money that has changed the game. Now guys do whatever they want with whomever. They come to a game in limousines with what they call their posses. Instead of their teammates they've got other people hanging around them all the time. There wasn't a lot of that back then. Most of us were good friends, and, especially on the road, we'd do things together.

But I also had time to myself on the road, and I had long been an avid reader. I would devour all kinds of books, from business to politics and social issues. We were, after all, in the middle of the 1960s, one of the most volatile periods in American history, so I'd often be alone in my room trying to make sense of it all with my books, newspapers and magazines.

And along with my mind I knew I had to take care of my body. I was now playing 36 to 38 minutes a game, and going mostly against guys who were bigger and stronger. Still, it seemed to me that some of those other guys weren't taking care of their bodies as well as they should, and when they were out on the town, I was in bed getting a good night's sleep.

It was an ingrained attitude I had more or less grown up with, and having a family to support, I felt I'd better take care of myself. Back then there weren't many guaranteed contracts, and if a guy had a few bad games or an injury, he might be gone. I'd already seen it happen. The league had 10 franchises with 12 guys on a team. Pretty much everybody could play, and there wasn't a big separation between the seventh through the 12th man. So if you didn't play well consistently or you got hurt, somebody might come in and prove himself, and you could be cut.

And then for many players, adding to the equation were all those women on the road. As a guy who credited his mostly smooth marriage with helping to keep his life balanced and healthy, I saw things happening that could cause trouble or at least serve as distractions. The fact was, very seldom did players have to chase women. It was just the opposite. They were always there, and after a game it didn't matter what city you were in, you knew the places to go. Yes, there were women at the game hanging around outside the locker room afterwards. But they also knew which hotel housed the team. They knew which clubs the guys favored, and they were always waiting there for both the single and some of the married guys.

Now most of them weren't building relationships. It was usually one-nighters. And I got a better look at how all this worked many years later when I was traded from Detroit to Washington. Because, hey, the same gals were there in the same places waiting for the Bullets players as well. So with every team you'd meet the same women in the same cities waiting for the players in town that night. Yeah, the guys might feel they were God's gift to the fair sex and see themselves as in charge, but these women just seemed to get a kick out of being with celebrity athletes.

Later, again when the big bucks became more prevalent, the issues could get more dicey. Then occasionally there'd be a woman who might decide it was time to become pregnant by a certain player. She'd figure either he would marry her or she would sue and grab some cash.

Of course, if any of this fouled up a player's life or got into his head, it could affect his concentration and lead to problems. So even though we were adults, we had bed checks. Teams saw the guys as investments they needed to protect, so our trainer the night before a game on the road would come around to each room and do bed checks. Around midnight he'd knock on the door, and the fellows who were really intent on having their fun would wait until he'd come and gone and then take off. It was pretty easy to beat the system, and after some years of this, teams gave up the effort.

• • •

Problematic players and inconsistent play were only two of the issues our player-coach Dave DeBusschere was dealing with in that '66–67 season. Was he a good coach? I'd have to say no, and I suspect Dave might have agreed back then. After a decent start in which we were winning almost as much as losing, the team began to sink lower and lower under .500.

Part of Dave's problem was that, as both the coach and one of the team's best players, he felt he had to be careful about handling his teammates. For example, in a lot of cases, a bench coach would have been calling plays for DeBusschere. But Dave didn't want to do that because he didn't want to seem selfish. And then there was the question of substitutions.

Ray Scott was a good player and filled the forward spot opposite DeBusschere, and I'm sure there were times Ray felt slighted by Dave. Maybe Ray was having a good game, and Dave brought John Tresvant off the bench for Ray, and Dave stayed in. Then you might see some looks, maybe a little conversation or some body language. Ray might have said, "Hey, I'm playing better than you. You should have come out, and I should have stayed in."

That kind of thing never really separated us, but those moments could be awkward and maybe made us less productive as a team. Finally, DeBusschere began to feel that his own play was being affected adversely, and you could tell he wanted that coaching responsibility lifted from him. With eight games left in the season—we would end up with 30 wins and 51 losses—the front office made the move. Assistant coach Donnis Butcher was given the top job, and DeBusschere went back to being one of the league's best forwards.

I was friends with most of the guys on the team but especially close with Eddie Miles. Because he was one of the team's stars and leading scorers, Eddie was even a role model for me. He took good care of himself, didn't drink much or smoke, and stayed away from drugs. He was married with five kids, a good husband and father, and our families were close.

Generally, except for the occasional miffed feelings over playing time, we were a pretty solid group both on the floor and in the locker room. But when the Pistons socialized after a home game or hung out together on the road, the breakdown was pretty much along racial lines. Usually Van Arsdale, DeBusschere, and Ron Reed, another White forward, would head out together, and the African American players had their own groups. From what I could tell, this was more or less how it was with the other teams in the league, reflecting, in a broad way, the American racial landscape at the time.

And it was the same in Metro Detroit, the area comprising the city and its suburbs and home to more than four million people. While most Blacks lived in the city (except in certain neighborhoods like ours which remained almost all White), the suburbs were largely White. The most infamous of those suburbs were Dearborn on the southwest edge of Detroit and Warren on the northeast. It was common knowledge that both were lily-White, and the stories of what could happen there were promptly passed along to players who were new to Detroit. The word was clear: be careful when you entered the confines of those two suburbs in particular, and don't let yourself get caught alone at night in either place. With the experiences that I and most other Black players had encountered growing up anywhere in the U.S., no more needed to be said.

Could you hear ugly things from the stands at Cobo? Yeah, there'd be the occasional racist gibe or epithet, but again from our personal histories we all knew that the best way to deal with it was to put it in the back of your mind and not let it affect your concentration.

• • •

Halfway through the season, the team found itself too often in losing streaks, but the talk of my taking Rookie of the Year honors was getting stronger. A lot of fans seemed to be coming out as much to see me play as to watch the Pistons. Part of it, I think, was that I always carried myself professionally. I was very confident but never cocky or arrogant. And I think people appreciated that I came to play hard every night, no matter the score. They could see that I was never just going through the motions.

Only a few other first-year players were starting around the league, but one of those was Lou Hudson, who was averaging in double figures for the St. Louis Hawks. With my natural competitiveness and all that early talk about the relative merits of Cazzie Russell and me still pushing my effort to prove I was number one, I hardly needed any extra motivation. But I'd watch the box scores and stat sheets to see how Hudson was doing, and if it looked like it might get close, I'd try to step up my game even further. And Cazzie? He was doing fine with the Knicks, coming off the bench and averaging 11 points a game. But he was never in the mix for Rookie of the Year.

I ended up winning the award going away, averaging 20 points and four assists. When people would ask me how it felt to win, I'd give them a grin and say it was a great honor because you can only get it once. Beyond the spotlight and my status as the Pistons' leading scorer, the most important thing was that I now had some major leverage when it came time to negotiate the next contract.

But even with the prospect of a heftier salary, I was already focused on a job for my summer months. Ironically, the best offer came from the bank that had turned me down for the mortgage on our home. The National Bank of Detroit's Aubrey Lee, who was probably the city's top Black in the banking field, had come to me, apologized for what had happened, and proposed to make it up to me. He said, "We'd like to have you with us in the off-season, if you're inclined to do it, and we'll put you in a training program."

In effect over the next several off-seasons, I'd be trained for and perform a variety of jobs at the bank. I started as a teller, and it was a great experience for me. I was dealing with people, which I was always good at, and dealing with money, and with my business background, I knew I'd be learning a lot that would become very important when I finished playing basketball. My dream was to run my own company one day.

So instead of spending my summer playing golf or doing speaking engagements and signing autographs, there I was every weekday working as a teller at the NBD branch at Greenfield and Puritan, right in our own neighborhood. Many of the people who came into the bank recognized the tall guy behind the window right away. I always had a lot of people waiting in line, so they could come to me.

• • •

On a Sunday in the middle of that first full summer in Detroit, on July 23, 1967, I turned on our TV set and learned that the city had exploded in what would become the nation's largest and deadliest civil disturbance since the Civil War. They were calling it a riot, and as the day wore on, what I saw on TV and heard from friends scared me to death.

Areas of the city that I knew, including that 12th Street neighborhood where, just one year earlier, my new teammates had taken me to a club on my first night in Detroit, were being ravaged by huge crowds who were looting businesses and setting them on fire. The early targets of people's rage may have been White-owned retail and grocery stores, but it soon didn't matter, and Black-owned places were hit as well. If there was stuff to grab and buildings to burn, the mob was on it. From my experience, the images on TV of large crowds looting and setting fires were hard to fathom. To see people who apparently didn't care, didn't seem to give a damn about each other or their own neighborhoods, was shocking and frightening.

It had all started early Sunday morning when Detroit police arrived on 12th Street to raid an unlicensed after-hours drinking club, what was known in those days as a "blind pig." There the mostly White police squad found a mostly Black group of 82 people celebrating the return of two local GIs from the Vietnam War. When the police made the fateful decision to arrest all 82, a large crowd of protestors gathered, and soon all hell broke loose.

That afternoon, when the Tigers' game was over at the stadium downtown, fans were told what was happening and to avoid certain areas of the city. Tigers' left fielder Willie Horton, who had grown up not far from 12th Street, went to the riot scene and tried in vain to calm the crowd.

On Monday and in the days that followed, the violence only widened and escalated, despite strict curfews and a large police effort. Gunfire was erupting in many places, and a running death toll began rising. I was asked if I would join some Black city leaders in going to the affected areas and asking for calm, but when I was told it could be dangerous, and knowing that even a local hero like Horton had been ineffective, I declined the request. By Tuesday, 4,700 U.S. Army paratroopers and 8,000 National Guardsmen were being deployed in the city, and in news footage of suspected snipers exchanging gunfire with troopers and of massive fires destroying whole commercial blocks, Detroit looked for all the world like a city at war.

Our own neighborhood remained safe and unaffected, but we could hear the tanks rumbling on their way to and from the Armory on 8 Mile Road. By the end of the week, the violence had finally been quelled and the troops withdrawn, but by then 43 were dead, more than 1,100 injured, over 7,200 arrested, and more than 2,000 buildings destroyed.

The negative effects of all this on the city of Detroit's future would be both significant and lasting.

6

PERENNIAL ALL-STAR

THE 1967–68 SEASON marked the beginning of the upstart American Basketball Association. All of us in the NBA were aware of this new league's potential for changing the landscape of professional basketball and what it could mean for our bank accounts. But not many of us were ready to test its uncharted waters. Still, the ABA was not exactly hurting for able players.

For example, the ABA's Pittsburgh Pipers had signed Connie Hawkins, a brilliant 6'8" forward, who as a freshman at Iowa had his name somehow mentioned in a point-shaving scandal. Never arrested or charged, he was nonetheless expelled and in effect banned from the NBA. For four years he had toured with the Harlem Globetrotters, and now he would have his shot with this new pro league. All he did in his first year was win the scoring title and be named MVP while leading his team to the ABA championship. Of course, all of the new league's teams were also eying the NBA's rookie crop, and in that summer of '67, the Pistons had not yet signed their number one pick, the country's top-rated college player, Jimmy Walker of Providence.

General manager Ed Coil asked me to come in and negotiate a new contract, so the team could concentrate on signing Walker. I was more than happy to. With the leverage of my Rookie of the Year honor, I quickly signed a two-year pact for $75,000 ($35,000 the first year and $40,000 the second), with a provision to renegotiate the second if I had another good year.

Yes, leading the Pistons in scoring and being the NBA's top rookie had facilitated a good contract, but starting my second season I knew they would also make me a marked man. Exactly how that would play out I was about to learn.

The first thing I noticed on the floor was that I was getting a lot more double teams. Defenders were leaving my teammates much more often to put another body in my way and make life more difficult for me. It didn't stop me from heading for the rim at every opportunity, but now I had to be a little more clever and creative in making my moves. And it also offered more chances for me to dish to my teammates and set them up to score. So my assists went from 4.1 per game as a rookie to 6.4 that second year. And from then on, for the rest of my career, I was always one of the top assist men in the league.

Still, as my team's scoring leader it was my job to put up points, so there was nothing that was going to stop me from driving the lane. And that's where I noticed another difference in the way opponents were dealing with me. Teams were getting much more physical with this skinny young guy on his way to the basket.

I never hesitated to go inside against the big guys who ruled that part of the floor, and they never hesitated to give me some physical abuse. On at least four or five occasions that year I had to leave the floor and head into the locker room where the trainer would need to stitch me up. I knew the big guys weren't trying to cut or hurt me, but when they'd whack you across the head or the face, sometimes it happened. Once in a while Aaris would say, "I saw you bleeding out there." And I would tell her, "Don't worry. They just take me in and stitch me back together. No Novocain or painkiller, they just sew me up, and I'm back on the floor ready to play."

Despite the extra attention, I was still getting my points, but it wasn't until we were well into the season that I actually realized I was among the league's leading scorers. Along with the game's superstars—Chamberlain, West, Oscar, and Elgin Baylor—I was right up there with them, averaging between 25 and 30 points. I had never even dreamed of being in such high-scoring company. But then halfway through the season, DeBusschere and I were named to the East Squad for the All-Star game.

At New York's Madison Square Garden I was thrilled to find myself on the floor with Chamberlain, Russell, Oscar and the East team playing against Jerry, Elgin and the NBA West. I played 20 minutes and scored nine points as we beat them 144–124, and back in those days the game actually meant something. Each of us on the East squad got $7,500 for winning, exactly half of my entire first year salary. But then the experience of playing on the same floor with all those icons was, as the saying goes, priceless.

As the season wound down, several of us were still in the scoring race. Playing against Oscar and West was always, of course, the ultimate challenge, but now there was an extra edge to it. They both could do everything. Jerry was probably a better outside shooter than Oscar, but Oscar had the size and the ability to get wherever he wanted to go, and he could just overpower you. With Jerry it was his quickness, his ability to get to the basket. He drove to the rim better than Oscar, and he was a very good defensive player.

With Jerry, I had learned to pick him up a little farther out on the court because of his speed and his jumping ability. His hops were as good as mine, and I could really jump. I wasn't going to block his shot, so I had to pick him up early to make him dribble more and try to direct him away from where he wanted to go. And back then, with the refs being a little more lenient, and if you were smart enough, you could be a little more physical. Whether with your hands or your forearm, you could contact the player in a way that you could basically feel where he wanted to go, and you could kind of re-direct him.

When I had the ball? Well, I was a little quicker and used screens to get open. Instead of Jerry, I'd try to get a bigger guy on me, and then I could isolate him and get to the hoop or pull up for a jump shot. That made things much easier.

As we finished the season, the race for most points scored was very close. But I ended up with 2,142, edging out Elgin's 2,002 and Wilt's 1,992. As for points per game, Oscar won the honor with 29.2. With 27.1, I hung on for second, again ahead of Elgin and Wilt. But even today I look at those numbers, think back to when I was 14 and watched that playground game between those two, and I simply shake my head.

The Pistons won 10 more games than the year before, made the playoffs, and extended the eventual league champion Boston Celtics to six games before bowing out. I averaged 28.2 a game in the playoffs, and when the All-NBA teams were named at season's end, I was listed on the first team along with Oscar, Wilt, Elgin, and Jerry Lucas. The fact that I had beaten out the perennial favorite Jerry West seemed to me incredible. But then I had come into my own in my second year. I really knew the pro game now, and my level of confidence was sky high. I didn't think anybody was going to stop me. They might slow me down, but they would not stop me.

So those first two years in the NBA could surely be described as a remarkable success—Rookie of the Year, league's leading scorer, NBA All-Star, and first team All-NBA—and I parlayed all of it into a renegotiated contract for my up-coming third season, moving from $40,000 to $75,000.

Nonetheless, after making our usual two-week visit home to D.C. to spend time with my parents, family, and friends, I was back at that NBD branch in our neighborhood for the summer and working again as a teller. Over the next several summers I would move up from head teller—in charge of all the tellers at that branch—to customer relations manager to assistant branch manager and then on to the overseas investment department downtown. It was good, solid training for me, and I'd eventually make great use of it. I'm sure some of my friends, who were spending much of their summers on the links, thought I was daft or foolish, but at one point this is what I told a writer for the *Washington Post*:

"The mistake most of us make is that we think we're going to play forever. Very few guys, I think, prepare for a second career. The lifestyle we lead, the position that the public puts us in as a successful athlete, makes us think we're invincible."

I had already learned that a dominant sports figure was likely to be placed on a pedestal. People want to get to know you, hang around you, do all kinds of things for you. And in some cases people will try to take advantage of you. They'll tell you how to invest your money. Or maybe they'll want to borrow money from you. They figure that you, as an athlete, are probably not that sharp. So you'll need to let somebody else manage your money for you. And a lot of guys I knew in the league got taken that way.

Frankly, a lot of athletes, with all kinds of money coming in at a young age, are not ready to deal with that. Today, some young guys are raking in so much that they can make a mistake or two and recover. But back then, while most of us were probably getting paid much more than our counterparts at that point in our lives, those other guys were in careers that could last 40 years. The average lifespan for athletes? Football, based on your position, maybe three to five years. Basketball was longer, maybe seven or eight. So you're making good money at a young age, and you assume that you're going to keep making this money for an extended period of time, but sports are so competitive. You've always got waves of young college guys coming after your job every year.

At the same time, you've got all these people saying you are God's gift to the game. You are sensational at this and that, and it's so easy to believe and accept it. Fortunately, I came from a well-rounded background. My parents never let me get a big head. Yes, I was a hell of a high school and college player, but my parents—neither of them with a high school education—always made it very clear that you've been blessed by God with this ability, but don't let it go to your head. They were pleased and proud of all the success I was having at every level, but they always said, "You've always got to treat people with respect and with dignity. It doesn't matter how good you are, or what they say about you. It doesn't matter how much money you make. People are people."

And their words never left me.

• • •

The violent turmoil of the 1960s seemed to boil over and scald all of us in 1968. With the murders of Martin Luther King and Bobby Kennedy, we lost two remarkable leaders we simply could not replace. It was a terrible setback for our country, which now seemed even more racially divided.

The sports world was one of the few bright and hopeful areas of our national life. Sports was an equalizer. It didn't matter whether your teammate was White or Black. And it didn't seem to matter to the fans whether the team was predominantly White or Black. Can you play and are you competitive? Those were the only important questions. But outside our sports arenas there were more riots, more murders, more distrust and unrest. And Vietnam, of course, was part of it as well.

I was thanking my lucky stars that I had not signed up again for ROTC in my junior year at Syracuse. I would have received some much-needed pay, but I would have been headed for service in the Army as well. Now with a wife and two children, my name was far down the draft lists.

As the Pistons started the '68–69 season, the big news was the trade of our All-Star forward Dave DeBusschere to the New York

Knicks. As with many trades, it came as another shocking notice that sports was also a business, and often heartless at that. In my rookie year, my roommate and good friend Ray Scott had been traded to the L.A. Lakers. The deal was supposed to be for another forward, Rudy LaRusso, but LaRusso didn't want to leave star-studded Los Angeles for lowly Detroit. He actually refused to come to the Pistons and held out so long that we finally had to accept a draft choice instead. Years later, Eddie Miles, again my roommate and my best friend on the team, was traded to the Baltimore Bullets. Eddie had just starred for us in a Sunday afternoon TV game, and in the locker room afterward he and the rest of us found out he'd been traded. I was stunned and devastated, because over the years he and I and our families had grown so close.

The Pistons made a lot of bad deals during my time with the club, but the DeBusschere trade may have been the worst. In exchange we got a back-up guard, Howard Komives, and Walt Bellamy, a center whose career was going decidedly sideways. But in New York the trade for DeBusschere became legendary. Along with Bill Bradley, Willis Reed, and guards Walt Frazier and Earl Monroe, he would lead them to two NBA championships.

Trades were generally a reminder that at any given moment we might become simply a commodity in the eyes of management. It was about this time that the stellar centerfielder Curt Flood was traded by the St. Louis Cardinals to the Philadelphia Phillies. Like Rudy LaRusso in the Ray Scott trade, Curt refused to accept the deal. But unlike the Pistons and Lakers, the Phillies and Cardinals refused to accommodate the player's wishes. Oh, and unlike LaRusso, Curt Flood was Black.

Famously, Curt took a stand, telling Baseball Commissioner Bowie Kuhn, "After 12 years in the major leagues, I do not feel I am a piece of property to be bought and sold irrespective of my wishes." Curt's career was effectively over, but he sued Major League Baseball over what was known as the reserve clause, a provision in every pro sports contract that kept players tied for life to the team they originally signed with. Naturally, we would all follow the progress of that suit all the way to the U.S. Supreme Court, where it would eventually lose in 1972. But the issue would be re-litigated three years later and the reserve clause would be gone for good, ushering in the era of free agency that has completely changed the face of professional sports.

Curt Flood was just one of many Black athletes who took stands in those days on important public issues and voiced their opinions in outspoken ways. It had started in a way at the 1968 Olympics, with sprinters Tommie Smith and John Carlos and their Black Power salute. Some of the guys I most admired were Jim Brown, Bill Russell, Kareem Abdul-Jabar, and Arthur Ashe, but the most famous and outspoken of them all was, of course, Cassius Clay, later known as Muhammad Ali.

As I've already recounted, when I first met Ali, his name was still Clay. It was back in 1964, when I was junior at Syracuse. We renewed our acquaintance years about this time in the late '60s in Pennsylvania's Pocono Mountains. By now of course, he was Ali, and he had a camp where he trained in the Poconos. And at that point I had a basketball camp nearby for youngsters 12 to 17. Occasionally we'd get together and got to know each other enough to say we were friends. In that setting he was a fun guy, very animated, and just loved people. He'd engage in a conversation with anybody, never looked at his stardom or fame as something that made him better than anybody else. That's how he lived his life. And much later, when Detroit put on a big day for me, Muhammad came to the city and was there for me.

As for the camp, I had gone into the deal with a partner named Howie Landa, who had been a small college player and coach and involved with other camps. We bought a hundred acres of land in the Poconos, and the camp became very popular and successful. We had eight or nine players over the years from our camp that ended up in the NBA.

In the beginning it was a place where I could go in the summertime and hone my game. But once I got exposed to it and saw how involved you could get with those young kids and the kind of impact it had on them, it became really important to me. We taught them not only basketball skills but life skills, and so I'd end up staying in the camp anywhere from four to six weeks without leaving. We got kids from all over but especially from cities like D.C. and Detroit, and places in New York and New Jersey. We probably had more White kids than Black kids. But for those Black kids from the different urban areas it was often the first time they'd been around White kids. Now they're living together in a cabin and bunking together. So it was a valuable learning experience for all of them. Many of them would come back and be counselors and stay in touch, and I've made lifelong friendships from those years up there in the Poconos.

• • •

Without DeBusschere that '68–69 season was a lost cause. We won only 32 games, but I had another good year. My scoring was off a bit, mostly because of some nagging injuries, but I still averaged 23.4 and my assists topped seven a game. In any case, I was about to engage in the most interesting and consequential contract negotiation of my career.

The ABA, with a full year under its belt, was going after players more aggressively and with some surprising success. Rick Barry, who was a scoring machine and truly one of the game's most gifted offensive players, was the first big star to leave the NBA and jump to the ABA. He moved from the San Francisco Warriors to the Oakland Oaks, which later became the Washington Capitols and then the Virginia Squires, and a lot of that had to do with his father-in-law Bruce Hale, who was the Oakland Oaks coach. And other good players, smelling the money being offered by ABA clubs, followed his lead. The ABA also had no rule restricting college underclassmen from entering the league, so while the NBA stuck to its policy of only accepting players after four years in school or once their class had graduated, the ABA had started to target and capture some of the talented younger college players—George McGinnis, Julius Erving, and George Gervin come to mind.

Was I watching all this with interests? You bet. So when I was approached by the ABA team in Washington D.C., I was all ears. Washington was my hometown and, thus, a perfect place for me to explore options. I could certainly try to use an offer from the Capitols to negotiate a better contract with the Pistons. About to enter my fourth year in the league, I was really engaged with and happy in Detroit. I didn't want to go anywhere else, but when the prospect of an offer from Washington appeared, I knew the leverage it might give me meant I'd try to use it to get a better deal from the Pistons.

Now the ABA surely did not yet have the glittering appeal of the NBA. Most still thought of it as a start-up league. Of the NBA's major stars—Russell, Wilt, Baylor, Oscar, Jerry West—none of them were headed to the ABA. So if you wanted to compete against the world's best players you needed to stay in the NBA.

Nonetheless, there were some deep pockets in the ABA, and there were many quiet conversations among NBA players about options and possibilities. We knew that some of the young guys coming right out of college were getting ABA teams to give them much more than their NBA market value.

I said little to my teammates about Washington's approach to me, but when the offer came in at $400,000 for three years, I knew I'd play things pretty close to the vest and let the Pistons think I was likely to go. I told Ed Coil that $400,000 was just too tempting to walk away from and that he'd need to match or come close to it in order for me to stay. In my heart I knew I didn't want to go anywhere. Detroit had become home for me at that point, and those first three seasons had been so good for me that I was not really tempted to leave. When Ed finally came back to say they'd give me $325,000 for next three years, I said we had a deal.

When I went back to the Washington owner, who was a D.C. guy, I told him that I'd heard he was thinking of moving his franchise to Virginia. When he didn't deny it, I said I was staying in Detroit.

So suddenly I was feeling much more financially secure, but that didn't mean much of a lifestyle change. I had learned to live on something less than what I had previously been making, always keeping clearly in mind that I would not be able to play forever. So rather than sliding into a more elaborate lifestyle, it was time to save some money.

Now I was in six figures per year, and we didn't need that much to live on, even with two kids. I easily saved half of my yearly income.

But they say everything's relative, and that was more evident than ever in the summer before our '70–71 season. With the first pick in the draft the Pistons chose St. Bonaventure's Bob Lanier, a big, bruising 6'11" center with a deft shooting touch. And with the ABA causing even more financial disruption, Detroit signed him for $1.5 million. That happened to be exactly 100 times greater than the $15,000 contract I had signed as a rookie just five years earlier.

Was I jealous? Resentful? No, instead I felt encouraged to think that if I continued to progress in my own career, I too might make that kind of money. And when I met the young guy, I liked him so much I couldn't be anything but happy for him. I know back then a lot of people thought we wouldn't get along. I was the star of the team and had just been named captain, and here was this mere rookie making so much money. But the bottom line for me was that this was a player who was definitely going to make us better. In fact, I had never seen a big-bodied center with that kind of shooting touch—an unstoppable sky hook and a deadly mid-range jumper—and tremendous rebounding skills. And then the Pistons put us together as roommates, and I really got to know the guy.

The problem for Bob at the start of our season was that he was playing hurt. In the NCAA tournament back in the spring, he had ripped a knee ligament in a collision with Villanova's Chris Ford. So after surgery he had spent the summer rehabbing a major injury and came into training camp with a still-less-than healthy knee. What I quickly learned about Bob was that he was a very sensitive, prideful guy. And at that point he simply couldn't play up to his own standards.

He had taken all that money but couldn't perform the way he wanted. Being inactive for so long his weight had blown up to somewhere between 290 and 300 pounds, and he still couldn't he couldn't jump off that leg properly. So it was really tough for him during the first half season or so.

In any case, we hit it off right away. I took him under my wing and told him a whole bunch of stuff, not just about basketball but how to handle himself in various situations. I went over everything about the city, where to go, what to expect. And I appreciated what he was going through because of the injury. For quite a while he was only playing 24 minutes a game and doing it basically on one good leg, so he averaged about 15 points a game his rookie season. Then in his second year, when he was healthy, he really blossomed into the 20 and 10 guy he was for his whole 14-year NBA Hall of Fame career.

In the process, Bob and I became exceedingly close, and we still are. Whenever we get together, the memories start flying. Some of them involve Bob's dad who moved from Buffalo to be with him in Detroit. Now his dad was a player, an older guy, shorter, maybe not even six feet, but he sure loved his son and loved being in the mix. So he'd hang out with us, go to all the games, go to the clubs we were going to, all of that. Bob was becoming a star, and his dad enjoyed everything that came with it.

Of course, I introduced Bob to my friends in Detroit, and there were a lot of them by this time. I was close to most of my teammates, and now that I was captain they were even more likely to come to me for advice and counsel about family problems and finances. I took my leadership role seriously as captain and considered it an honor that the team, and especially my teammates, had that kind of respect for me.

I also had friends in the business world, at the banks and the car companies, and developed close friendships with guys on the other sports teams in town, particularly Willie Horton and Earl Wilson on the Tigers and Mel Farr, Lem Barney, and Charlie Sanders with the Lions. We'd get together after games and go to each other's homes, our families became very close, and all of them turned into important, life-long relationships.

And always there were the Motown folks I'd gotten to know. The ones I was closest to were my old D.C. neighborhood pal Marvin Gaye and the Four Tops. Duke Fakir, Levi Stubbs, Renaldo "Obie" Benson, and Lawrence Payton had formed their group way back in high school, and in addition to becoming superstar entertainers they were all avid card players. When I introduced them to Lanier, I found out that Bob loved to gamble. And soon we'd be getting together on a regular basis for a friendly game of poker. I didn't play cards—I'd come along just to observe the action, listen to music, and get something to eat—but Bob and the Tops got along famously.

There often seems to be an affinity between athletes—pro athletes especially—and entertainers, and I think it's because in the end they're all performers. Whether you're a dancer or a singer, or an athlete, you are performing for the public. The difference is as athletes we're competing against each other, whereas, entertainers, strictly speaking, are not. In an arena, a stadium, a theater or a club, we are both there live performing for an audience. We athletes do it in competition against each other. And I supposed in a sense you might say entertainers compete against themselves, to see if they can match or better their best performances. But ultimately for both of us it's all about performing for an audience, and both jobs can be difficult and pressurized and constantly subject to instant feedback and criticism.

I'm not sure a lot of people understand this. They probably don't even think about it, but an athlete's every move on the court is being immediately evaluated by thousands of people, and many of them will let you know in real time, and in no uncertain terms, what they think. And then after the game the media, the commentators and sports writers, will also tell you how you did. That pressure of instant evaluation is all part of the game. It's part of the deal.

But the worst thing you can do as an athlete, or perhaps as anybody who's performing in front of the public, is to start reading too much into your press clippings. So many guys after a game are looking at the stat sheets and wondering what's going to be said about them. What's going to be written. And when some guys get criticized, they take it personally and can't deal with it.

That's one of the things that I never did. I never took it personally. As a young man coming into the league, I may have been a little more mature because of my background. So I always looked at the sportswriters, announcers, and commentators as a part of the game. If they had something negative to say I would obviously think about it and maybe not like it much, but I never took it personally or kept chewing it over and over.

But there were players who would read or watch those reports the next day and get very upset. And that's probably one of the worst things you can do. You can't control what others say or think, and you're only putting additional pressure on yourself. So now you've got more things, maybe too many things, you've got to think about. I mean as a basketball player and as an athlete in general, when you've got too much on your mind, when you've got too many thoughts swirling around in your head, you start reacting to them and don't do what's natural. You start trying to do things that are unnatural, and your performance is likely to suffer when you play that way.

That's certainly the way it was for me, and many others I've had conversations with about what can affect performance have said the same. But like many things in life, keeping yourself focused by living with some measure of self-control is often more easily said than done.

7

ANOTHER DAMAGED EYE

AS WE EMBARKED ON THE '71–72 SEASON, our Pistons club had lots of reasons to feel optimistic. The previous season we had finished eight games above .500 (up from a woeful 20 games under the year before). As captain, I had been among the league's scoring leaders, averaging 27 per game, and I had developed some real chemistry with my backcourt mate Jimmy Walker. My roommate and pal Lanier had continued to build up the left knee that had given him so much trouble his first year, and he, and all of us, were looking for great things from big Bob. And then there was our strong, athletic rookie forward, Curtis Rowe, from the three-time national champion UCLA Bruins.

Yes, our training camp was, for the first time since I'd arrived in Detroit, filled with optimism, and it didn't hurt that we had a bunch of guys who genuinely liked each other. The importance of camaraderie on an NBA team should never be underestimated.

On October 5, about a week before the season opener, we traveled to New York's Madison Square Garden, always one of my favorite places to play, for an exhibition game against the Los Angeles Lakers in the first game of a double-header.

In the third quarter, we were close on the Lakers' heels, and as usual I was playing full-bore even though the game meant nothing. Coach Butch van Breda Kolff would have been happy to let me sit, so he could get a longer look at some of the younger guys trying to make the squad. But unlike many of the vets who preferred to take it easy in the preseason, my standard routine was to play these exhibition games to the hilt, thinking it would only help to hone my competitive edge.

So with a quick surge I came off a pick and raced past a former Piston teammate of mine, Happy Hairston, and then it happened in an instant. Happy stuck out a hand trying to slow me down, and his index finger caught me square in my right eye, my one good eye. It was strictly an accident, but I was on the floor, covering my face with my hands and cringing in pain.

The trainer got me off the floor to the bench and gave me an ice pack to hold on the eye. That helped reduce the pain, but my vision remained blurred, so I wondered, naturally, if this might be serious. I was still wondering, and frankly worrying, the next morning on our flight back to Detroit. So I went straight to Henry Ford Hospital, only minutes away from Cobo, to have the eye examined by their ophthalmologists. Their diagnosis was that the eyeball had been scratched, something that would likely heal within a week or so, with the blurring clearing up over time as well.

I was reassured, and a week later back at the Garden in New York I was in the starting lineup as we opened the season against the Knicks. Maybe I wasn't yet at 100 percent, but I kept that to myself. Yes, most of my shots were from close in, but I scored 24 points, and we won 91–84.

Two days later back in Detroit I'm driving down to practice at Cobo with Jimmy Walker in the car. We're on the freeway, and all of a sudden I can't see out of that right eye. Now, of course, I had very little vision in my left eye, and so I told him, "I've got to stop. I can't see." I managed to pull onto the shoulder, but it was so sudden. One minute I could see, and the next minute I was blind. I didn't feel pain or anything. I just couldn't see. And so I told Jimmy, "You've got to drive."

I didn't know what to think except that it must be somehow connected to that eye injury. When we got to Cobo, Jimmy had to lead me inside. At practice we told van Breda Kolff and the trainer what had happened, and they decided this time to take me straight to the University of Michigan Hospital in Ann Arbor. They had to call Aaris and let her and my family know what had happened. So I'm sure that there was panic with them, but I wasn't aware of it. My focus was on getting to the hospital and finding out what the problem was.

A team of doctors met with us at the hospital and examined the eye. The lead surgeon was Dr. Morton Cox Jr., an associate professor in the University's School of Ophthalmology. He shined a light in my ailing eye, and I couldn't even see the light. It was a grade 1 detached retina, Dr. Cox said finally, and he went on to explain that I had suffered a partial tear of the retina from its supportive tissue. It needed to be treated quickly before it tore away completely, resulting in a permanent loss of vision. They would admit me immediately to the hospital and would need to operate first thing in the morning.

Through all of this, as you might expect, I was deeply concerned and frankly scared. The only reassuring thing I heard was the doctor saying, "Yes, we can reattach the retina." But he would not yet give me a prognosis, so there was no word about what my sight might amount to after the operation.

The docs told me they would call and talk to my family and to the Pistons, but they'd be careful about what they said. They knew I was the team's top player and that the press would be all over this injury. Later I'd learn that enough information would reach the media for them to report that the injury could jeopardize my career.

Padded patches were placed over both of my eyes, and I spent the night in the hospital, unable to see a thing, alone with my thoughts, worries, and fears, and saying more than a few prayers. I wondered if I'd ever see my wife's face again, if I'd manage to see my daughters grow up, and whether I'd ever play basketball again.

In the morning they prepped me for surgery. The Pistons had done some research and told me that Dr. Cox was one of the premier surgeons for the kind of procedure he was about to perform. So I tried to have positive thoughts until they used anesthesia and put me out. Then Dr. Cox and his team operated for about 90 minutes and reattached the retina.

After I came out of it, my eyes were firmly bandaged, so I didn't know what to think. But then I had a good talk with Dr. Cox. With great bedside manner he told me the operation went very well. He said, "We reattached the retina with silicone thread, and it's going to be stronger than it was before." I'm sure he didn't want to leave me with lots of negative thoughts and so was very reassuring, but in fact he did seem to be genuinely pleased with how the surgery had gone. He said that, of course, we couldn't know for sure, but he was hoping for a full recovery.

They would know more when they removed the bandages for the first time, but that wouldn't happen for another three days. They did not want that eye moving at all right now, and I did have a lot of swelling. The nurses used ice to bring the swelling down, and about all I could do was sit in my room and listen to hospital sounds. I'd hear when the nurses came in, and occasionally they'd tune the TV into news and sports.

And then I learned that my medical crisis had become a local news event, and there were real concerns in Metro Detroit about whether one of the NBA's top 10 players would ever play the game again.

Finally, they took the bandages off and took a look at the eye. They had warned me they would need to shine a light in the eye and that was going to be painful. But when that light hit my eye, the pain I felt was excruciating. Until that moment I had really felt nothing, no pain at all. But even though it was so painful, I could actually see the light, and that's when I knew I was going to be able to see again. I didn't know how well, but I could finally see the light, and that was the first step back.

Both eyes were again carefully patched, and it would be another few days before they would release me and I could go home. I'd been getting lots of calls, from Aaris, of course, Lanier and my other Detroit teammates and friends, but one afternoon, a nurse gave me the phone and on the other end I heard, "Hi, Dave. It's Jerry West."

To say I was pleasantly surprised would be such an understatement. Jerry said he just wanted me to know how so many people were thinking about me and pulling for my full recovery. He hoped I understood how much I meant to the league and how I was a guy that everybody respected for playing the game the right way. He said he always loved playing against me and was looking forward to doing it again. I thanked Jerry and told him how much his call meant to me. I was deeply grateful.

All the well-wishers left me thinking that even if this were the end of my playing days, I could tell myself that in my five seasons in the league I'd made my mark: First team All-NBA, Rookie of the Year, three All-Star games, and a scoring title. And then I'd think back to just a week ago, when so much more seemed possible and even likely.

Whenever the Pistons had a day off, Lanier would show up at the hospital, and we'd talk. Bob tried to be reassuring, but I knew it was an open question as to whether I would ever play basketball again in the dominant way I was used to. Not even Dr. Cox knew for sure. There were just so many potential issues with things like peripheral vision and depth perception.

Finally the day came for the hospital to release me. The whole team of physicians came in to see me, and Dr. Cox was again reassuring. But an older doctor, the team leader, then told me it was their carefully considered advice that even if I fully regained my sight, I should not play again. Their reasoning was simple: if I ever suffered another blow to the eye, I would probably never be able to see again. Playing, said the doc, would just not be worth the risk.

They also told me I would need to keep these pads on my eyes for the next couple of weeks at home, so that the eye didn't move at all and the healing process could continue. And even after the pads do come off, they said, "We don't want you looking at anything at home. You cannot read. Do not look at TV. Keep your shades down so that there's no light. Just stay in a dark place."

I did exactly what I'd been told and a week later went back to the hospital in Ann Arbor so they could check on the eye's progress. There was still some swelling, and when they shined the light in my eye, it was painful again. But they seemed satisfied with the way things looked and told me again it was going to take some time for the healing process to happen. Of course, I had been thinking a lot about the advice they had given me to not play again. I said nothing to the docs, but I knew for certain that if I could see, I was going to play.

Another week and another visit to Ann Arbor for another exam. This time, finally, they told me I could go home and take the pads off. But they emphasized again: no reading, no TV, no sitting under a lamp, and no bright lights at all, so no going outside. Basically, I couldn't go anywhere or do anything except sit in a chair in a dimly lit room. With the pads off I still couldn't see much of anything, so I was just sitting there all day at home with the usual troubling and frustrating thoughts. Am I ever going to be able to really see again? And if so, will I be able to see well enough to be able to play again?

Aaris and I spent a lot of time talking, and all my teammates and a lot of other friends came by to visit, and that was great. I realized again how many wonderful friends I had made in Detroit, and it was clear that all of them were concerned about me as a person, much more so than me as a player. I told them about the prognosis the docs had given me, that my sight would return and that I would need glasses or contacts. But I still told no one the story about my left eye and how little I could see with it.

Finally, one morning I woke up, opened my eyes, and I could see something. It was very blurry at first, but I could see with that repaired right eye. And so I began to move around the house a little.

Naturally it helped that I knew where everything was in the house. But little by little over the next week or so my vision in that eye gradually improved. The first time I left the house, it was just for a short walk outside, and there was a little trepidation. Light from a lamp in the house couldn't compare to the natural light we had outside that day. But there was no pain or discomfort, and seeing bright sunshine once again felt like a blessing.

It was another week or two before they told me I could go down to Cobo to watch my teammates practice. And another couple of weeks—after I got fitted with contacts and glasses—before I could practice with them. I also had prescription goggles made, designed to protect the eye, but the first time I tried them on I knew immediately that they restricted my peripheral vision so much I wouldn't wear them to play.

In any case, it was so great to be back on the floor again with my teammates, but we were all such close friends that in those first few practices the guys were clearly scared to get too close to me. It was like, "Don't touch him, don't touch him." After a while I managed to convince them I wasn't worried about the eye and neither should they, and then we were all going after each other again at something like full speed.

How was my eyesight? Well, I could tell pretty quickly that, yes, the peripheral vision in that right eye was not what it had been, and I seemed to have lost some depth perception as well. But the fact was I was rusty and kind of out of shape, and it would be some time before I could really make a judgment on the true state of my play. I just knew it felt so good to be out there competing. There was a huge weight off my shoulders, because I knew I could play again.

Maybe I'd have to be more of an assist man, at least as I continued to adjust to shooting the ball. I spent endless hours in the gym after practice and eventually began to see some improvement, though my outside shot was still lacking. Maybe I'd have to go to the basket even more and maybe pull up for more short jumpers. But because I felt I needed to focus even harder than I had before at the foul line, I was becoming a better free throw shooter. And I was also more motivated on defense, since I wanted to be as complete a player as possible.

My game was starting to come around, and I felt game ready. On the morning of December 28, Dr. Cox finally gave me the okay to play that night against the New York Knicks. "The healing is as complete as it's going to be," Dr. Cox told me, and he saw no reason why I couldn't play "a little bit" that evening.

While I'd been gone the Pistons had floundered. Coach van Breda Kolff had been fired and replaced by my old friend Earl Lloyd. Whether and how much I would play would be up to Earl, but then from the beginning he had always been in my corner. That night a rare sell-out crowd at Cobo celebrated my return with a standing ovation that made my stomach flip a bit in the pre-game intros.

Once again the Knicks had one hell of a team, with that great backcourt of Frazier and Monroe. But that night, going against those two, I ended up playing 40 minutes and scoring 21. After the game I sat in the locker room and told reporters, "The eye didn't bother me at all." To myself I thought, "Well, yeah, I can still do this!"

Over the 45 games still left in the season, my shooting percentage was down a bit, but my assists were up, and I was still able to average 22.6. The loss of the first two and a half months had cost me another All-Star appearance, but given the darkness that had descended as the season opened, I was deeply grateful for the chance to continue playing the game I loved so much.

8

THE TRADE

I'VE GOT GOOD NEWS AND BAD NEWS about the 1972–73 season, the year after I suffered the detached retina that had threatened my career. First, the good: I played all 82 games and put up numbers comparable to the years before the injury—22.4 points and 7.8 assists per game. I was once again an All-Star, and so was my good friend Bob Lanier, who had another great year, firmly establishing himself as one of the league's premier centers.

And the bad news? The Pistons once again struggled through a losing season (40 wins and 42 losses) and once again failed to make the playoffs. Seven games into the season, the team's management decided on another coaching change, firing my friend and longtime advocate Earl Lloyd and replacing him with my old roommate Ray Scott. At least under Ray's guidance we were one game over .500, and with five straight wins at season's end, there were enough signs of life that we could look ahead to the '73–74 season with some optimism.

In 1973, I signed a three-year contract worth $450,000, and it was a measure of the trust and good faith between Fred Zollner, Ed Coil, and myself that they agreed I would have the right to renegotiate that contract the following year, depending on my performance in the season ahead. I had also asked them to withhold a portion of my salary as a convenient way to take care of some improvements I had in mind for our family home. Both the right to renegotiate and the withholding deal were part of a side agreement, not written into the contract. Little did I know that this seemingly unremarkable arrangement would eventually become a major reason why I would end up leaving the Pistons for another NBA city. But now I'm getting ahead of my story.

A few years earlier, when we had learned our third child, Aleisha, was on the way, Aaris and I had decided we needed a new home with more space. Frankly, I had also become worried about the safety of my family in Detroit and about the quality of the city schools our girls would attend, and so I found a much larger home in the adjacent suburb of Southfield, near 12 Mile and Lahser roads, about four miles from the city of Detroit's border. It had been built a year or two earlier but had never been occupied, a beautiful home with five bedrooms and five baths, 4,200 square feet on three-quarters of an acre—more than enough room for a nice new pool that was the major reason for the withholding deal I had arranged with the Pistons' management. It was a home where our family could live in very comfortable fashion, but, more important to my own peace of mind, I could be much more assured that my wife and daughters would be safe and secure while I was away on the team's extended road trips.

While we were now living outside Detroit, the city continued to be at the center of my focus and activity. By now wherever I'd go in the city, I'd get what you might call All-Star treatment. I was always recognized and treated well, although this was not anything I expected or felt I simply deserved. I had been raised to never let myself get big-headed or feel so special that I couldn't relate to so-called average, everyday folks. And I made a point of relating well to everybody, from the customers I would serve at the bank during the summer, to the business people, city leaders, and politicians I was getting to know.

One of those political leaders who sought me out around this time was Coleman Young. I had first met him when he was a state senator, and now he was running for mayor of Detroit. I had no personal interest in politics, but I had always stayed on top of the news and always read everything I could get my hands on about the many tough issues facing the city. It was, after all, only a half-dozen years since the riot that had ripped Detroit apart.

I knew something about Coleman Young's background: a lieutenant with the famed Tuskegee Airmen during World War II, he had worked in the early Civil Rights Movement and in left-wing politics and became a hero in Detroit's Black community for standing up, in ways both staunch and colorful, to the House Un-American Activities Committee during the McCarthy era. I thought he had a real chance to become Detroit's first Black mayor, and I knew he wanted to get my endorsement for his candidacy. The only problem was that I had already committed my backing to another Black candidate, a former District Court Judge and my personal attorney at the time, Ed Bell.

Nonetheless, I said yes to a meeting with Coleman at our home in Southfield, along with a couple of our mutual union friends, Buddy Battle and Marc Stepp. We sat in our living room, and when I told them my endorsement had already gone to Ed Bell, Coleman looked at me and asked, "Are you sure about that?"

I said, "Yes, I'm sure. I've already made that commitment."

Coleman gave me another look and said, "Well, I'm glad you stuck to your word to Ed, because had you changed your mind, I don't think I could have ever trusted you."

I nodded, and then he smiled in that charming way of his, and said, "But when I beat him, then I want you to support me."

I said I would, and I did.

In the primary, Coleman beat Ed and several others as well, and in the general he won against the White former police chief John Nichols. Both the city and the country were in such turmoil, racial and otherwise, that I think Coleman Young turned out to be the right man at the right time in Detroit. In the Black community, which was rapidly becoming a strong majority in the city, he was seen as the kind of leader who would stand up and fight for those who had never even had a role in the game. Others worried about his outspoken ways and his profanity, but he was in fact a consummate politician who cared deeply about the under-served.

The changes he made in the public safety arena—police and fire—were long overdue. Those two departments were predominantly White when he came in and had been functioning as a kind of occupying force, which had been one of the major factors in the '67 riot. When he placed more African Americans in those crucial positions and especially when he reached out to the largely White business community and formed important alliances that helped to spur development in Detroit that served to benefit everyone, Black and White, you can see why he ended up running the city for 20 years.

That day he came to my house to ask for an endorsement he did not get, I had a sense of the enormous job he was asking to take on, and I knew it would never be the kind of task I'd be anxious to pursue.

Here I am (far left) in my freshman year at Syracuse University with some classmates, including Donnie Cronson (second from the right) and John Mackey (far right).

In action against the Davidson Wildcats and guard George Leight (20) in 1965.
(Malcolm Emmons/
USA TODAY Sports, Imagn)

Shooting over Archie Clark of the Philadelphia 76ers during a game in '68, early in my career with the Pistons.
(Focus on Sport/Getty Images)

Driving past Norm Van Lier of the Bulls during a 1974 NBA playoff game in Chicago.
(FHJ/AP Images)

*Here I am holding
the trophy after being
named MVP of the
NBA All-Star Game
in Philadelphia on
February 4, 1976.*

(AP Images)

*A game against
Wes Unseld and the
Washington Bullets
during my short stint
with the Celtics.*

(Photo by Focus on Sport/
Getty Images)

Me at the White House with President Regan in 1984. I was being honored as Minority Small Business Person of the Year.

Me with mayor Coleman Young and Muhammad Ali. This was in 1987, in celebration of "Dave Bing Day" as declared by Mayor Young. I was being honored for committing the necessary funds to reinstate all athletic programs in the Detroit Public School system after they were eliminated due to significant school budget restraints.

Forty-seven of the 50 Greatest Players in NBA History assembled in Cleveland during the halftime ceremony of the 1997 All-Star Game.

Me, Oscar Robertson (center), and Lenny Wilkens (right) chat during the 50 Greatest Players ceremony at halftime of the '97 All-Star Game.

(Mark Duncan/AP Images)

Celebrating my mayoral victory on Tuesday, May 5, 2009.
(Paul Sancya/AP Images)

A press conference announcing the demolition of Detroit's renowned Brewster Projects, which was home for many Motown greats, including Diana Ross, Mary Wilson of the Supremes, and Della Reese.

Mayor of Detroit: 2008–2013.

A 2010 meeting with President Obama to discuss federal financial support for Detroit during my time as mayor.

Congratulating BINGO mentee Orlando Evans, a member of the first Bing Youth Institute graduating class, in 2018.

My family (left to right, first row): my grandson Alexander; my daughter Bridgett; my wife, Yvette; me, holding my great-granddaughter Delilah; my daughter Aleisha; (second row, standing): my granddaughter Caris; my grandson Denzell; my daughter Cassaundra; and my grandson Kenneth.

• • •

A Pistons franchise record of 52 wins against 30 losses: that's what we accomplished in the '73–74 season, Ray Scott's first full year as a head coach. It was a personal triumph for Ray, who was the first Black coach to ever be named Coach of the Year in the NBA, or in any professional sport for that matter. Quite an honor, but our success was not, of course, an overnight thing.

Over the past year, Ray and the Pistons management had instigated a number of changes that helped make a difference. The first and most important came a year earlier, when the team traded a second-round draft pick to the Atlanta Hawks for a tough, versatile forward named Don Adams. Players called him "Smart," not only because his namesake was a Hollywood actor who gained fame in the popular TV show *Get Smart*, but more so because he had been an excellent student at Northwestern University and enjoyed a reputation of being very basketball-savvy, rarely making a mistake on the court. He was one of the NBA's top defensive players, a rugged rebounder, and could perform well at a number of different positions. For these reasons and more, Don had quickly become an important Piston and one of my best friends on the team.

Another addition making a difference was John Mengelt, a hard-nosed, high-energy guard, whose dive-on-the-floor and fly-into-the-seats style earned him the nickname "Crash" and made him popular with the Cobo crowd. And then there was George Trapp, a guy we called "Instant Heat," who always hit the floor ready to singe the nets.

In our highly competitive Midwest Division, we spent the season chasing the conference-champion Milwaukee Bucks and the Chicago

Bulls and, despite our franchise record 52 wins, ended up in third place. Making the playoffs for only the second time during my years with the Pistons, we took the Bulls to a deciding seventh game before ending the season on a sour note with a loss, 96–94, that was particularly hard to take.

Nonetheless, as we geared up for the 1974–75 season, I felt we were a team with a lot of upside and great chemistry. "It was really starting to come together," my pal Lanier would say later. "We all got along and had each other's backs. And then we win 52 games and we're starting to get a little more national exposure. Things were looking up."

Coach Ray Scott's words were even stronger: "We were poised for greatness."

And then in July of 1974 the Pistons founder and owner Fred Zollner sold the team. The buyer was a collection of a dozen businessmen, but the lead investor was a native Detroiter named William Davidson. The owner of Guardian Industries, one of the world's largest glass suppliers, Davidson, like Zollner before him, was an auto supplier magnate. About owning a professional sports team he knew little or nothing, so he would have to learn on the job, and ultimately, from my perspective, that would end up hurting us.

The trouble started not long after the sale went through, when general manager Ed Coil, who stayed on to help ease the transition, informed me that the new owners would not honor that side deal I had made with Fred Zollner to renegotiate my contract and for the team to withhold a relatively small portion of my salary. I had decided this was a good time to go ahead and put in that pool for Aaris and the girls, but when I asked for the amount that had been withheld—about $30,000—I was told that Mr. Davidson felt no obligation under the law to provide me with the money. It was, after all, strictly a side deal, almost a gentlemen's agreement, and not written into the team's contract with me. And it was the same with my deal with Zollner to renegotiate our contract.

Of course, I understood the legalities of it, even without counsel from my attorney Ed Bell, who had not really been involved in any of my previous contract negotiations. But the unfairness of the situation seemed crystal clear to me. First I was shocked by what I was hearing, and then I was angry.

The past season had been the best in Pistons history, and I had played well, with 18.8 points, 6.9 assists, and playing 39 minutes per game while missing only one contest all year. Surely I had earned the right to reopen the contract. As for the $30,000 withheld, that was my money, I told Coil, money that he knew very well I had already earned, money that was due to me under the explicit agreement I had come to with Mr. Zollner.

But that was just the point, said Coil, because William Davidson felt he was under no obligation to honor any arrangements or compensation agreed to by Zollner, who was now entirely out of the picture.

I didn't blame Coil, with whom I had always had a good relationship. I knew he was only the messenger. But given my position as captain and team leader and my status in the league as a perennial All-Star, I couldn't believe the new management would not see the fairness—and the obvious wisdom—of honoring the previous owner's arrangements with me. Yes, we were not talking about a great deal of money, certainly compared to the millions the new owners had just anted up for the team, but to me that was all the more reason why I should be given my due.

Frankly, I felt incensed about the whole mess and devalued by my new bosses, and I made my feelings clear to Coil. I told him, "If this is how these people are going to treat me, then we're going to have a problem."

But what to do about it?

My answer was a holdout during training camp that might give me some leverage. I talked with my teammates, and all of them were supportive and understood that I would do nothing that would ultimately harm our team and its chances for a good season. And that was especially so with my roommate at the time, Don Adams. I had been rooming with Lanier for two years, but when we acquired Adams, I roomed with him as a way to help him feel comfortable and fit in. And not only did that happen, but the two of us had become fast friends.

Now as training camp approached, I knew that Don was still without a contract. He was disgruntled with the Pistons' offer of $60,000 and was trying to get to $80,000. He felt that as a starter, a major role player, and a guy who was being touted for the league's all-defensive team, he was definitely underpaid. And so when I told him about my situation and that I was not going to come to training camp on time, he said, "Well I'm probably going to do the same thing." So now you've got two-fifths of the starting lineup that's not going to be in training camp, which was definitely going to be a problem for our new owners.

Again, we had a very close-knit team. They understood what was going on and they all sided with both of us. Don was a popular and solid teammate, and I was the captain and highly respected by all the guys. Looking at my situation, they said this is a guy who never poses a problem, comes to work every day, practices hard, just like he plays, he's one of the league's top players, and you're treating him like this?

Of course, Scott, our coach, got wind of what we were talking about and met with both Don and myself one-on-one, emphasizing to each of us that our first responsibility was to our team. And before training camp opened, he also called a team meeting at a posh restaurant across the street from Cobo Arena. Later he would say: "I told the entire team that day—but it was really intended for Dave and Don—that we had a collective obligation to focus primarily on what was best for the team first and what was best for themselves individually second."

Scott was caught in the middle. As coach he was part of management and needed to do their bidding, but he also needed to maintain a good working relationship with his players. He tried to stay away from the issues we had with ownership, and he did not get involved in any kind of ego trip. All he wanted as a coach was to get his players into training camp and get them ready to play.

September 19, was set as the first day of training camp. We had until midnight to report to a dormitory on the Eastern Michigan University campus in Ypsilanti, west of Detroit. Don and I said we weren't coming. Management said that if we failed to report, there'd be suspensions and fines. Midnight arrived, and we did not.

On the first day of camp, the Associated Press quoted Scott as saying: "Dave has a valid contract. He's very important, but not more important than the team."

Ed Coil spelled things out: In addition to being suspended, we'd each be fined $500 a day for the first 10 days, and if we still weren't back, the fines would get steeper. Oh, and if Don didn't come in the next day, he would be immediately traded. The possibility of a trade wouldn't come up with me for a while yet, but then I had an ace in the hole in that regard.

The pressure on Don was intense, and I understood when he told me that he would have to end his holdout after less than a day. But I felt I had more clout and leverage, and so I continued to stay away from training camp. Everyday I'd work out on my own, usually at Detroit's St. Cecilia's, a gym that for years had drawn the best players in the city for spirited pick-up games. After almost two weeks, word finally came from management that I needed to end my holdout and come back to the team, or they would trade me.

"Go ahead" was my quick response. I had a no-trade clause in my contract, and I could veto any deal they might try to make. But on October 7, our confrontation got splashed across TV and the newspapers. The headline in the *Detroit Free Press* was "BING: 'PAY ME, OR TRADE ME.'" The story quoted my attorney Ed Bell: "After failing to get any consideration from [the owners] on Bing's contract interests, Dave has determined that he is willing to waive the no-trade clause in his contract and accept a trade to another team."

Basically, I was calling their bluff, knowing they could not send me off to anyplace I didn't want to go. *The Free Press* piece, like other media reports, cited salary numbers that were inaccurate and made me sound rather greedy. After so many years of good will in Detroit, that was not something I appreciated.

And so we had come to a kind of stalemate, and I finally decided I needed to think like a business person. I was unhappy and still angry about what the owners had done, but they were showing no signs of a change of heart or direction, so what was my next move?

Was I going to sue them? Stay out the whole season? Neither made any sense. So I told myself, just suck it up, come back in, and play as hard as possible. We've got a good team, and we don't need to allow this to split us apart. I told the Associated Press I was returning for my teammates:

"They've all asked me to come back. We feel that with or without me we're a great team. But with me we're a better team. I respect my teammates as individuals and I respect being part of this team and that's why I'm back."

The holdout had cost me about $6,000 in fines, but I returned in time for all of the exhibition games. And then we got off to a pretty decent regular season start, winning seven of our first 11. In that stretch I showed no signs of rust or funk, averaging 22 a game. There were ups and downs as we moved on through the season, but by February 1, we were 10 games above .500 and feeling pretty good about ourselves.

And then the bottom dropped out, and we lost 10 of our next 11. There are usually many different factors contributing to a losing streak, but one constant is that enormous pressure builds on both players and coaches.

About half-way through that losing streak, we went into Milwaukee and got bombed by the Bucks, 130–109. Bob Lanier had family in Milwaukee, and afterward his dad, his aunt, and a couple of his female cousins came to the hotel and had some dinner with Bob, me, and Don Adams. Some Detroit reporters and, of course, Ray Scott were staying at the hotel and were also eating in the restaurant. And at one point, the coach sent word to our table that, "Hey, you can't have girls in here."

Bob told Ray, "But these are my cousins, and it's not the first time they've been with us." But Ray was upset, very pissed off. It had been one of those games in which nothing had gone right, and we had gotten crushed. So Ray says he's going to fine us if those girls stay with us there in the hotel restaurant. And it became an ugly thing. Bob is angry. I'm upset. But Ray is saying, "I don't like what I see. You guys didn't play well, and here you are having drinks and eating here in the hotel and having a great time with these girls."

I guess he felt the visual for the media of us enjoying ourselves didn't look good. But again we made it very clear: "Man, you know these girls. They're Bob's cousins, and this is not the first time you've seen them." But obviously he was still stewing about the game, and the whole thing had turned into a lot of bad feelings.

Back in Detroit a few days later, we're at practice at Cobo and, as we're getting ready in the locker room, Don's not there. So what the hell is going on? Where is Don? And then we hear that Don had been called to the front office. When we came out on the floor to practice, Ed Coil called us over and into the stands to say that Don had been cut.

Not traded. Cut.

All of us are looking at each other and thinking, *What the hell is this?!*

So we practiced, and then in the locker room, the media came up to me, confirmed that Adams had been cut, and asked what I thought. Naturally I was very upset. Next to Lanier, Don was my best friend on the Pistons. I knew Don's wife was eight months pregnant with their first child, and we as families were very close. So I'm worried about him, I'm worried about her. And when the media asked me what I thought of the move, I said, "It's the dumbest thing I've ever seen. Yeah, he's under contract, and they have the right to trade him. But to just cut him, and he's a starter on this team, and we get nothing for him? I've never seen anything so dumb."

I was so concerned about Don that I left Cobo and went straight to his home. And I'm trying to think of why they would do such a thing. They probably thought that this is a guy who's pissed off over his contract, and so they're not getting his best. I imagined that's how they rationalized it. But to cut a starter just didn't make any damn sense.

So I don't know where he is, and I get to his home, and he's not there. And now I don't really know what to say to his wife. She has not seen nor heard from him yet and clearly has no idea of what has just happened. We're sitting there talking, and I'm just trying to pass the time, just trying to play this by ear. Of course, there were no cell phones back then, and there was no way to find out where he might be. She asked where he could have gone, and I said we had to practice at Cobo, but I don't know where he went from there. This went on for an hour, and it was terrible, one of the most uncomfortable hours of my life. And then the news about Don being cut came on TV, and she's looking at me, and I have nothing to say. I couldn't say anything.

So finally Don came in and saw me there. We exchanged looks, and there was a connection between us because of the pain I saw in his eyes. He looked at his wife, and he knew that she knew. And he just left without saying a word. So I had to call my wife and let her know where I was, and what was going on.

Don finally came home later that evening, and needless to say he was devastated. I stayed at his home until he came back, and it was a sad scene. The big issue with him was that their first child was about to arrive, and all of a sudden here he is without a job. And his pride was hurt, because it's one thing to get traded—we all understand that's a business deal. It's quite another thing to be a starting player and get cut. For what reason? We just could not come to terms with it.

And then I got a call from Ray telling me not to say anything negative about the team or about this deal. I said, "Right, so you guys own my contract. You don't own me. I'm going to say what I see, and I think this move is worse than the dumbest thing I've ever seen." I told Ray that, yes, they had a right to get rid of Don, but they had hurt the team by cutting him instead of trading him and to get something of value in return. They got nothing for him, and that was just plain stupid.

The next day I talked to the Associated Press: "Here was a guy who was a starter, and now he's axed. How can a lesser ballplayer feel secure under these conditions? To cut him is a hell of a slap in the face. That's like saying he's not as good as anybody else on the team, and I don't believe that."

Back at the start of the season I had tried to keep my contract issues out of the public eye, but now, as captain, I felt obligated to speak out about what they had done to Don. And that's when my relationship really went south with both the coach and management. A lot of our fans were probably surprised and unhappy to see this new side of me. But our whole team felt the same way. We had a tight-knit group of teammates. We were good friends. Our families were close. And this thing they had done to Don and to our team, really, pulled everything apart for us. All of a sudden, as a team we looked at management, Ray included, and saw things altogether differently.

As a team leader I felt I had a duty to voice my opinion, and actually I was a little upset with Bob Lanier, because he and I were the stars on this team, and I spoke out and wanted him to do so as well. He didn't, and that bothered me. But it didn't change our friendship. I was hoping that he would offer his honest view, because I didn't want to be out there all by myself. But I simply felt it was the right thing to do.

Our losing ways continued after Milwaukee, and a few days later our coach really lost it. During a close loss to Kansas City, Ray got so angry over what he thought was a bad foul call on John Mengelt that he picked up a chair from the bench and tossed it across the floor. He was ejected, and that was kind of emblematic of how the rest of the season went.

From a team that had won a franchise record 52 games a year earlier, we slid back down to 40–42. My personal numbers were up slightly from our record year, but because I had held out at the start of the season and had been outspoken about the team's mismanagement, especially with what they had done to Don Adams, much of the media in town and some of the fans decided I must be the reason why the team seemed to be falling apart in the last several weeks of the season. But I knew I was giving it everything I had.

Lanier would say later, "I'd go over to Dave's house, and he would feel a little down because it seemed like everything and everybody was kind of piling on him. But that just made him even stronger and more determined. He knew he had done the right thing standing up for what he believed was right."

But I also knew that the heart had gone out of the whole team. I mean you played hard because as a professional that's what you're supposed to do. But our heart wasn't in it now. We rallied a bit in the final days and somehow made the playoffs in a best of three set against the Seattle SuperSonics. After splitting the first two, we lost in Seattle, 100–93, and the season was mercifully over. Ultimately, the whole experience had been so awful and disheartening that I finally decided I no longer wanted to play for the Pistons.

Word got back to me that management had concluded I was a locker room lawyer, a disruptive force on the team. I knew they were looking for a trade, but because of that no-trade clause in my contract, I had to approve whatever deal they wanted to make. So they came to me and said, "Where do you want to go?"

And I said, "You guys make a deal and come back to me, and I'll reject or approve," which they didn't like. So there were three teams they came back with: the Los Angeles Lakers, the Boston Celtics, and the Washington Bullets. I chose my old hometown, D.C.

I knew Ray Scott liked the Bullets' young guard, Kevin Porter. The Bullets had gone all the way to the NBA finals that year, before losing four straight to Golden State. With me at guard instead of Porter, I thought the Bullets might have a good shot at the title in the coming season. I figured that's how Washington might see it, and I was right. On August 28, 1975, the Pistons announced they had traded me to the Bullets in exchange for Porter.

But it's one thing to know in your mind that something is for the best, and quite another to feel that in your heart. When my old friend Lanier found out about the trade, he came over to my house, and the two of us just sat there crying. He was telling me that I needed to stay, that the two of us could still be the nucleus of a great team and that I needed to turn around and nix that trade. Today we still have that conversation, and Bob still tells me, "It pains me to this day."

Yes, I could have vetoed the trade. But it would have been a crazy environment for me to stay in Detroit. I just didn't want to be here after what they had done to me and what they had done to Don. That tore our team apart, and I never could have been effective if I had stayed.

With our once strong relationship now in taters, Ray Scott and I would not speak again for about five years. But there's an old saying: "Time heals all wounds," and that's how it would be with Ray and me. At the wedding of one of our friends, we ran into each other and let bygones be bygones.

As for Don Adams, he was picked up by the St. Louis Spirits in the ABA and finished the season there. They had Maurice Lucas and Bad News Barnes, so they were a pretty good team. He and I were in touch all the time, and since his wife and their new baby stayed in Detroit, Aaris and I would look in on them regularly. Don would eventually end up with the NBA's Buffalo Braves, but he kept his home in Detroit, and we remain good friends to this day.

9

THE YEARS IN EXILE

WITH MY TRADE TO WASHINGTON not finalized until late August, the question was: How should I handle this with the family? With all the kids about to start school in Southfield and no time to find a suitable home in D.C., I wasn't prepared to move the whole family. So the decision was that Aaris and the girls would stay here, and I'd get an apartment there. Of course, my parents wanted me to come back and stay with them, but at 32 years old, I wasn't about do that.

I did find a very nice apartment relatively close to where I had grown up, but on the Maryland side. And now I had things to do that I had not ever had to think about before—like furnishing this apartment. Even though I had family and friends in the area, I was really all by myself for the first time. So it was an adjustment.

And then there was the other major adjustment—to my new team, the Bullets. Fortunately, I'd played in All-Star games with Wes Unseld and Elvin "Big E" Hayes, and I knew all the other players. They made it easy, welcomed and accepted me right away. General manager Bob Ferry and coach K.C. Jones knew they were getting a better player, and frankly, both seemed happy and excited about the deal. That's not a knock on Kevin Porter, but I was definitely a better player. And this was a team that had just won 60 games and competed for the NBA championship. So I was pleased with the prospect of finally playing on a team with a real chance to go all the way.

But at the same time, I knew I had to adjust, because I was coming to a club with two bona fide All-Stars in Wes and Elvin and potentially a third with shooting guard Phil Chenier. So as an All-Star myself, I knew I should not come in and try to dominate. I needed to figure out how my skills and personality fit into this talented squad, and I tried to make it as easy as possible for them. They made it pretty easy for me as well, and it all went quite smoothly.

Actually, being away from Aaris and the girls was the hard part. It was a tough time, with lots of phone calls back home. With the kids in school it was difficult for them to come to me, and with a busy 82-game schedule, I couldn't get back to them very often. So it was a tough adjustment. And the only good thing was that I had family in D.C., along with all the people I grew up with there, and we reconnected.

Once the season got underway, I quickly realized that Phil Chenier was one of the good guys, and he became like a little brother to me. He was a very good player, a great shooter, and a strong defender. We were about the same size, but since he was a shooting guard, I really became the team's point guard. I averaged 6.0 assists, but only 16.2 points; I didn't have to score a lot with Chenier and Big E filling it up.

I made the starting All-Star team that year, but honestly, in my own mind I wasn't sure I should have started. In several previous years I had been better, but I had the rep and the name, and I think the fans and everybody else knew that I had changed my game to fit with what Washington needed and that I was no longer going to be a prolific scorer. I was happy to have once again made the All-Star team, but it felt like I had something to prove once the game started, because I had misgivings as to whether I should have been there as a starter. That was probably a little extra motivation, and playing with the East team, we beat the West 123–109. I scored 16 and was named the Most Valuable Player.

Unfortunately, that was a season highlight, because as a team, the Bullets slipped from 60 wins to a record of 48–34. To be very honest about it, K.C. Jones was a truly nice, easygoing guy, but I wasn't overly impressed with his coaching ability. Actually, the guy who did a lot of the coaching was the assistant, Bernie Bickerstaff. Unfortunately, K.C. was under a ton of pressure that year because his team had gotten swept by Golden State in the previous championship series. And now we ended up winning 12 fewer regular season games, and then in the first round of the playoffs we lost to Cleveland in seven games.

While I feel we had a better team, with more talent, we didn't play up to our potential. And, frankly, I think we also got outcoached by Lenny Wilkens, the Cavaliers great tactician. Still, K.C. was really well-liked by all the players, and when Abe Pollin, the owner, made the decision to let K.C. go, it did not sit well with us.

And then Pollin turned to former Bulls coach Dick Motta, and things went from bad to worse.

For my second year in D.C., I moved Aaris and the kids down there with me, because I had time to make adjustments, to find a good home in a very nice area, Potomac, Maryland, and with a great school system for the girls. So I moved everybody to Washington, but I never sold our home in Detroit. I was so entrenched there, had met so many good people and made so many close friends, that I kept the Southfield home. I knew we'd be coming back to the city, because it was home.

Dick Motta turned out to be the antithesis of K.C. Jones: a good Xs and Os guy, but really hard to play for. I did not like him as a coach, because, instead of using the talents of the very good team we had, he wanted everybody to play like his old Chicago Bulls. He wanted Chenier and me to play like young caution-to-the-wind guys, diving on the floor and into the seats, and we didn't take to Motta very well.

My position was: I've gotta be me. But he wanted changes and traded away Truck Robinson, a good young player who Elvin Hayes felt shouldn't be playing so many minutes because it took shots away from Big E. So Truck went to Atlanta for a guard named Tommy Henderson. Then Motta came to me and said, "Tommy's a younger guy, and yeah, he can't score like you, but he's a true point guard, so we're probably going to start playing him. Basically, we want you to come off the bench and be the third guard."

I told Motta I would accept that as long as I was going to keeping playing meaningful minutes. I said, "I'm at the end of my career, and I can deal with that." And so that's what I did. But as my floor time dwindled and another less-than-wonderful season wound down, I knew I wasn't coming back.

If you think it sounds like there were chemistry issues with the Bullets that year, I won't deny it. But I think it had more to do with the coach than with the players. Some of the younger guys would come to me and say, "We really respect you for how you're handling this." And Tommy Henderson told me, "I know I can't outplay you, but he wants me to start. He wants me to play. And if you can help me, please do."

And so even today I get a Christmas card from Tom Henderson that basically says, "I just really want you to know how much I respect you for the way you dealt with me back then, because you could have made it very difficult for me."

At the end of the season, we again made the playoffs but were beaten by Houston, with Moses Malone, Rudy Tomjanovich, and Calvin Murphy. And that's when I said I'm not coming back.

Basically I retired because of Dick Motta. I was ready to leave the game rather than play for someone who didn't know how to use me or get the best from a good team. I had made my peace with retirement and was focused on moving our family back to our home in Detroit.

And that's when I got a call from Red Auerbach.

Red, of course, was originally a D.C. guy, and I had known him for a long time, first as the coach of the Boston Celtics and then as their general manager. Obviously I had played against his teams my whole career. But he'd always come back to Washington in the off-season, because he just kept an apartment, or a condo, in Boston. So he called and found me at my parents' house and said, "I hear you're going to retire. You're not going to come back and play with the Bullets."

I said, "That's right."

And he said, "Well, you know you just played on the wrong team." I chuckled, and he went into his pitch:

"Dave, I need you to think about coming up here with the Celtics. You can still play, and we need you. I can't make any promises to you about starting, because I've got Jo Jo White and Charlie Scott. But if we had a third guard like you, we're going to be right back in the mix. I've got an All-Star in Curtis Rowe; Dave Cowens, an All-Star in the middle; and an All-Star in Sidney Wicks. I've got three guys in the frontcourt that are all All-Stars. I got Charlie, Jo Jo, and with you in the backcourt, another three All-Stars. And if I can get Havlicek to come back, that makes seven."

Now all of that was true, but the problem was that all of us were *former* All-Stars, because all of our careers had obviously started to change at that point. Havlicek was 37. I was 34. So I didn't say yes right away, but I felt good when I hung up. I knew I could still play, and I didn't want my career to end on a sour note because of Dick Motta. And so I made my mind up pretty quickly that this was going to be a good shot for me.

I called Havlicek, because we knew each other quite well, and he said, "It would be great to have you on the team, but the only advice I'll give you is, if you're going to come, just don't come to training camp. Training camp will kill you."

When I got back to Auerbach, he told me, "I can't pay you what you're used to getting, because I'm going to play you as a third guard."

I said, "Red, if I come up there, it's not about the money. It's about the opportunity to play on a good team."

So I signed a one-year contract with the Celtics for $150,000. I went to Boston and missed the first week of training camp, but then I called Havlicek and said, "I think I have to come in. I don't want to miss the whole camp." Once again I was coming into a new situation and adjusting to a new team, so I really felt the need to get started.

Now Cowens and I were friendly, and Jo Jo and Charlie and I were all good friends. From All-Star games and in other ways, we knew each other very well. So there I am in training camp, and, hell, I still could outplay Charlie and Jo Jo at that point in my career. And, yes, the Boston camp was competitive as hell. And compared with other training camps, it was tougher. We ran and ran and ran some more. The Celtics were an organization that just wore you out, and you had to be in shape. And so soon enough I was in shape and able to adjust.

But as we got into the season, things weren't going all that well. We were falling short of the way we thought we should be playing. Now that was a time when drugs had become pretty prevalent, particularly cocaine. You had old timers like me, Cowens, and Havlicek, and we'd go out after a game and have a couple of beers while we'd get something to eat, but none of us really got into drugs. I won't name names, but with some of the other guys, drugs were pretty common. Cocaine started becoming an issue from about 1976 forward, and it was the new drug on the market, a potent booster. Marijuana was already in the league, but you didn't hear a lot of guys talking about cocaine until around '75, '76, and then it became the drug of choice, particularly for a lot of the younger guys. So to put it simply, we had players on that team who were into cocaine. How did it affect their game? I don't believe, at least I don't have knowledge, that guys played high, but on off-days or after a game, there was no doubt the guys were into it.

I'm not a doctor, and I don't know the impact that it would have on you physically. But those who used said it was like speed and gave you a real quick high. And then you'd come down.

So I recall a specific stretch of the season when we were losing a lot. Tommy Heinsohn was the coach, and K.C. Jones, my former coach with the Bullets, was the assistant. We had lost a game by 25 or 30 points, and our guys in the locker room were just horsing around, like it was no big deal. Sidney Wicks and Curtis Rowe, the California guys, were talking loudly about where they were going to party. And Auerbach came in and went completely off. And the next day he traded Charlie Scott for Don Chaney, who had a hurt leg and couldn't play, and Kermit Washington, who was serving a 60-day suspension for punching Rudy Tomjanovich of the Rockets and breaking his jaw. Red was so pissed off that he wanted to break up the team right then and there.

And then Jo Jo got hurt—his Achilles tendon. So all of a sudden the starting guards are gone, and we have a new starting backcourt of Havlicek and me. He's 37 and I'm 34, probably the oldest backcourt in the history of the NBA. But we were both playing well. Coming off the bench, I'd been averaging 13–14 points a game, and Havlicek was still getting his 20–21, so we still had a good back court. But we were also chasing around the likes of Calvin Murphy, Gail Goodrich, Tiny Archibald—all these small, fast guys—and that was tough.

We played that season out, and near the end Havlicek announced his retirement after 16 years. By then I also knew I wasn't going back to Boston, but I was not about to step on his announcement. So publicly I kept quiet, but I did tell Red that I was not coming back. This was it for me.

I hadn't moved my family to Boston. I had kept them back in Detroit, and thank God for that, because I really saw Boston back then as a pretty racist city. So I looked at everything and said it's time for me to get out right now. I've had 12 seasons and really re-established myself this past year with the Celtics by playing well.

But Auerbach said, "No, I want you to come back. You're probably trying to get more money, because you did play well, and now I'm losing John, so I don't really have a leader on this team. And you know you're a leader. You really get along with all your teammates. They all respect you and know you still can play. So let's figure out how you can come back."

I said, "Red, I'm not trying to hold you up. I'm not asking for any more money. I just want you to know that I'm not coming back, so when you come to draft time, you can do what you need to do."

In the 1978 draft, Red and the Celtics ended up picking a guy named Larry Bird, and they would soon be on their way back to greatness.

Yes, Red was right: I knew that physically I could have played competitively for another couple of seasons. And, yes, for a dozen years I had been fortunate enough to be spotlighted in professional sports, a dominant culture in American life, excelling at one of its favorite games. I had racked up 18,327 career points, 5,397 assists, seven All-Star game appearances, and one NBA season individual scoring title.

But to me the game had always been about much more than fame, honors, or statistics. It was about being with my teammates and closest friends through thick and thin, testing myself in game after game against the best in the world and embracing the thrill of competition as an essential feature of my life. And now all that would be entirely gone.

But I had always prepared myself for something beyond basketball. And so I didn't know exactly what I was going to do, but I felt reasonably certain that I could handle the adjustment and make the transition to the next big thing in my life.

10

DOWN TO BUSINESS

DURING MY FIRST SUMMER IN DETROIT without basketball in my future, I certainly had a lot of people wanting to talk with me about… yes, basketball. Friends, ex-teammates, a coach or two, and just folks I'd run into around town—all of them wanted to hear from me directly about whether I was really leaving the game behind, and, if so, what would be next for me. And then many of them had a suggestion: Had I ever thought about coaching, and if not, why not? After all, I was a smart guy, knew the game inside and out, and had the kind of personality that allowed me to get along with everybody. The consensus was I'd make a great coach, but the consensus didn't include me.

Over all my years of playing the game I had never seriously considered coaching. When I did actually entertain the idea, I usually reminded myself that most great players do not end up coaching. And the reason for that, I thought, was that great players have a God-given athletic talent, and so they experience the game differently and play it as only they can. My thought was that they'd be prone to the biggest mistake that you can make as a coach: comparing other players to yourself. "All right, I'm a great player. Faced with this situation, this is what I would do, so that's what this player should do." But that player, of course, doesn't have the same God-given talent the great player had. And so I believed that to excel at coaching it would take a very different kind of mindset.

Now the role that did appeal to me belonged to the guy who ran the show, assembled all the pieces, and put the team together: the general manager. But while we already had several Black coaches— Bill Russell (obviously the exception that proved the rule about great players and good coaches), Al Attles, Lenny Wilkens, and the Pistons' Ray Scott and Earl Lloyd—Blacks in front-office positions were still few and far between, and my sense of things told me it would be a long, uncertain process for anyone, however smart or adept, to move through the ranks to that top spot.

Naturally, my old Piston pals, guys like Bob Lanier and Don Adams (who had just retired from the NBA team in Buffalo), were always calling me that summer to join them in workouts and pickup games down at Cobo Arena. Telling myself I needed to stay in decent shape and listening to my body say, "Hey, man, you know this is what we're supposed to be doing, what we've always done at this time of the year," I'd go down to Cobo and get into it with them. And then the guys, especially Lanier, would be yapping at me about how I still had it, how I could still play better than most, and how the Pistons could sure use what I could bring. What I really needed to do was forget this silly retirement thing.

And then one day at Cobo, I looked over at the sidelines, and there was Dick Vitale, who had left the college coaching ranks to take over the Pistons. And now he was joining the chorus: "Damn, Dave, you can still play! How about coming back and helping us out."

Dick and Bob and all the rest of them were not telling me something I didn't know. I was sure I still had enough game to play and contribute. But I also knew that I had made the right decision for me about my future, and so I said again, "Thanks, guys, but no thanks. I've hung them up for good."

Little did I know that in the not-too-distant future an opportunity would appear almost out of nowhere that might put the reins of an NBA franchise in my hands.

But for now, the question for me was what kind of work was I going to say yes to. From my teenage years, I had dreamed about running my own business. In effect, my dad was an independent contractor, always working on a variety of construction jobs—on homes, churches, apartment buildings—and in a way he was his own boss and a kind of entrepreneur. And I saw all of that and said to myself, that's what I'd like to do one day—run my own company.

In a couple of past off-seasons, I had taken part in a Chrysler Corporation dealership training program, learning the intricacies of owning and operating a car dealership. Mel Farr, the former Detroit Lions running back and a good friend of mine, had made a real success of doing that and was still urging me to get into it. But the problem was the more I looked at it, the less it appealed to me. I saw a lot of things that Mel had to do to promote his name and his brand—all the over-the-top TV advertising with Mel flying around with a superhero's cape—and I knew that wasn't my style. I was not that outgoing guy who loved seeing my name publicized. I was much more laid back. So I just didn't see that being the way I wanted to go.

Ultimately the call that would really change my life that summer came from a guy named Ron Kramer. Ron had been an All-Pro tight end for the Green Bay Packers and later with the Lions. Before that he'd been a three-sport star at Michigan and achieved the improbable feat of leading both the U. of M. football and basketball teams in scoring for two years. And after his playing days were over, he joined a local company called Paragon Steel where he was now a vice-president. Over the years, as Ron and I had become friends, he let me know that Paragon and the steel business had been very good to him. With the Big Three automakers headquartered in Detroit, he said there'd always be a powerful demand for all types of steel and steel products.

Now Ron was wondering if I might be interested in a job with Paragon. The owners, a pair of brothers named Warren, thought, with my high-visibility in the community, I'd be perfect for a sales position. Ron said Paragon had four or five other former pro athletes working for them in sales because they could always open doors that other guys could not get into. I thanked him for the offer but said the one thing I knew about the steel business was that I was completely ignorant about it. I wouldn't feel comfortable trying to sell for the company without a good understanding of the business. Was there some kind of training position available in which I could learn from the ground up and then work my way into sales and marketing? Ron said he thought that could be arranged, and before long we had worked out a deal.

I started in the warehouse and observed all the ins and outs of shipping and receiving, learning the importance of paperwork and scheduling. Paragon was not a direct automotive supplier. They supplied two sub-suppliers, and so you had to get to know the companies that were their customers and what their needs were. From a processing standpoint, from a timing standpoint, scheduling was critical and so was paperwork, because when your invoices said you were shipping product out, you had to make damn sure that every detail of the order was correct—the specifications and processing of the steel, its weight and of course the delivery date.

You had to be precise about all those things, but once you got the basics down, it was pretty repetitive. And so after four months, I moved inside to the accounting department to learn its routines, and after another few months it was on to inside sales, where you had to follow the order and its paperwork into the warehouse, into shipping and receiving.

Finally, I moved into outside sales, which had you actually going to the customers. That's what I enjoyed the most, because we're talking a blue-collar industry here, and a lot of the solid, unpretentious people I was meeting seemed impressed with getting to know me. Because I was still in training, I was always with another Paragon salesperson, and we'd take people out to lunch or dinner and talk about their business and what their needs were. Mainly I needed to convince them I was serious about this, so it wasn't difficult to be well-received and accepted.

Not long after I started with Paragon, I was asked by the popular Detroit area sports broadcaster George Blaha if I'd like to do color commentary with him on Michigan State University basketball games. Thinking it might be fun and a chance to keep my name in front of Detroiters—you never knew how that might help my effort to forge a business career—I said yes. Usually the games were at night, so after working all day at Paragon, I'd drive an hour and a half to East Lansing and cover the game. Often I'd also spend some time with my two older daughters, Cassaundra and Bridgett, who were in school at MSU. For the away games there was more travel, mostly to Midwest cities where I could establish or cultivate what might turn out to be business contacts.

I enjoyed myself, felt comfortable on the broadcasts, and apparently did the job well-enough, because the next year George invited me to work with him covering the Pistons' games. Now there were more games and more extensive travel, flying around the country to NBA cities. In my second and last year doing the Pistons' games, the team had drafted Indiana star Isiah Thomas, who quickly turned into a rookie sensation. He and I got to know each other pretty well in his first season, and he would constantly call me after a game and ask me to critique his play. That was Isiah, always trying to improve and get better at whatever was important to him, and that was an attitude we shared, and something at the core of our relationship that is still going strong after nearly four decades.

• • •

During those two years with Paragon while I was learning how to build my own business in the steel industry and also working for MSU and the Pistons, my marriage to Aaris was failing. I think we had actually been growing apart for some time, and now it was coming to a head. Of course, she had been a young mother for a long time and certainly a very good one, but she had never given herself a chance to grow. Throughout our marriage she had never worked and never taken the opportunity to go to college, get a degree, and perhaps carve out a career for herself. Frankly, I think she became comfortable with the lifestyle provided by my being a professional athlete. We were never really hurting for money, always had enough to live a pleasant life. But now I think she had gotten to the point where the thought was, "You've had your career, and now it's time for me to live my life."

It wasn't ugly, but I felt the way things were going, it wasn't going to work, and so I initiated. I moved out of our home and into a place in downtown Detroit. And then after a year or so, I moved back home to try again and see if we could work something out. But it was soon obvious that we were inevitably going in two very different directions. Aaris got a condo in Southfield, and I stayed in the home. While Cassaundra and Bridgett at Michigan State said they preferred living with me during the summer months away from school, Aleisha, our youngest daughter, wanted to stay with her mother. But after a year, she said, "No, I'm coming back home." And then all three of the kids were with me.

• • •

Over my first year and a half with Paragon I had learned a lot about how the company ran its business, and I began to think about how I might be able to start my own firm. But when I raised the subject with friends, I often got a lot of pushback. The economy is so slow, they'd say, the time is not right. They'd ask, why steel and the auto industry? Both of them are struggling. And when I said I'd be committed to centering my business in Detroit, the response was, "Hey, the city is in a steep decline. It's not a place to start such a risky venture."

Nonetheless, I saw an opportunity and actually liked the timing. When I told Ron Kramer and the Warren brothers about what I was planning to do, I said I understood that times were tough, but in a good climate or bad there would always be a lot of risk. Yes, the upfront investment was huge, because you're talking plants and heavy-duty equipment, and steel itself is a very high-priced commodity. But I thought because of those things I had certain advantages. I had some money to invest. I had contacts. I had majored in economics and business, and I had all that good training at Paragon. And one of the key things I had learned along the way was that the Big Three automakers—GM, Ford, and Chrysler—all seemed to be committed to programs that would help minority suppliers.

From my vantage point at Paragon I had looked around and found very few minorities anywhere in the business. It wasn't surprising, despite those Big Three programs, given the risks, the hefty investments, and the high costs. Most minority firms couldn't deal with all that, but I figured I could do this. It was a challenge, but one I felt up to. I had saved at that point somewhere close to $200,000. I wasn't ready to put all that money into the company, but I would need to invest almost half of it.

I was pleased with the response from Kramer and the Warrens. They knew I wouldn't be doing exactly what they did and so wouldn't be competition for them. Paragon supplied structural steel plate to the automotive industry. That was not production steel, those big rolls of steel that I'd be dealing with. So they wished me well and understood how I could benefit from the auto companies' intention to grow their minority supply base.

But then they suggested setting me up as an adjunct to Paragon, as a subsidiary. In effect, they would do all of the work and have me function as a kind of figurehead. Of course, there was no way I was going to do that. I felt I had the smarts and the work ethic to do this on my own. And so I declined their offer, and when I left, it was on good terms. We remained friendly, and they let me know if I ever needed to call on them for something, they'd be there.

And even during my last few months at Paragon, they allowed me to bring in a couple people I would need to get started. And so I hired a young lady, Rae Withers, who was going to be my administrative assistant. She was suggested by Earl Lloyd, who had worked with her at the Police Athletic League. And also Bennie White. He was my little brother, a really solid young man who was 14 when I first met him at my basketball camp in Pennsylvania. I had begun mentoring him there and that continued back in Detroit. He got along well with my daughters and became like their big brother. He'd gone on to play at Michigan State, and now I was bringing him into the world of business. Today our relationship has continued for almost 50 years.

When I finally did leave Paragon, I took Jim Ivers with me, one of their top accounting and finance guys. I knew it was going to be important to have that kind of experience, so I had told Ivers about my plans. He was the accounting manager at Paragon, we had a good relationship, and when I said I'd like him to come with me, he was ready to make the move. The fact is, back then in 1980, with the business climate so uncertain, when you looked at it from Jim's perspective, he was doing a very risky thing. But he had gotten to know me over those two years and understood I was serious. Despite the risks, he saw an opportunity for himself.

So Jim Ivers, Rae Withers, Benny White, and me—those were the four employees that constituted Bing Steel when we incorporated. But I also needed the expertise of lawyers and accountants to help set up the company and establish a business plan. My lawyer was Harry McDonald, with a boutique law firm in suburban Birmingham, and Plante Moran covered the accounting.

To get started, I wasn't in a position to afford a warehouse and all the equipment we would need, so I rented some office space at the Chrysler Center in downtown Detroit. I had to start strictly as a broker, moving steel from one customer or supplier to another, and used the relationships I had forged while at Paragon to arrange to buy the steel. Because it took me a while to establish a bank line of credit, I had to quickly tap into some of that $80,000 plus of my own money, so I soon had skin in the game.

In addition to my savings, I was still receiving deferred income from the NBA, about $75,000 dollars a year, since I had not taken all of my money upfront during my two years in Baltimore and my last year in Boston. So I would have that deferred income over the next five years to take care of my family. But for equity in the business, I really needed that line of credit. And because they thought I had a good business plan, the National Bank of Detroit finally began extending us substantial credit. NBD, of course, had been the first bank I had gone to in my rookie year in Detroit to try for a home mortgage, and they had turned me down. But now the reception was much different. A lot of the people I had met and worked with at the bank during those seven off-seasons were now in a position to make decisions. So once again it was all about people and relationships.

Initially I would get an order from a car maker, and I'd go to the warehouse of a steel company I knew through Paragon. I'd place the order with that company, and they would schedule the processing of the steel (contracting to sell it to me, of course, and not to one of my competitors) and then deliver it to my customer. As I mentioned, Bing Steel began as a broker, and actually for our first two years that's all we were.

My very first customer was GM. I went to Bob Stone, the vice president for purchasing I had gotten to know at Paragon, and secured GM's order. Then I placed it with Kasle Steel, a big supplier, and they processed that order. And finally I set up all the shipping arrangements to General Motors. And that's how we got started.

At Ford, it was more of the same with their vice president for purchasing, Clint Lauer. He sent the word down to the company's individual buyers to work with me, because Ford, like GM and Chrysler, wanted to promote their minority supplier program with companies they felt were worthy of support. They all understood and were comfortable with Bing Steel's plan moving forward. I had told all of them that starting out I had no warehouse or equipment or stock. But I would get them exactly what was needed, when it was needed and for a good competitive price.

Now of course the supplier I chose would set his price for the steel and processing as high as possible, and so the upshot of all this was that the margins I was working with were always very thin. I was dealing with 1½ or 2 percent margins, razor thin.

So it was tough to make a profit, and, God forbid, if you made a mistake, if you supplied your customer with the wrong spec of steel, or with the wrong cut or processing. Those things were all established up front, and everything had to be precisely delivered, or you would lose the order. There were no computers back then, of course, and if a mistake was made, you wouldn't find out about it until the very end. And then it was too late. You'd have to eat the steel or try to find somebody else that could use it.

Now you were also at the mercy of your supplier to give you exactly what you had asked for. And you had to have trustworthy relationships with the people on the receiving end in your customer's plant. I would have to go to those plants to check on our orders, because certain people, if they were of a mind to, could do some pretty ugly things that could seriously screw up your deal. They might take receipt of the steel but say they didn't get what they had ordered. They might mishandle a coil, dropping and damaging it, and then claim that it arrived like that. So there were a number of ugly things that could happen, and some of them had a racist tinge to them.

Also, early on, despite those initial orders from the Big Three, there were some folks I had come up against who wouldn't give me the time of day. You could almost hear them thinking, "This guy knows nothing about steel, or about the business." And some of the buyers in the industry would make me wait forever in their lobby before they finally asked me to come in and try to sell my product. I suppose it was a test to see whether or not I was really serious, so I just kept coming back.

But, frankly, during our first six months in business I was seriously wondering whether this was going to work. We weren't consistently getting the kind of orders we needed. There were doubts and trust issues because we were a rank newcomer, and our customers were testing us with jobs that were just little bits and pieces. The bottom line was starkly clear: we weren't getting enough good jobs to make the kind of money we needed to make, and because my margins were so thin, I couldn't make a profit on a lot of the orders we did manage to get. And so my overhead was killing me even though I was paying only the other three employees while I took no salary myself. I was living strictly on that NBA deferred income.

When I looked at where we were after Bing Steel's first six months, I thought I'd made a big mistake. In short, we had lost a lot of money, more than half of that roughly $90,000 from my savings that I had put in to start the business. So it scared the hell out of me.

But when I talked to people who really knew the business, especially those with the Big Three who I was sure wanted me to succeed, I was reassured. They said we were doing things the right way, and losing money our first year was not that surprising or unusual. Yes, it could be frightening, but it was just something you had to get through. It was going to take a while to be accepted in the club, they said. And when I thought about it, I knew the easiest thing to do when things don't go your way is to quit. So I simply had to summon the wherewithal and the staying power to keep at it.

Basically at that point I was working non-stop, putting in 14–15 hours a day on my business. And then after that long day was done, I'd often have a Pistons game to cover, so I'd either drive out to the Silverdome where the team was playing by then, or if it was an away game, fly out of town. But after two years of the Pistons gig, I finally had to leave it behind—I was just too damn busy.

In a typical day back then I'd be up at 5:00 AM and head from my home in Southfield to our office downtown by 6:30 or 7:00. The employees came in around 7:30 or 8:00, and then we'd be attacking the paperwork, checking on our customers and with our suppliers. I was on the phone a lot, and then I'd be out of the office much of the day. Most days I'd be at lunch with one customer and at dinner with another as well. There was a lot of that, developing relationships, letting people get to know me. And it certainly helped that I had always felt confident in my people skills.

I had never allowed myself a big head about my success as an athlete and had always tried to be down to earth and real around others. So in my experience people saw that and felt they could develop trust with you pretty quickly. People would gravitate to you if you treated them with dignity and respect regardless of where they were in life. That was a mantra for me: Treat people like you want to be treated and give people credit for what they do and what they bring to the table. I'm talking about doing the right thing as a human being. But it's also the smart thing to do in terms of building trust which is indispensable in starting a business and making it happen.

• • •

Now by this time, Aaris and I were going through the divorce, and I knew that too was going to cost me money I didn't have. I had to explain to her that, given what I had put into the business and the difficulties it was currently going through, we were mostly living on that deferred income. We agreed that she would get half of the assets, but she had to understand that I didn't have the liquidity to pay her half of what the assets were at the moment, so I would have to pay her over a period of time.

At this point I had not been dating at all. I'd been telling myself I was just too busy, but in the summer of '81 I met someone who forced me to reconsider. Along with my friend Lem Barney, the Lions' great all-pro defensive back, I had agreed to be a celebrity name for a golf and tennis outing that was part of a fundraiser conducted by Southwest Detroit Hospital. The proceeds would go to a program for indigent people with medical needs, because the hospital was in the heart of Detroit, and most of the people it served were very poor. So Lem was the draw for folks who wanted to play golf, and I was the guy for tennis.

Afterward there was a dinner at the Michigan Inn attended by all the participants and several people from the hospital, and of course Lem and I were moving around the room meeting and saying hello to everyone. Now this was the second year in a row we had done this fundraiser, and I recalled the previous year encountering a strikingly attractive woman from the hospital. She had said her name was Yvette, I said it was a pleasure to meet her and that was about it. I was in the midst of trying to sort out my marital troubles back then, and I wasn't ready for anything at that point.

Now I spotted that same beautiful woman sitting at a table with five or six other people. There was a fellow sitting next to her, and I thought maybe he was her date, but I went over and asked if she was with someone, and when she said no, I asked her to dance. I was then in the final stages of the divorce, and after we danced I thought this might be a good time to try dating again. She gave me her phone number, I called, suggested dinner at a French restaurant in Southfield, and we hit it off quickly.

Yvette had graduated from Wayne State in Detroit and had grown up in the city with her parents and two sisters, one of whom was her twin. She was working at the hospital as a physical therapist, but was also studying optometry at Ferris State, which was about 90 minutes from Detroit. I found her smart and easy to talk to, with a good innate business sense. And we were soon into a serious relationship.

Not surprisingly, my daughters, who were all living with me that summer, were at first a bit standoffish with Yvette. But they knew I had not been dating and that if I brought someone home now, they could be sure this was a special person. Soon enough they understood this was someone important to me, and Yvette did as well, because it wasn't long before she thought better of making that long drive to Ferris State every week.

• • •

In Bing Steel's second six months I think our customers began to feel a little more comfortable with us. And then it finally started to pay off. We were getting more jobs with a little more volume, and we began to break even. We ended the year with about $1.7 million in sales, and while our loss for the year was about $80,000, the first $60,000 or so had come in the first six months. Then our losses began to dwindle, and now I knew we were heading in the right direction. Why the turnaround? Mostly I think people in this a small community of companies that constituted the steel business in Detroit began to see that I was a totally serious player. Once they got to know and trust me, they saw that I was a good opportunity for them to move their product.

Actually, we had begun to do well enough that I finally decided we needed more employees, certainly someone else knowledgeable in steel and steel sales. And so I brought in another salesperson who had worked for Paragon. He handled inside sales, and I was the outside guy. Also, he helped train Benny White and solidified the work done inside the office. And then in year two I hired two other people who had experience in the business.

Year two was when Bing Steel began to make some money. So we were growing but I knew the pace of that growth would need to increase if we were to really establish ourselves as a viable company. The business plan I had put together was based on a clear-eyed perception that the growth we needed could not really happen if we remained just a broker. We needed to be a full-fledged business and not just a buyer of product and services from other companies. So from a development standpoint I knew that what we needed to grow was a warehouse.

In Detroit, west of downtown near Michigan Avenue and West Grand Boulevard, I found an old warehouse to lease that would serve our purpose. It was about 35,000 square feet, had been used for steel, and included cranes to move the steel around. Now I could go out and buy my steel directly from the mill. And that quickly increased my margin, because now I'm buying directly from the mill and not from another supplier. I could bring my inventory in, and once I secured an order, I could move it to somebody else to process it for me. That was a good first step, but with our next move we would need to obtain the kind of heavy-duty equipment required to process or cut our steel to size.

The auto makers were still very much invested in helping us grow as a minority supplier, and that's why General Motors came to the table with us at this point and said they had an important piece of equipment available for us. Pontiac Motors told me, "We've got a slitter that we will sell you at a discount, and we'll help you get it installed." What that slitter did was cut steel. Those big rolls of steel coming from the mill would go on the slitter to be cut to the size the customer wanted. The customer didn't need that big roll of steel. He needed it in a smaller width, which the customer would then use to make parts with.

So obviously this was an opportunity that could make a major difference in our business, and we got engineers involved to prepare the warehouse floor for our new slitter, digging a deep pit to mount and support it securely. And in year three, with our warehouse and slitter on line, our business really took off. Our margins at that point were still pretty slim, but now we had some serious volume. And, as any basic business class will tell you, volume can make up for slim margins. Now not nearly as dependent on other suppliers, we could do on our own the work we'd been forced to pay other companies to do.

· · ·

It was about this time that I received a call from my mother saying that my dad had suffered another stroke. He'd been rushed to the hospital where the doctors quickly operated to relieve pressure from bleeding on the brain. Mom said the prognosis was not good.

Two years earlier Dad's first stroke had left him partially paralyzed on his right side. He had a speech impediment at that point and was speaking very slowly. Despite the partial paralysis, he could still get up and around, but it was very difficult for him, and he had stayed at home with my mom as his fulltime caregiver. But in those two years after the first stroke he was a changed man—very angry and often depressed. He had always been a devout Christian, but I think he couldn't accept the fact that something like that had happened to him. It was that tough old question: Why do bad things happen to good people? For my mother, with constant 24/7 responsibility for his care, it had been a deeply difficult time that she met with what I thought was a quiet heroism.

I flew to D.C. to join her at the hospital along with my older sister, Dorothy, who had come in from Indianapolis, and my younger sister, Brenda, and my brother, Hasker Jr., who still lived in D.C. Basically they were all looking to me for a decision about whether or not we should take our dad off life support. When I spoke with the doctors, they said it was very unlikely he would ever regain consciousness, and if we took him off life support, he would definitely not survive. They also told me that Dad's strokes could probably be traced back to the head injury he had suffered on that construction job more than 20 years earlier, that it was likely the injury had left him with a weakness in the brain that eventually led to the strokes.

Finally, I made a decision, and within a day and a half after they unplugged the life support, Hasker Bing passed away at the age of 67. As always, I looked back at his life as an inspiration, a model of hard work, responsibility, and loving support for his family, friends, and community.

After making funeral arrangements I came back to Detroit to bring my daughters and Yvette back to D.C. for the funeral. Afterward, my mother continued to live in D.C. Throughout her life she had remained in good health, never seeing a doctor, except when she was having her children, until she left us in March of 2017 at the age of 93.

• • •

If I had to name one regret about my dad's life, it would be that he did not live long enough to see the extent of my business success. After his first stroke in 1981, I did have a chance to tell him about the early progress of my business, and though his speech was somewhat impaired, I think he understood that we were doing better each year.

But now as we moved into year four, things had really started to hum for Bing Steel. We needed more people in the warehouse to handle shipping and receiving and with the slitter more people to do the processing. We had gone from four employees to 19. And then came a gratifying surprise in a call from the White House.

The Reagan Administration had named Dave Bing the National Minority Small Businessman of the Year. Our automotive customers—Ford, Chrysler, GM—had made recommendations to the Department of Commerce as to their outstanding minority supplier. So off to D.C. I went to pick up the award from President Ronald Reagan in a ceremony at the White House.

The honor quickly put me in a bright spotlight in Detroit's business community and its political arena. Suddenly I was being asked to join the boards of outfits like DTE Energy, Detroit Renaissance, and the Economic Club of Detroit, and I was now rubbing shoulders with CEOs, presidents, and top public officials.

So, yes, that award brought more recognition and notoriety that helped greatly with the trust we needed to keep adding new customers, but we still had to put in a full day, every day, and we just kept plugging away. In that fourth year we saw some major growth, and by 1985 we were doing about $40 million in annual sales. We had added another warehouse with another slitter and, of course, more people. We were now trucking shipments of steel to 53 customers, not only to the Big Three but also to firms like Deere & Company. And the number of our employees was at 63 and growing.

Now all through this there were still people telling me that I really had to get out of Detroit. About hiring more people, they would say, "Detroit is going through really tough times and just doesn't have what you need." They'd point to the city's inferior public schools and say, "You've got to go to the suburbs to get the right kind of people to help you grow." Well, that's not how I saw it. I knew what we needed most were people willing to work hard, and that the city of Detroit had a lot of those people—either unemployed or underemployed and often disrespected. I felt all they needed was an opportunity, but very few businesses seemed willing to give these people a chance. I was in a position where I could, and I didn't want to be only a minority owner. I wanted Bing Steel to reflect minorities throughout its ranks.

The mostly White industry had many workers with the expertise and knowledge we needed. The learning curve for a lot of the people I brought in was often steep, but I was willing to pay the price for the training it took to bring them up to speed. After all, it would help not only them but also their families as well as the city, because now there'd be fewer people unemployed and on the dole, and more tax-paying citizens. There's a saying: "Doing well while doing good." And that's very important to me. I saw no reason why we couldn't do both.

Now as for doing well, I knew customers like Ford Motor Company were right when they told me, "You can only grow so much in steel. With processing you can make a lot more money. You need to get into stamping and start making parts." But I didn't know anything about that end of the business. So I worked with a Ford program that linked a small minority-owned businesses with a larger White-owned firm that could serve as a mentor. This led to my connecting with Toronto-based Magna International, a major supplier with annual revenues of $1.7 billion. And together we formed Superb Manufacturing to make stamped underbody parts such as hinges, brackets, and gas tank pans.

Basically, it was a five-year agreement with Magna for a joint venture, after which I would be a completely independent owner. Magna held 40 percent of Superb and were in charge of engineering and manufacturing, which was their strength. And I owned 60 percent and took care of administration and sales, while we learned stamping and the manufacturing end. The only hitch came when I couldn't talk Magna out of their fears about locating in what they saw as the depressed, high-crime city of Detroit. I finally swallowed hard and found a plant in the northern suburb of Sterling Heights.

Once in operation, Superb recorded first-year sales of $2.4 million, and over the next few years we remained in Sterling Heights. But in that time frame I bought a large parcel of land in Detroit that would become very important to our growth as a company.

I had gone to Mayor Young and told him that I wanted all my companies in the city of Detroit. So the mayor and his right-hand guy, Emmett Moten, showed me some land right next to the old Chrysler Headquarters in Highland Park, an area of Detroit once full of housing but now only vacant land. It was close to all the freeways, so it would be easy for the trucks to get in and out, and our transportation costs would be lowered. Obviously they gave me a great price on the deal because I was going to create jobs in the city of Detroit. I would call the area North Industrial Park.

Now as Magna and I had set up a good working relationship, they got to know me better and had confidence in my ability. I would go to Toronto to meet with their owners and develop strategies, and when I told them I now owned property in Detroit and we needed to build a new plant there, they said okay. By then they had seen that our joint venture had big-time benefits for both of us, and they were getting lots of additional work from all the car companies.

So now that we needed to build a new plant, I figured why not do it myself. I started a construction firm called Heritage 21, with that name being a throwback to the days when I had first started working with my dad. But it also made good financial sense. That plant for Superb was no small undertaking: $5 million, 56,000 square feet. And while the construction of the building was a substantial project, there was also all that equipment we needed to install, because with stamping plants you've got those big presses that require foundations that are anchored 20 feet in the ground. Nonetheless, why not pay my own company to do the work instead of some outside firm?

Superb's move to our new plant meant losing some money early on, because we had to put so much into the new facility. So it took a while to build the business base for Superb, but at the same time, Bing Steel was making money. Of course, Superb had become one of Bing Steel's customers. We were supplying all of the steel it needed, and as a result, Bing Steel was still growing. Now it didn't help that the automobile business at that time was taking a serious downturn, so Superb took about three years before it reached the volume and kind of business that it needed to make money.

But from early on we looked at stacking companies with vertical integration as the way to go. So we had Bing Steel, then we had Superb Manufacturing, and now we had Heritage 21 Construction. In North Industrial Park, we had the Superb Manufacturing stamping plant. And after a couple of years of using their plant manager and engineering people, I was able to attract some additional talent to replace them. And then in another year or two we replaced a couple of engineers and more operations people with workers we trained. And by the time the Magna people had left entirely, Superb's revenues had grown 10-fold to $20 million. It was an easy transition for us that worked out well.

•   •   •

The Bing Group, as we were now called, was also becoming something of a family firm. When Cassaundra, my oldest, graduated from the business school at Michigan State, she moved right into our operations area and took a bit of the load off me. Bridgett had majored in communications, but it wasn't long before she too joined the Bing

Group, working in human resources. Aleisha was just starting her college education at Syracuse, but in four years she would also be destined to lend her skills and know-how to the administration area of our business.

As for Yvette, we lived together for a year or so before getting married in 1986. It was a sizeable wedding at our church, Hartford Memorial, one of the largest in the area. Yvette's twin sister was the Maid of Honor, and I had two Best Men, Lem Barney and Bob Lanier. Afterwards we had a reception downtown in the restaurant atop the Renaissance Center with about 200 friends and family.

And right after we got married, Yvette also joined the Bing Group. Among other things she was in charge of was payroll, but it wasn't long before she noted that our growing business had an increasing need for janitorial services. For a while I was building a plant almost every two years, and we were going outside to have somebody come in and clean up. And then one day, clearly understanding our preference for vertical integration, Yvette said, "Maybe I can start my own company to provide our janitorial services." And so with my encouragement she did just that, forming her own firm to do what was needed in all our offices and plants.

Now almost three decades later, Yvette still has that business going strong. She's made it a great success with about 40 employees servicing some 80 banks.

11

THE MEASURE OF SUCCESS

ON MARCH 4, 1985, a freak of nature started a series of events that nearly ended up changing my life. A heavy, late-season overnight snowfall followed by lots of rain collapsed the roof of the Pontiac Silverdome, the 82,000-seat football stadium that for several years had been doing double-duty as the home of the Detroit Pistons.

With the last month of their season still ahead, the Pistons were obviously in need of a place to play their remaining home games. Detroit's mayor Coleman Young quickly rolled into action, directing his staff to secure an agreement with the city's pro hockey club, the Red Wings, to allow the Pistons to share their six-year-old Joe Louis Arena on Detroit's riverfront for the rest of the season.

Coleman, in case you were wondering, was not acting simply out of the goodness of his heart. He had been disappointed and angry six years earlier when Pistons owner Bill Davidson had decided not to join the Red Wings in moving to Joe Louis, and instead chose to head out of the city and into the suburbs and to put his team in a facility, the Silverdome, not at all suitable for basketball.

Now the Pistons, with a cast of new characters led by their remarkable young point guard Isiah Thomas, were a team on the rise, and their fans were filling the seats for these re-scheduled games downtown. Not surprisingly, the mayor's mind was churning with thoughts of new options and possibilities.

One day I got a call from the mayor's office, asking if I could come in for a meeting. I never passed up a chance to spend time with the city's leader and most interesting character, and as we sat across from one another, he, as usual, got right to the point. Number one, did I think I could put together a group of investors with the clout and wherewithal to possibly buy the Pistons from Bill Davidson? And number two, did I know of any other NBA team that might be up for sale?

On the latter, I told Coleman that I would need to do some scouting around, but I was fascinated with the idea of possibly bringing a second NBA team to the Motor City. I thought it unlikely that Davidson would be willing to sell his team, but in either case, over the past several years of doing business in Detroit, I had made lots of connections and won the trust of some of the business community's major players, so I felt there was a good chance we could assemble a collection of high-rolling movers and shakers in the city to make a run at bringing the NBA back downtown. We both agreed that for now any move on either score should be discrete and held close to the vest.

Back at my office, the first call I made was to an old friend, my freshman-year roommate at Syracuse, Frank Nicoletti. Frank and I had stayed in close touch over the years and followed each other's careers. Now, with a high-powered law firm in Manhattan, Frank was one of the most well-connected guys I knew and, given the elite circles in which he traveled, perfectly positioned to pick up the kind of info we were looking for. I told him about my chat with Mayor Young and asked if he'd keep an eye peeled for signs that an NBA team might be on the market.

Then I stared making some local calls, and it wasn't long before an impressive group of powerful business types were ready to support either a move to bring the Pistons "home," or to make Detroit the only town besides New York and Los Angeles to feature two NBA teams. Among those I had quickly enlisted were moguls like Max Fisher, who had been instrumental in making the Renaissance Center happen along with other major developments in the city; brewery owner Peter Stroh; and real estate magnate Al Taubman, the owner of the U.S. Football League's Michigan Panthers. They had all agreed to be part of a consortium of investors ready to pursue either project.

About other available NBA franchises I soon learned that both the Atlanta Hawks and the Golden State Warriors were on the market. It might take only $7 million to buy the Hawks, but there was a problem with moving them away from Atlanta, because Ted Turner's regional cable network had an ironclad contract keeping them there. And the Warriors already had a very interested prospective buyer.

Urged on by Mayor Young, our investment group was quietly using a back-channel approach to certain parties affiliated with the Pistons ownership. Davidson, the majority owner, was avoided, but his friend Peter Stroh made the mistake of asking him what kind of cash it might take to secure a sale, and Davidson exploded in anger. He vowed the team would never move back to Detroit as long he had control, and soon announced that he was planning a new facility in a distant northern suburb, an arena that would soon turn out to be the Palace of Auburn Hills.

That might have been the end of it, but then I got a surprising call from California. Frank Nicoletti was out there on a golf vacation and found himself playing a round at the Olympic Club outside San Francisco in a foursome that included a fellow named James Fitzgerald.

Unbeknownst to Frank, Fitzgerald just happened to be the majority owner of the NBA's Milwaukee Bucks. After their round, the four were sipping Scotch, and Fitzgerald casually announced that he was looking to sell the Bucks. Originally from California, he was suffering with some health issues and was tired of the weather in Milwaukee and of empty seats and losing money. The city couldn't be bothered to upgrade its inadequate arena, and what he really wanted to do was move back to northern California and buy the Golden State Warriors.

Frank couldn't believe what he was hearing, and told Fitzgerald he just might have a buyer for the Bucks. With the mention of my name, Jim Fitzgerald got excited, knowing that the NBA was more than anxious to have a Black franchise owner, and figuring that my involvement might pave the way for his purchase of the Warriors. Thirty minutes after his surprising call, I phoned Frank back and told him Mayor Young wanted to meet with us, like, immediately.

In the meeting I set up, Coleman was his usual colorful self with Frank and me and waxed eloquent on what he said was my ability to swing a deal that would bring a second NBA franchise to the city of Detroit. But afterward, Frank still wondered if that was really a feasible option. To date, only New York and Los Angeles had shown enough fan interest to support two NBA teams, and while fan involvement with the Pistons had demonstrated some new life lately, it seemed far from certain that Metro Detroit could keep two clubs afloat.

Nevertheless, when my old friend Frank returned to California for another meeting with Fitzgerald, he carried a purchasing offer for the Milwaukee Bucks of just under $15 million. It was a very substantial bid indeed for a team in one of the smaller NBA markets, and Fitzgerald was impressed.

On our end, Peter Stroh had dropped out, doubtful about Detroit's ability to support two teams, but I had stepped up my own pledged involvement to about 10 percent, or $1.5 million. The mayor and I were hopeful the offer would make a deal happen, but then came another roadblock. Bud Selig, the owner of major league baseball's Milwaukee Brewers, had a TV network arrangement similar to Ted Turner's down in Atlanta. And by stalling the sale, Selig was hoping the threat of losing the Bucks to Detroit would galvanize investors behind a new arena and more support for the team.

For a time, the deal seemed dead, but early in 1986, Jim Fitzgerald called Frank Nicoletti and got the wheels turning again. By then, however, our investor group had suffered more defections and diminished support. Max Fisher had dropped out, and Al Taubman had cut back his financial pledge. With the mayor's urging I was ready to raise my stake above 20 percent, which would then make me a managing partner. But we still needed more financial clout.

It came when Coleman and I met with the Little Caesars Pizza king Mike Ilitch, the owner of the Detroit Red Wings. Mike quickly saw the advantage of an NBA club filling the seats at Joe Louis Arena for 41 dates every year, and he agreed to take a minority stake in this new pro sports venture in Detroit. So we were back in business. Nothing had changed in Milwaukee's lack of civic or corporate support for a new arena, and Fitzgerald felt he was closing in on his dream of ridding himself of the Bucks and buying the Warriors.

In May of 1986, Fitzgerald signed a purchasing agreement, which essentially meant that the Milwaukee Bucks would soon be moving to Detroit. NBA commissioner David Stern was reportedly ecstatic at the prospect of the first African American franchise owner and vowed to move quickly to expedite the sale's ratification. I even had some preliminary discussions with Milwaukee team officials about whether or not to keep the Bucks name, but until all the t's were crossed, the i's dotted and all of the $15-million purchase price was ready and accounted for, we all vowed to keep the deal well under wraps.

And then Jim Lites delivered a cold shower to his father-in-law, Mike Ilitch. Married to Ilitch's daughter Denise and managing the outfit that owned the Red Wings, Lites had been doing his due diligence with some dispassionate market research, and the news was not good: any new NBA team in town could expect to fill an average of only 4,000 seats per game. At that rate, the operation would be a serious money loser.

The mayor and our investor group tried hard to convince Ilitch that a second NBA franchise would mean great long-term benefits for the city and for everyone involved, but despite his major commitment to the development of downtown Detroit, Ilitch said no, he was out. And in the wake of that defection, the whole effort finally fell apart in that summer of 1986.

In Milwaukee, Jim Fitzgerald still ended up with what he wanted. Faced with the open threat of losing their NBA team, a couple of well-heeled corporate investors finally stepped up to build a new arena in the city and to put together a financial package that out-distanced our own offer for the Bucks by a few million dollars. In the end, Milwaukee kept its team, and Fitzgerald took his cash off to California and secured the Warriors.

As for me, I remained convinced that in the long run we could have made a new NBA club work in downtown Detroit, but of course we'd never know. What soon became clear, however, was that my reputation among the area's top corporate power brokers had received a significant boost. My business savvy, negotiating skills, and devotion to our troubled city's best interests were all now unquestioned.

• • •

As a new decade dawned, the Bing Group's annual revenues were climbing to $61 million, and in 1990, *Black Enterprise* magazine called with the news that we had placed eighth on their list of the top 20 Black-owned industrial and service companies in the U.S. It was a position that everybody at our company was proud of, including all of our employees. But, as it had been from the beginning, our goal was simply to continue growing. We had not really set our sights on being No. 1, the largest minority-owned company. We just wanted to keep on growing and keep giving more people opportunities for employment. That was very important to me, but that's not to say I'd get soft-hearted, or soft-headed about the process. Here's a quote from a *Sports Illustrated* article that definitely set the record straight:

"George Trapp... was one of Bing's Pistons teammates, and after they both retired, Bing hired Trapp to work for one of his auto parts companies. Trapp wasn't getting his work done. Bing fired him. What about Campy Russell? He was another friend from Bing's NBA days. Bing hired and fired him too. Curtis Rowe, same thing. He played most of his career with Bing, went to work for him at Bing Steel, then got fired. Bing told them all, and dozens of others, when they were hired: Do your work or you're gone. It needs to be reciprocal. If they wanted a free ride, they were on the wrong track."

These were all friends and former teammates who were on hard times or into drugs, and they needed help. And so I let them know up front, I couldn't help them if I didn't hold them to the same level of professionalism, expectations, and work ethic that I had for everybody else. So I had told each of them: You've got to abide by the rules here, and if you don't, you can't be here.

Earlier in 1990, I had received another gratifying call, one that I had been waiting on for some time, from Springfield, Massachusetts. The folks at the Naismith Memorial Basketball Hall of Fame were pleased to inform me that I had been elected to the Hall. They wanted to be sure that I could attend the induction ceremony and explained that I would need to have a Hall of Fame member introduce me.

The first person I thought of was Oscar Robertson. Since that first game I'd played against him in my rookie year some 23 years earlier, Oscar and I had always been close, and when I called and asked if he would be my guy, he gladly and graciously accepted. So on a festive and moving evening in February, Oscar told the audience filled with some of the greatest players of all time: "Dave is the perfect example of professionalism, class, dignity, and humanity."

The other NBA inductees with me that night were the amazing Earl "the Pearl" Monroe and the great Elvin "Big E" Hayes. All three of us had played at times for the Bullets, either in Washington or in Baltimore. Of course, the Bullets wanted me to go in as a Bullet, but I had played in Washington only two years, and it was a no-brainer that I'd go in as a Piston.

Seeing Oscar that night, along with so many old friends, got me thinking about the arc of my career, how it reached all the way back to those outdoor courts in D.C. and the gym at Spingarn High, and how I was currently in the middle of a campaign to help young players just starting out in the game.

The Detroit Public Schools were in such dire financial straits that they were planning to drop all school athletics as well as music programs. Thinking back on what school sports had meant to me and for so many other young people, I vowed not to allow that to happen. The DPS superintendent quoted me a figure that the system needed to keep the programs going, and I sat down and wrote a personal check for $600,000.

Then I joined others in pressing for a vote in the state legislature to authorize a referendum to underwrite and maintain those athletic and music programs. But in the meantime, while we were waiting on the legislature, Isiah Thomas, the Pistons, and I went out and raised almost $400,000, and when the state finally agreed to the referendum that ultimately passed to give the Detroit district what it needed to keep school sports and music alive, we gave the funds we had raised to the DPS to cover some of their other educational needs.

And my cashed check for $600,000? I kept it as a reminder of what can happen when people finally join together and do the right thing.

But when I was writing that check, I was not only thinking of the importance of school sports in general, but also of a series of boys and young men I had been mentoring over the years. I've mentioned the first one, Benny White, who had gone from my basketball camp in the Poconos to Detroit's Northern High School to Michigan State and acquired a college education in the process.

The next youngster I connected with had come to Detroit from Alabama when he was 13 years old and also enrolled at Northern High. He was already about 6'3" or so, but he had a 16 or 17 shoe size, so you knew he was going to keep on growing. The coach at Northern said, "I've got a kid who doesn't know his father and moved up here to live with his aunt and uncle. He could really use your help."

Now, because he was new to Detroit, the kid had no idea I had been a basketball player. Initially it was just about a Black man trying to help a young Black boy, and I made it clear that while I'd offer help, he was going to have to earn his way. I'd bring him into my business and give him a job there during the summer. In fact, it took him the better part of that first summer to ask me why I seemed to be pretty popular. And then in my office he saw some old basketball plaques, and he asked me, "So you played?" And I said, "Yeah, I played." Nobody had ever told him anything about that, but once he learned my story, our relationship was really cemented, and we became very close. Every summer I would send him to Syracuse for a summer basketball camp, and he fell in love with the place.

And so Derrick Coleman wound up being an All-American there, and then he starred in the NBA for 15 years.

And after Derrick it was Jalen Rose. Actually, I had known Jalen from the beginning, because at the time Jalen was conceived and born, his dad, Jimmy Walker, was my backcourt mate with the Pistons. I was aware of the boy thereafter, because I knew his mother well. But once Jalen grew up and started playing as a ninth grader at Detroit's Southwestern High, his coach, Perry Watson, who was a good friend of mine, came to me and said, "I know you know Jalen, but now he needs some advice, he needs some direction. And in the summer he's going to need a job to make a little money." And so I did the same for Jalen that I had for Derrick. And we remain close to this day.

Jalen had never known his dad, never met him. But as he became a good high school player and then starred as a freshman at Michigan as part of the Fab Five, Jalen wanted to meet his dad. Of course, he knew I had played with Jimmy and asked me if I could set up a meeting. But Jimmy didn't want to do that. He was living in Kansas City at the time, and he never wanted to meet Jalen because he had never provided for him, number one, and the worst thing he thought he could do now would be to come into his life. Jimmy told me, "He's going to think I want something from him now that he's become a very good player and got national recognition. I don't want him to think that I want something from him."

Jalen got as far calling Jimmy and having a few phone chats with him, but then Jimmy got sick and died from complications from lung cancer. And when he passed, Jalen and I went to Kansas City for the funeral. I think Jalen was hoping to at least see his dad laid out at the funeral home. But we learned when we got there that his remains had been cremated.

At one point back in his days in Detroit, Jimmy had married here, and he and his wife had a daughter, who I ultimately introduced to

Jalen. But Jimmy was just one of those loveable but incorrigible guys, and he fathered an unbelievable number of kids all over the country.

As I said, I'm still close with Jalen, though I probably see him more often these days on ESPN than in person. I'm especially proud of his charitable and philanthropic work and served on his board when he first opened his school, the Jalen Rose Leadership Academy, a tuition-free, public charter high school in northwest Detroit.

Now at the same time I was trying to help save school sports in the city, I got involved in a cause that reached back to the opposite end of the continuum: the plight of retired players from the early days of the NBA. My good friend and former coach, Earl Lloyd—the NBA's first Black player—would often tell me about what it was like back in the day, well before the NBA had a pension plan. In fact, the league had two decades of players with no access to a pension, and now they were getting older and were often in ill-health.

So I got on the phone and called Oscar, called Dave DeBusschere and a couple of others I knew to be good, caring men, Dave Cowens and Archie Clark. And I said, "Let's meet and talk about getting the league to provide a pension plan for all these ex-players in their seventies and eighties and in some cases with major health issues. Some of them are not doing well financially, and we've got to do something to help these guys out."

The response was great from Oscar and the others, and we all decided to go to New York to meet with NBA commissioner David Stern. But once we told him what our issues were and what we wanted, he gave us a lot of pushback. The league's bottom line seemed to be that nobody knew those old guys, and, quite frankly, most people didn't give a damn about them.

So it took us six or seven years of arguing, trying to convince the league to invest enough money so these ex-players could participate in the pension plan. When we first started there were 117 former players alive with no pension. By the time we finally reached an agreement with the league, we were down to 77 guys, because so many of them had passed away.

It was about that time, on the NBA's 50th anniversary of its founding in 1946, that the league put together a list of its 50 greatest players. A panel of selected coaches, GMs, players, and media members made their selections, and it turned out that four of us who had worked on the pension deal—Oscar, DeBusschere, Cowens, and me—were on the list. Frankly, I was elated and considered it actually a greater honor than the Hall of Fame. The list was announced at a major affair at the All-Star game weekend in Cleveland in February 1996. It was a great weekend and wonderful to see so many of my old friends, great players I had played with and competed against.

• • •

In the mid-90s, our business was booming, in part because Chrysler had announced that it wanted its top-tier suppliers to buy at least 5 percent from minority firms. And when the other car companies followed suit, we began to really notice a difference. There had been a lot of Tier One suppliers hesitant about doing business with minority companies, but when that edict came down from the Big Three, there was now another avenue of growth that we had not previously enjoyed.

At the same time, there was also a move generally to consolidate and reduce the total number of suppliers that the car companies and their Tier One suppliers were dealing with. But finding other minority companies we might work with was very difficult, because most of us were first generation and relatively new. And all of us were usually strapped for cash. So joining forces with another minority company was a difficult proposition. After our great success with Magna, I had come close with a couple of joint deals—with Worthington Steel in Ohio and Woodbridge Ventures—but ultimately neither came together. And another, with Rouge Industries, lasted only three or four years.

And then in '96, Lear Seating came along, one of the top three auto seat manufacturers in the world, with $7 billion in revenues. Lear's CEO Ken Way was a Detroit guy, and we had been selling them steel. Lay said they were happy with us as a supplier, and since their business was growing, they saw an opportunity to get us involved in seat assembly.

"Would you be interested?" asked Lay.

"Absolutely," I responded.

Our new joint venture was called Detroit Automotive Interiors, and we were soon building a new plant in North Industrial Park. At the time we had two plants in the Park, and both were Magna operations, stamping and assembly. But that parcel of land I had originally bought from the city was about 30 acres in total, so we built our first seat assembly plant there, and two years later we built another plant for headrest assembly also in North Industrial Park. And once underway, it became very clear very quickly that total seat assembly meant big bucks. Its gross was unbelievable.

Overall, the Bing Group's growth was very rapid, and in 1997 we took in $183 million in revenues, almost triple what we were making in 1990. And we were learning that there were big differences between employing 100 workers and now more than 700.

At the start, of course, we were non-union, but as my employees grew in number, the unions, both the UAW and the Teamsters, started coming around. When we were a relatively small company, I pretty much knew everybody we employed by their first names. But as we grew, and working with so many more people, we couldn't have the same kind of relationship. Early on we had profit-sharing plans for the employees, and when the company made a profit, everybody shared in it. There was kind of a top-down family relationship, but when the unions came in and started making promises to people in terms of hourly pay, and with all these union rules, then there were some problems.

And then I had to get much more involved in conversations and negotiations, because the unions obviously wanted to come in and make us a union shop. I felt we didn't need a union, because in my view we were taking people off the street and giving them a great opportunity, paying them a very competitive wage, and offering them in some cases profit sharing as well. So as we grew, we were doing all these things for our people, and then the union came in out of the blue with promises I couldn't live with nor could they keep.

Huge wage increases, I knew, were out of the question in a company that was not flush with cash, because it was needed to continue building facilities and equipping them properly. Growth was my focus, so I could continue to employ more people. The union debate sidetracked me a bit, but ultimately, when both the Teamsters and the

UAW were successful in coming in, we did not have a negative relationship. Things weren't all that different except that people had to pay union dues (while, in my view, not getting much or anything for them), and our ability to grow wasn't impacted in any substantial way.

In its June 1998 issue, *Black Enterprise* named the Bing Group its Minority Company of the Year. With the growth and the success we were having, the magazine had recently listed us at number three in the country, but this new honor was huge. Everybody would take notice of something like that, and it meant more customers and more orders.

And increasingly those new orders were coming from outside the car business. I had finally begun making inroads at appliance makers like GE and Whirlpool and with the office furniture manufacturers Steelcase and Hayworth, selling them steel for their products. I had started courting them, because the automotive industry had always been so dominant that the major companies dictated price and, frankly, everything else. And by now we had been around the block enough times to know how cyclical the automotive business was. You might have three years of growth in the auto industry, and then you could be whipsawed into a downturn.

The only real option was to make connections with other industries that weren't so cyclical. So I went to Grand Rapids, Michigan's furniture capital, and did the same thing that I had done with the car companies. The top people I met with there were by now aware of our respected position in the industry generally. And they were also starting to have some of the same goals in terms of minority involvement. So this was a new playing field with real potential.

With all our new growth, we had begun to find it difficult to hire enough people to fill our jobs, because a lot of minorities didn't have the skill set or the background those jobs required. So in the summer of '99 I went to Ford Motor Company and said, "We've got to start training people, because the folks I'm bringing in now don't know anything about the industry. And we're starting to have quality problems that none of us need or want. So let's build a facility and start training people, not just for me but for other minority companies as well."

So Ford and the Bing Group teamed up to build the Detroit Manufacturing Training Center. We supplied the land in North Industrial Park, and Ford provided $3 million to build and equip the facility. And when it was up and running the center offered 400 students per year free eight-week training sessions in areas such as welding, injection molding, and computers. It was another example of actually doing well and doing good.

Everything seemed to be humming along nicely, and then on August 13, 1999, a fire started in the 60,000-square-foot plant we shared with Lear. It started during the second shift, about eight o'clock at night. I was at home and ran back down there, but by the time I arrived, the whole facility was gone. There had been a lot of cardboard in the area of the plant where the fire ignited, and it spread so fast that even though the fire department got there quickly, they couldn't save it. The sight of that plant, which had been such a productive place just hours earlier, basically burned to the ground was unbelievably painful.

Investigators ruled it had been deliberately set, possibly by a disgruntled employee who had been seen by a supervisor in the area where the fire had started. He reportedly had a drug problem and had recently been disciplined. This was after the union had come in, and I didn't know the employee or what his problems were.

Three months later, in December, a second fire occurred at Detroit Automotive Interiors, the other plant we had with Lear, this time destroying more than a quarter of the 135,000-square-foot plant. Once again, a disgruntled employee was suspected, but this time only a portion of the building was damaged, so the plant could remain in operation while that area was repaired.

Nonetheless, workers from the facility that had burned in August had relocated to this larger plant, and many would now have to move again. Lear's attitude was: Okay, we've got one plant ruined, another damaged, and a lot of product destroyed. How are we going to take care of our customers? Lear's can-do answer was that while we rebuilt the first plant on its original foundations and repaired the second plant, we would have to transfer a large number of employees to a Lear facility deep in the suburbs. And so for a lot of our employees that was an imposition, and for those who didn't have cars it was a major problem. So while construction proceeded on the plants, we were bussing people between North Industrial Park in Detroit and Auburn Hills.

It was not an easy time for any of us, but despite these setbacks, our company had a record year in 1999, with revenues reaching $304 million. The Bing Group now employed more than 1,100, and our joint venture with Lear continued to be a gift that kept on giving.

In the celebrated millennial year of 2000, Lear found a new opportunity in Berne, Indiana. Lear had acquired another company, and a plant in Berne was part of the deal. Now at this point we still weren't doing business with any of the so-called transplant or overseas companies, like Toyota, Honda, and BMW. But this Indiana plant's primary customer was Toyota. So for us, joining Lear in Berne would open important new doors, and for Toyota it meant satisfying some of the minority mandates established by the three major American car companies.

From a strategic standpoint it made sense for our joint venture with Lear to buy that firm and its plant, but now for the first time, I would have to spend business hours outside the Detroit metropolitan area. On a regular basis, I needed to drive down to Berne, outside Ft. Wayne, because the people at that plant needed to see me as their new owner. They knew Lear, but they didn't know me, and all of a sudden they had become a minority company. There were very few minorities on their workforce, and they needed a comfort zone. But once they got to see me and know me on a consistent basis, it worked out well.

• • •

In the summer of 2002, we became involved with an initiative that I saw as a way to give back to our community. I had formed a company called Dogwood Ventures to build homes in a residential neighborhood adjacent to North Industrial Park. The area had been lined with homes in the past but now included a lot of vacant lots, and my vision was to build it up and help it out. Working with me on Dogwood were Coleman Young's former right-hand guy Emmett Moten and Kirk Lewis, the president of one of our Bing Group companies, and a fellow with whom I went all the way back to when I was playing for the Pistons and he was a ball boy. The idea had come from conversations I had with some of our employees. They told me they'd like to live close to their workplace in North Industrial Park, but there were no suitable homes nearby.

So why not build homes in that adjacent neighborhood? Why not build nice, brick, four-bedroom homes and try to sell them? And, of course, lots of people told me I was crazy. They said, "You can't build really nice homes in this area, because people can't afford them, or won't invest in a neighborhood with tough inner-city problems." But my thought was that if people have good jobs and decent incomes, let's give them an opportunity. Let's build these homes and see whether or not there's a market out there.

So I built two attractive brick homes, with four bedrooms and a six-figure price tag. We worked with church and community groups to get the word out, and both homes were purchased quickly for the asking price. And soon there was a lot of interest both from my employees as well as from people in that neighborhood. And all of a sudden folks were saying, "Hey, this makes sense. Now the value of our property is going to increase, because it's close to that well-kept North Industrial Park. And now people are moving into our neighborhood and groups are partnering with the neighborhood elementary school and doing some things for our kids." So people who had wanted to move out now said, wait, maybe not. Maybe things are starting to turn around.

Actually, I wasn't interested in making money on this project. The goal for me was to not lose money. But if we were making anything from those homes, then we'd take that money and reinvest it. So we started buying vacant land, lot by lot, and we ended up building and selling more than 30 homes over a three-year period. And people in the media began coming to me for comments like these about the beleaguered city of Detroit:

"Running away from a problem never solved a problem. Detroit had its issues before. It will continue to have its issues, but solutions can only come from those who have a deepseated love for this city and a relentless drive to see the city improve. I'm not naive enough to believe that I'll see all the problems facing this city corrected in my lifetime, but you've got to start somewhere: building my business within the city of Detroit, employing Detroiters, and showing what could be accomplished with a little initiative and a lot of hard work and sweat."

About this time, I got involved in the charter school effort in Detroit. I read in one of the papers that mayor Kwame Kilpatrick and the Detroit Public Schools had been offered $200 million from a very wealthy philanthropist named Robert Thompson, who wanted to start a series of charter schools in the city. Thompson felt that Detroit's public schools were so mired in failure that the only way to improve them was to set up a competing system of charters that would use dedication and innovation to give the city's kids a real shot at quality education.

The DPS and Kilpatrick administration were more than willing to take the money, but with the union brass of the Detroit Federation of Teachers digging in their heels, they refused to allow Mr. Thompson to have any input as to how it was spent. At one point the union even threatened a lawsuit claiming that charters would violate the public trust by siphoning resources away from its schools. Thompson finally said, "Thanks, but no thanks."

So the matter was at a standoff when I called and met with Bob Thompson. I found him to be a man with a deep and generous concern for Detroit's young people, and I think he saw me as someone who cared not a whit about the tangles of politics but with a respected voice and a presence in the city. Of course, when I came out publicly in support of Thompson's charter school plans, I was quickly reviled in certain circles in the Black community. But I was neither surprised nor put off by all the flack. All I cared about was welfare of Detroit's children and their chance at a better education.

So I enlisted the help of the head of Michigan's Department of Commerce, Doug Ross, who was himself a former Detroit teacher, and he helped us find a way to make Bob Thompson's vision a reality. Today there are five Thompson sponsored charter schools in the city and the first one has my name on it.

They say timing is everything. I say, even if it's not, it's always pretty damn important. Take our experience with the Watermark, a project that we announced in the spring of 2007. Like our Dogwood development, building homes next to North Industrial Park, it involved housing, but at the very opposite end of the spectrum. Emmett Moten had told me about a parcel of land owned by the city right on the Detroit River just east of downtown, and so I had taken an option on that land with the idea of perhaps putting up high-end condominiums. And the more I thought about it, the more I saw the city making a concerted effort to develop its long-neglected waterfront, and the more I heard people talking about a possible revival of the downtown area, the more I liked the idea. This could be another way I might be able to contribute to the city I had been committed to for so many decades.

So I exercised the option, and with a new entity we called Spingarn Development, we put together a major marketing piece, hiring planners, architects and interior designers to come up with a 110-unit, $60-million luxury project on the river, the likes of which Detroit had not seen before. We constructed models for the townhouses and the units in a nine-story tower, everything beautifully designed and fitted out with top-end features, along with the promise of spectacular views up and down the river. And when we went public in May 2007, we were greeted with excitement and enthusiasm.

Yes, our prices were high, from $350,000 for the smaller units to over a million a piece for the four penthouses. But I was quoted at the time as saying, "I feel very confident that with the product we're going to present, we'll be very competitive." And sales moved fast from the beginning. Businessman Roger Penske took one of the penthouses, and Derrick Coleman took another. The other two went to DTE's Tony Earley and the African American auto dealer Greg Jackson, and soon we had sold more than 40 percent of all the other units.

Earlier we had changed our corporate name from the Bing Group to Bing Holdings to better represent what I saw as a kind of mothership for all our investments, like the Watermark. My plan was to use it as a resource center to more easily acquire the funding I might need. Our revenues in 2007 were approaching $700 million, we had a workforce of close to 1,500, and the future looked bright indeed.

But anyone with a basic understanding of the recent economic past knows that we, along with almost everyone else on the planet, had failed to see some very dark clouds on the horizon. And a hard rain was about to fall.

12

NEVER SAY NEVER

WAY BACK IN 1992, just before Christmas, mayor Coleman Young, who had helmed Detroit for nearly two decades, was thinking about who he'd like to see take over the city's top job when hizzoner finally stepped down. Coleman asked me to his office one day to share his thoughts and sound me out. First, he told me it was clear that I cared about the city and was popular with its people. I had my ego under control, was honest, had leadership skills and the right heart for it. The only question for him was whether I really wanted the job and all the responsibility it entailed. If I did, he said he'd marshal all his political and financial clout behind my candidacy, and he had no doubt, given the extensive community good-will I had banked over the years, I would win in a walk.

I thanked the Mayor for his assessment and his offer, but said I would need to pass on the opportunity. When he asked why, I told him, "I have hundreds of people who are entrusted to me at the company. I can't abandon them. I have a responsibility to them, and I don't have a succession plan in place right now that would afford me the opportunity to pursue other interests."

Coleman smiled and gave me that pleasant growl of his. "God-damn, that's absolutely the right answer."

I think there were many other movers and shakers in Detroit who agreed with Coleman's view, but I was still building my businesses and strongly felt I could play a more effective role for the city outside of politics. The idea of my running for the job would reassert itself over the ensuing years, and while I would continue to say no, I would often also add, "I won't say never."

So a decade and a half passed, and, in fiscal terms both locally and nationally, things had definitely changed for the worse.

Worries and fears about an economy grinding down and then turning into a major tailspin started in 2007 and got louder and more insistent throughout 2008. As business at Bing Holdings began to drop off, loans became harder to come by, and money was increasingly scarce. The car companies were coming to their supply base and demanding price reductions. The threat was: "If you don't give us the price we need, we'll quit your business and turn to somebody else." But with our already narrow margins, there was no way we could give them what they wanted without major losses. It was getting very dicey indeed.

Yes, it had happened before. The auto business had always been cyclical, but this downturn felt different, as many small suppliers were facing serious economic peril, and for the first time, I wasn't sure we'd be able to survive. Now we were all becoming sadly familiar with previously esoteric terms like "housing bubble" and "credit default swaps." Massive issues with subprime mortgages turned into a full-on international banking crisis with the collapse of Lehman Brothers in the fall of 2008. By then we were headed into what became known as the Great Recession, the worst financial disaster since the 1930s and the Great Depression.

I hardly have to tell you what all this did to real estate projects like the Watermark. Inevitably it dissolved with considerable investment loss. Our businesses, which had been humming along for years, were suddenly looking at customers cutting back big time and outstanding bank loans (for those plants we had been building) all coming due.

The whole auto industry was crashing, General Motors and Chrysler were heading for bankruptcy, and the support that we had been getting as a minority company was gone. As for the banks, they, of course, treated us like anybody else loaded with debt. When they called the loans, you had no choice.

So we started losing money as an entity in '07, and now I had to consider my options. If I hung on, I was pretty certain to lose a lot more money. But I was deeply concerned about my 1,400 employees. I could try to find some bargain-basement deals where I could sell and not lose as much. But then so many of the people I was employing would be thrown on the scrap heap, with little hope of finding another job. For a while, probably for a lot longer than I should have, I didn't go out to the market to try to sell. I continued losing money, trying to keep my people employed for as long as I could, always hoping against hope that somehow things would turn around. So we continued to supply our customers and continued to lose money. After successfully building the business for nearly three decades, it was a very disheartening time. I stayed in business at least a year longer than I should have. It was well into '08 when I finally said, "I can no longer do this," and we started to wind down.

Now almost simultaneously with all this, the area's business community had begun hearing more and more about our young mayor's scandalous and corrupt behavior. I had originally thought highly of Kwame Kilpatrick, a whip-smart law school grad from a politically active Detroit family, married with three young sons, and a guy who had seemingly entered politics for all the right reasons. I had supported his run for mayor, but then in '07 we began hearing lots of rumors. It basically started with talk of an affair with his chief of staff, a woman I knew named Christine Beatty, and from my vantage point that didn't bother me nearly as much as all the whispers bouncing around the city by then about pay-to-play. Word was that in order to get a meeting with the mayor, you had to pay his father, and by dangling city contracts they were fleecing people right and left.

In January of '08, the *Detroit Free Press* blew the lid off the scandal when it published thousands of text messages between the mayor and Beatty that not only documented their extra-marital affair, but put them in serious legal jeopardy for perjury and fraudulent behavior involving a secret $8.4 million payoff to keep a couple of Detroit cops quiet.

With the media now out in full force and on the hunt, all kinds of sordid corruption began to surface. Some of it centered on Kilpatrick's relationship with a buddy named Bobby Ferguson. When it came to any demolition or construction job going on in the city, Bobby had to be involved. And his contribution was pretty much limited to paperwork, never having to do much of anything to get paid.

The stories of sex and corruption were coming in rapid fire succession now and making Detroit seem like a laughingstock. At that point, with all these rumors swirling and everything happening in the media, the subject was always coming up in the business meetings and conversations that I was having. Detroiters generally were upset, but they all saw Kwame Kilpatrick as a native son of the city, and nobody was confronting him. It was obvious to me that this had to stop, and so I requested a meeting.

Kilpatrick and I had always had a good relationship, and I was old enough to be his dad. I said, "As you certainly know, there are a lot of negative things being reported about you lately, and you are clearly losing all the support you once had. Very frankly, I don't see how you can regain the trust and support of your constituents. I've been in conversations with a lot of different people, both in the business community and in the general population, and I have to tell you, a helluva lot of people in Detroit think that you need to leave office."

He said that he was sorry that I felt that way, but he had to do what he had to do. Actually, I think he had a pretty realistic sense of how people were thinking and talking in both the business circles and the wider community, but he seemed to feel that, because he was such a large and dominating personality, he could really get away with this stuff, that it was just a matter of time until people would stop digging up dirt, and all of this would blow over. Maybe he would back off from what he was doing, and it would all eventually go away. But, of course, that never happened.

On March 18, 2008, the Detroit City Council called for the mayor to resign, and six days later Kilpatrick was indicted in federal court on eight criminal felony counts, including perjury, obstruction of justice, and misconduct in office. Still he would not step down, vowing a fight to the finish and claiming that he was the victim of a media witch-hunt.

The City Council then requested that Michigan governor Jennifer Granholm, a Democrat, declare Kilpatrick unfit for office and force him to step down. But she chose to wait for the mayor to finally see the light and do the honorable thing. Over the next several months, certain leaders in our business community tried paying him to leave office, with four or five loans of $50,000 to $75,000 dollars for a total of close to $300,000. He needed the cash because of the lifestyle he was living, and as far as I know, he never paid the money back.

In the meantime, with Kilpatrick's political demise seeming inevitable, many of us in the city's business and community leadership were looking around at possible candidates to replace our wayward young mayor when the time finally came. In my own personal survey, I saw no one I thought was a good fit. The most obvious choice was the president of the City Council, Ken Cockrel Jr., but to me he was strictly a politician, and that was not what I thought we needed. Actually, none of the people I was talking with then thought he was the answer. We all thought we needed somebody who wasn't tied to the politics of the city. And with all the hard, ugly decisions that would have to be made, the typical politician was not likely to make them.

At that point, in all those conversations I was having with business colleagues, friends, and other leaders in town, many of them kept coming back to me as the best possible choice. But I was going through our whole business exit at that time, and I certainly did not need or want another job. "No sir, not at all," I'd tell them. This was supposed to be my time to find the best way to get out of the business, while taking care of as many employees as possible. And then my plan, and dream, would be to just retire and enjoy life. I had lately taken up golf, and we had a beautiful vacation home down in Hilton Head, South Carolina. Besides, I'd say, I don't know anything about politics or running a city, and so I had what anybody would consider legitimate doubts about taking this job.

In fact, we knew Detroit was constantly losing its tax base and had gone from 1.3 million people down to 700,000. A lot of major businesses had moved out of the city, the suburbs were growing, and the city was dying. Unemployment was very high, and so was crime, and there was no end in sight to any of this. Certainly, no one, least of all me, had a magic wand or a silver bullet we could employ to change things for the better. It was going to be a really difficult, long-term project.

So it took two or three months of meetings with business folks and community people, where there was a lot of cajoling resulting in pretty much a groundswell, with everybody saying, "Hey, Dave, face it, you're the guy. You've got a good relationship with all kinds of groups in the city. People trust you. You've got a great business background. You've got community involvement, and that's what we need right now. We've got to restore trust in this city."

Now when I really thought about it, my bottom line was that I cared for the city and its people. And looking at the perilous situation Detroit was in, it was going to be hard for me to point my finger at Kilpatrick and say, "You didn't do this, you didn't do that." And then I turn around and do nothing about it.

So I felt that I could be helpful to my city and its people, but it was not something that I wanted. Based on all of those conversations, I knew in my mind how difficult it was going to be and the tough impact it would have on me and my family. Just for openers, the first thing I'd be forced to do, once I made a decision to go forward, was move into Detroit. I hadn't lived in the city for close to four decades.

As for my friends, Bob Lanier was not living in the Detroit area, but he knew what was going on. And as my name surfaced, the question from Bob was, "Are you nuts? Why in the hell would you want to do that?" The reactions from Jim Boeheim and Frank Nicoletti were similar. But my pals in Detroit, Lem Barney and Mel Farr, encouraged me to run. Mel was especially forceful, saying I was a natural fit and that the city might not make it through this turmoil without somebody (namely me) it could trust implicitly.

Emmett Moten and Charlie Beckham, two guys who had been close to Coleman Young, were good friends of mine, and they were pushing me, saying I was the right person at the right time. But the fellows who finally made the difference were Tony Earley from DTE Energy, Roger Penske, Gene Miller from Comerica Bank, Judge Damon Keith, and civil rights pioneer Art Johnson. They were all longtime friends and supporters, all had my deep respect and moved me to make the decision to go for it.

Once I thought through what I was doing, I brought the family together and talked to them about the decision. By that time, I pretty much knew what their response would be, and there were no surprises in that meeting. We were a close-knit family, and Yvette and my kids knew my heart as the leader of the family. They knew I really cared about people, especially those who had done nothing to cause their own misfortune. I thought I could help, at least give them a voice. So I made that decision, knowing it was going to be hard on all of us, because I thought I could make a difference. I explained that the first thing I'd have to do was move out of our beautiful home in suburban Franklin and establish residence in Detroit, probably in an apartment downtown.

Yvette said, "I feel you. I know you've made up your mind here, and I don't think you're going to change it. I'm certain that you're up to the challenge, and I do think you are a good person with your heart in the right place, but I'm not ready to move yet. You've still got some exploring to do, and I'll be with you for that, but I've got my own business to run, and I'm not ready to leave our home."

In June, I gave the *Free Press* an interview that was a step toward going public. I said, "The unfortunate thing for those of us who are strong supporters of the city is that it becomes more and more difficult to circle the wagons and become protective. It's just a matter of time before those people, regardless of how much they love the city, find options to move, and we could see an outpouring of whatever middle class we still have here. That's a death knell because we've lost so much of our middle class. You can't have just all poor people and think the city's going to do well. And that's what's happening right now. And we've got to change that."

I also had words for our embattled young mayor: "Do we have capable people in the city that can change things? I think so. But what we don't need to happen is to split the community more than it is split right now. It's not about Black and White. It's not necessarily about city and suburb. It's about credible leaders right now and, unfortunately, we've got a problem there."

And I basically called him out: "I don't think we can prejudge the legality of what the mayor is going through. But whether he's guilty or innocent is not the issue to me right now. It's the harm that's being placed on the citizens. And I don't think anybody can deflect that. I just think… the political leadership, the business leadership, the educational leadership have all got to sit down at the table and figure out a model that works for everybody, and tough decisions have got to be made."

Finally, in September of '08, Kilpatrick agreed to a plea deal with the feds and left the mayor's office. He spent 99 days in jail and then found himself charged with other offenses and later sentenced to prison for 28 years. So on September 19, according to the city charter, he was immediately replaced by Cockrel, the president of the City Council, with a special election scheduled for the following May in 2009.

Now to establish residency I had to make the move to a furnished apartment down on Jefferson, near the river, east of downtown. And I'll tell you, from the start it was pretty damn lonely. I was all by myself much of the time, except for occasional visits from Yvette, and the weekends I'd often spend at home in Franklin. That was a tough time, separated from my family and spending the better part 14–16 hours a day just canvassing the city, learning as much as I could and meeting with as many people as possible.

Canvassing Detroit, meeting with individuals and community groups in every sad and neglected corner of the city, was a deeply sobering experience for me. I found so much anger, squalor, and despair in so many neighborhoods that I caught myself wondering if this could really be a major city in the wealthiest nation on earth.

Charlie Beckham, Emmett Motten, and Kirk Lewis were helping to set up the meetings with community groups. Also helping were Jim Stapleton, a guy with a lot of political connections, and Ed Tinsley, an ex-banker and a strong numbers guy. We'd have a meeting at a community center or in someone's home. And people who didn't know me would get a chance to see what I was about.

And so I learned over and over just how bad it was for those who lived in this once dynamic city. They were unemployed or under-employed, couldn't feel safe in their own homes, couldn't trust the delivery of basic city services and worried about the kind of education their children were getting in their schools. But I also heard again and again from so many people about how happy they were that I was running and trying to help. I learned for the most part that I had a very good reputation as a solid, down-to-earth person who cared for people and had done some positive things in the city.

And once we started to prepare for the interim election primary in February 2009, I learned that I'd be up against a lengthy list of can-didates, many of whom no one had ever heard of, but also including Cockrel, the sitting mayor who had a strong political background, and Freman Hendrix, who had been the deputy mayor under Dennis Archer. I knew Freman as a good guy with a solid reputation. So while lots of people told me I was the favorite, it seemed likely to me that this was not going to be a walk in the park.

The two top vote getters in the primary would move on to square off in the special election scheduled for May 5. But there was so much basic political stuff I had no concept of, so much inside governmental experience that both Cockrel and Hendrix possessed that I lacked. And I felt I had to get myself on a fast track to an understanding of the intricacies of city government.

On February 24, about 15 percent of Detroit's eligible voters cast their ballots and gave me 26,337 votes, Cockrel 24,677, and Hendrix 21,208. Cockrel and I would be facing each other in May.

This time, as the special election approached, I was much more confident both about what I was doing and that I would get elected. As a businessman I had always been well prepared. I had a work ethic better than most. And once I gained the knowledge I needed about the task in front of me, I was sure I was going to be competitive. So even though Cockrel certainly had more insight into the politics of the city, I had really prepared myself to get as much knowledge as I could to go head to head against him. In his six months in office he had brought in a new police chief and a deputy mayor, but there was little else anyone could see in terms of positive change.

Our campaign team was that same small group of people I'd been meeting with on an ongoing basis: Kirk Lewis, Emmett Moten, Charlie Beckham, Jim Stapleton, and Ed Tinsley, along with Kilpatrick's deputy mayor, Anthony Adams; Doris Biscoe, formerly a news anchor at Channel 7 with whom I had gone to high school in D.C.; and Bob Warfield, who had been VP for News at Channel 4. On election night, they were all with me at the Fort Shelby DoubleTree Hotel downtown, along with family and friends and many who had convinced me to run and offered crucial support. Generally, the feedback we were getting was that it would just come down too how many percentage points we'd win by. But in fact I was still pretty much a political novice running against a guy who had been in politics most of his adult life.

Again, only a slim portion of Detroiters went to the polls, and the results were in quickly: my 52 percent to Cockrel's 48. I was sworn in six days later, with little in the way of pomp and circumstance, and would be mayor of the City of Detroit until the regularly scheduled general election in November of 2009. Here's some of what I said in my first inaugural speech:

"Today marks the beginning of a new era for Detroit. For quite some time, many have talked about the need to bring change, and today that change is before us.... We will no longer be defined by the failures, divisiveness, and self-serving actions of the past. We are turning the page to a new time in Detroit, focused not just on the challenges we face, but the opportunities we have to rebuild and renew our city.

"As you all are well aware, we have a number of significant issues to address in the next four years. We can't hide from those challenges or look for quick fixes that compromise our future. And that's why from day one, I've made the tough but necessary choices to put our city back on track:

"Implementing a tough new ethics policy and setting higher expectations for my administration.

"Making leadership changes to improve our public safety departments and to reduce crime in our neighborhoods.

"Addressing our budget crisis and the need to right-size city government with a data-driven and long-term big-picture approach.

"But this is just the beginning. Many more difficult decisions lie ahead. And at a time when we will be asking our citizens for sacrifice, it is incumbent on us to lead by example. Change starts at the top. That's why my appointees were the first city employees to take the 10 percent salary cut through furlough days. This is an important contribution to help get our fiscal house in order.

"And one of our most important challenges will be restoring trust in city government. Detroiters have been through a difficult time, and their confidence in government has been understandably shaken. But I believe we are on the path to regaining that trust with a transparent and open approach to governing. The public has a right to know what we're doing and why we're doing it. We must also repair the image and perception of Detroit. By changing the way we do our business, by improving our tone, and by sharing the progress I know we will make, we will be better positioned to attract the investment and jobs we need. I come from a team background and understand that I cannot do this job alone.

"Change is never easy. But no matter our differences, we must always remember we're working toward the same goal of building a better future for Detroit and Detroiters."

The speech got good reviews. Obviously, I was trying to convince people in Detroit that we were their agents and that they needed to buy into our agenda. I didn't want people working in city government to see their position as simply a job, as little more than a way to earn an income. They needed to take on responsibility, to be held to account, because in my view there were too many in city government who were taking advantage of the city.

With less than a week of transition between my victory and our new administration taking office, we got little or nothing from Cockrel and his people in terms of briefings or reports on where things stood after his seven months on the job. Frankly, I believe he thought he was going to win, so there was no reason to prepare even basic info for us. And that's why I needed to move as quickly as possible to assemble key data on budgets, expenditures, and plans for each department. Getting all that information together would take a good bit of time and effort, but we couldn't do much of anything without it.

Off the bat for me was getting to know the leadership already in place. I couldn't come in and make snap personnel decisions. I needed to sit down with department heads and find a way to gauge their attitudes and values, to assess their strengths and weaknesses. That would be the first step in the crucial process of finding and evaluating accurate data on how each department was doing financially. Then, ultimately, it would be a question of whom to keep and whom to replace.

I was bringing in some new people from the outside who didn't know city government at all. Charlie Beckham was one of the few who knew it inside and out, and he was an old and trusted friend, one of my tennis-playing buddies from the old days, along with Mel Farr and Lem Barney. So I felt comfortable relying on Charlie's experience and expertise. But when he came in with me there were more than a few whispers.

Back when he was one of Coleman Young's top people, he had run into trouble in connection with the infamous Vista sludge-hauling bribery case back in the '80s. There had been a payoff in a multi-million dollar city contract that had nearly taken down the Young administration, and it had put Charlie in prison for a couple of years. But I had known Charlie pretty well back then and didn't think he was really at fault. It seemed to me that he had been basically a fall-guy for Coleman. I was a firm believer in second chances and placed him in an important position in our new administration, but eventually, when those whispers became loud enough to serve as a reminder of Kilpatrick's fraud and corruption, Charlie took himself off the team. In the end, we both knew that our number one priority had to be restoring trust in the office.

So now I had to get to know some of the pivotal people in city government and, just as important, let them get to know me. I began by meeting with each of the department heads one-on-one, and I quickly found that there were a number of good people in city government. The standard line I had heard from Detroiters was that city workers were a bunch of thieves, or people who didn't know what they were doing, or people who didn't care. But I discovered many who didn't fit that picture, and what happened with Kwame had disappointed and demoralized a lot of them.

There were also others, however, who had clearly been co-opted, and when they had seen Kilpatrick getting away with certain things, he had then served as a model. My consistent message, of course, was that this was just unacceptable and certainly not the way it was going to be from now on. So at each meeting I always underscored the importance of ethics. If you were caught doing anything wrong, you would be gone. It was as simple as that. And as it played out, those who could cut it stayed and those who couldn't were fired.

Also, from the beginning I tried to set the tone for what I was about. I didn't want anyone to think I was coming in there to walk on water, appear holier than thou, or be something other than a member of our team. So knowing from the start that cuts would be unavoidable, I announced I would take no salary beyond a dollar a year. I wanted it to be obvious this wasn't about money for me, because I already knew we'd soon have to trim staff, salaries, and benefits.

Of course, all of this meant that I was actually paying to be mayor. After the election, I moved out of that first apartment, but not into the Manoogian Mansion, the mayor's traditional residence in the city. Kilpatrick's hard-partying and carelessness had left it trashed and in need of a major make-over. Instead I moved into an attractive place on the river, a condo in the Shoreline complex, east of downtown, which was expensive at $3,500 a month. Yvette and I were still on the schedule we'd established when I had moved into the city. Maybe once during the week she'd come down to the condo, and then over the weekend a lot of times I would go to our home in Franklin, depending on what was going on in the city and what my commitments were.

Fortunately ours was a good strong relationship, so we didn't have any major disconnect.

As for Bing Holdings, we had begun closing down in 2008 and would finally finish in '09. Because I was so busy in the mayor's office, my daughter Cassaundra (who was our CFO) and my attorneys and accountants were responsible for shutting everything down, and it was a bittersweet thing for all of us. We had enjoyed a great run, and for a while we hoped against hope that something might happen to turn things around. But the industry continued to struggle, and over our last year in business we lost roughly $7 million to $8 million. If we had closed down a year earlier, we could have avoided that kind of loss, but then most of my 1,400 employees would not have been able to get a job anywhere else. At least now, as we headed for 2010 and with the economy beginning to pick up, they'd have a shot at finding other work.

• • •

Being alone in the condo was not fun, so one of the things I usually did was take my mayoral staff out to dinner in small groups of two or three people. We'd have conversations that we had no time for during our busy workday, and it was a way for us to get to know each other and build the team. At one of our favorite restaurants, I'd always pick up the tab with a personal credit card. I never I had a city card, and my staffers got a good feel for me as a fellow trying to serve the city for the right reasons. They all knew I was not in this for any kind of self-aggrandizement. And when it came time to cut their salaries—within 90 to 120 days—it was for them neither a surprise nor something to gripe about. The great thing was that, as hard as we were working, they took these cuts and nobody quit. So they were doing more work and living on less.

At the same time, it was harder to convince outside talent that we needed them to come into city government. Who wants to come in at a less-than-competitive salary and work harder? So it was a tough sell, but I actually got turned down only a few times, because, I think, people felt so strongly about trying to bring the city back out of its pain and trouble, and they were willing to take a risk.

Among my most important staffers at that time were Bob Warfield, who was handling communication, and Kirk Lewis, the executive in charge of Public Safety, with police and fire under him. Bob was key in getting our message of change and new hope out to a community used to news going from bad to worse. And Kirk had also brought in a couple of top accounting managers whose background and savvy began to make me feel more comfortable with the quality of the financial data I was getting.

Most of our time in those first six months was spent on collecting and evaluating information. That was the priority, because as a business person I knew that you could only make solid business decisions based on good, hard data. But back when we first started, we had nothing like that.

So we had to go into each department and meticulously audit what each of them was doing and what their budgets were, turning over every rock and looking into every crevice to find accurate and comprehensive info from numbers that had sometimes been hidden or fudged. We asked repeatedly if we might be able to move some money from this to that, or from one department to another.

Unfortunately, what we eventually found was that there were huge issues within every one of the city's departments, because all of them were spending way more than they had in their budgets.

Everybody was in a serious deficit situation, and the word from my finance people to all of the department heads was simple: "You can't continue to live like this. You can't spend more than you have. There are things that you may need or want to do, but you can't do them."

So once we got to the bottom of things, the view was bleak indeed. Essentially, we were bankrupt without filing bankruptcy. We were over $17 billion in debt if you included long-term liabilities, meaning the pension fund and the benefits. Benefits alone represented 107 percent of payroll. And so it also meant that we could not maintain the employee base. We had over 14,000 employees on the city's payroll, and we couldn't afford anywhere near that number. My biggest fear was that we were soon going to face a payless payday. Nothing could be worse than that.

Frankly, I was already sure the only way out of this was bankruptcy. I knew now there was no way that we could generate enough revenue to be successful running the city. The tax base had dropped dramatically. The population was still shrinking. All the services that we needed to provide for the city's businesses and its citizens were beyond what we could afford.

As we began to formulate a plan to move forward, all the decisions we were confronting from an economic standpoint were negative. The choices were between the heartbreaking and the impossible, and all of them were going to have a negative impact on Detroiters, folks who were already dealing with a graduation rate in their schools of 20 percent, an unemployment rate of 27 percent, and a median income of $28,730, lower than in any major city in the country.

Yes, there were times when I wondered, "What the hell have I got myself into?" But now there was no turning back.

13

MISSION IMPOSSIBLE

I **F I'M HONEST,** I'd have to say there wasn't much I actually liked about this new job of mine. It seemed that every day brought a different crisis to deal with. But because we had established good working relationships with our staffers, nobody shirked their responsibilities, and we just moved from crisis to crisis.

Since I was used to starting at 6:30 or 7:00 in the morning, I continued to do that in the mayor's office. I was usually the first one there, so I would make coffee for everyone. I had soon learned that people in city government usually didn't start work before 8:00 AM. And because there were no expectations and nobody checking on them, I would walk the floor, so to speak. I wanted to see who was there and who wasn't. And so when I found people who didn't like to come to work on time or left early, I explained that their approach was not acceptable. Start early, start on time, and work all day. That was my expectation for everybody. So while some were soon dismissed, work habits and the on-the-job atmosphere started to change.

Practically every hour through the day I'd be meeting with somebody, trying to identify their department's problems and find solutions. And the people who witnessed my approach and work ethic saw what I expected of them and understood that I wasn't the kind of guy who would simply tell them what to do, and then just sit around or go off and do something more pleasant. I was down there in the foxhole with them.

In no time, it seemed we had ploughed through most of those six months of the interim term, and now we had to prepare for the full-term election in November. First up was the August 4 primary, with a half-dozen names on the ballot, most of them basically unknown. My only real competition came from Tom Barrow, an accountant and businessman who had run and lost in the past. I made sure that trend continued, getting more than 68,000 votes to his 10,302.

We faced off again on November 3. I respected Barrow, but by now I was confident enough with the experience of the past several months that I didn't think he could beat me. The worst thing that he could say about me was that I was a suburban carpetbagger, but I knew most Detroiters wouldn't buy that.

Still, while I had been honest in my public statements about the massive difficulties the city faced, I had carefully avoided making any of the major moves I knew would be necessary but were likely to anger and disappoint almost everybody. I had cut about 400 government jobs and terminated some union contracts, but most of the tough stuff would have to wait until after we had been returned to office and had four years ahead of us.

On election night, we were back at the Fort Shelby DoubleTree with basically the same collection of family, friends, and supporters along with key staffers. But up from D.C. were my 85-year-old mom and even a couple of my boyhood pals who had arrived to take it all in with me. Yvette and I sat on a couch and watched a documentary on Barack Obama's rise to the White House, while the others all followed the vote tally.

When the results finally came in from the typically small percentage of Detroit voters, I had 56 percent to Barrow's 41. In my victory speech, I said: "Thank you, Detroit. Thank you for the chance to finish the job that was started several months ago. Together we can now put Detroit back on the right path. Thank you, for your confidence. I see progress, and I know we are headed in the right direction."

I believed those words, but I also knew we were in the grip of a massive fiscal disaster. Our once proud city wasn't even close to having the resources it needed to make life reasonably livable for its citizens and viable for its business community. Yes, we had won the chance to fix things, but all we had ahead of us were crushingly difficult decisions. Yes, we had a plan, but its implementation would be another order of business altogether.

With a good look at the city's books, I knew we were surely headed for a financial collapse. We had an annual revenue stream of a little more than a billion dollars. You couldn't even come close to running the city on that. The interest on the debt alone exceeded a quarter of a billion dollars a year. There was clearly no way we could continue down that road.

During the campaign I had not talked about being a one-term mayor. But now we were in a position where almost every choice we confronted would result in a painful decision for the people of our city. Whether it was cutting payroll or cutting benefits or negotiating with the unions over 56 different contracts, all of it posed a terrible ordeal, and we didn't even have enough staff to tackle it either effectively or efficiently.

The work to be done was so tough and unpleasant, so likely to anger and disappoint so many Detroiters, that I felt it could only be done by a one-term mayor. All those deeply difficult decisions would simply not allow a mayor to be popular enough to run again. So in my mind there was no doubt I'd be a one-term mayor. And the fact was that being mayor was not something that I had wanted in the first place. Yes, I thought I could help, but now I was facing only heartbreaking decisions that were certain to negatively impact lots of vulnerable people.

Clearly I needed to find help for Detroiters from outside the city's coffers, and there was one obvious place to look. I had met Barack Obama the first time at a fundraiser for him in Chicago during his first campaign. Jesse Jackson and I were good friends, and he introduced me to this remarkably impressive young leader.

Soon after I was elected, I called the president in D.C., and he offered congratulations and said he was pleased with my election. He knew something about me because he was a basketball fan, but he also knew I was a political novice, facing very tough times in the city of Detroit. He promised to support us, saying, "Let me know what you need, and I'll give you whatever help I can."

Of course, I told him I knew what he was facing and would never go to him for something I thought was impossible for him to give. But over the next four years, the Obama Administration was extremely supportive, and Barack and his team leaned over backwards to help our city in several different ways.

As for the other branch of city government I had to deal with, I had a pretty decent relationship with most of the nine City Council members. But Charles Pugh, a former news anchor at the Fox-owned station in Detroit, was the Council's top vote getter and therefore became Council president. And I think in his mind at that time he was already envisioning a run for mayor. So he really made it much more difficult in my opinion than it should have been in our relationship. And early on I found that I couldn't really trust him. We would meet and formulate an agenda, and then within 24 hours, he had changed the terms we had agreed on. So I came not to trust him.

Gary Brown was a former cop who had come in second on the ballot. We got along, but I soon came to suspect that he too had political ambitions that included my job.

Now the key people in formulating our plan to move forward were Chris Brown and Kirk Lewis. Chris was my chief operating officer, a very bright guy who had been with DTE Energy and had been recommended by my friend Tony Earley, who ran DTE. Chris was a very aggressive guy, didn't play politics at all, and didn't much care whether you liked him or not. He wasn't afraid to make hard decisions.

Kirk was chief governmental and corporate affairs officer and a much easier-going person. He was a relationship guy and had been with me at Bing Holdings for a long time. In fact, I had known Kirk since he was 12 years old when he was a ball boy with the Pistons. Later, he had grown up in my company, so we had a long-term relationship, and now he was our key guy in dealing with the State.

As for the plan, we knew we didn't have nearly enough money to support every department. So putting a budget together was somewhere between difficult and a nightmare. Because some departments, as important as they might be, were not close to the funding levels they needed to operate properly, we had to decide which were the most crucial departments. Some were obviously key, like Water and Sewage and Public Safety (Police, Fire, and EMS). And some were well down the list, like the City Airport, which we couldn't really support properly, and Recreation, which I knew played an important role in the life of the city but would need to find some creative funding sources.

Of course, we had several other departments that provided vital services. One was Homeland Security, because Detroit is located right across the river from Canada and serves as an entry point into the U.S. And another was Transportation, which included bus service but also all the vehicles involved in general services, such as trash pickup, snow removal, and grass cutting.

And then there was Planning and Development, because we had so much neighborhood blight and so many vacant homes that were a major public safety issue. Most of them were crime scenes in waiting, with squatters and people with bad intentions preying on school kids.

Of course, we needed to reduce the number of those homes that were so far gone they needed to be removed, but we had to focus on certain areas. We couldn't do it across the whole city and had to be very focused on the location of schools. So we concentrated on danger points, the areas where school kids were walking to school past those vacant and beyond-repair houses. But knocking those kinds of homes down and getting rid of the debris was a very expensive proposition, and that's where HUD became an important partner to us. We had substantial financial support from Obama's Department of Housing and Urban Development, which we used to deal with blight.

Something similar also happened with Transportation. A very popular project was that M-line, which was three-and-a-half miles of rail from downtown up Woodward to the New Center area. Carolyn Kilpatrick, Kwame's mother, was still a congresswoman, and she was the key person in getting us the first $25 million dollars of a federal grant which allowed us to move forward with the with the M-line. So we got good help from the Obama Administration on the transportation side as well.

But we were facing so many difficult and painful decisions. Every time I went out to a meeting in the community, I felt people needed to hear the true story and an accurate picture. There was no sense in telling folks, "Hey, the cavalry is coming, so just hold on and we're going to save you and your neighborhood." We had to let people know that we were making some very tough decisions that were going to negatively impact them. And at least give them the truth, so that they could make an informed decision for themselves. I was not going to be able to come in and spread the little bit of money we had across the whole city. But it was hard to tell people, "We've only got so much money, and I can't spread these very limited funds across the entire city, because then we won't be helping anybody."

Did we have some kind of timetable in mind? Well, yes, we had a five-year plan, but in working within our budget for the year, we had so many unexpected crises confronting us and demanding the kind of resources we didn't really have. So needing to deal almost daily with serious issues right in front of your nose made taking the long view difficult indeed.

Unexpected crises seemed to be everywhere we looked, and in the spring of 2010 we encountered one early on that revealed problems internally that were about the last thing we needed at that point. In one of my first appointments I had named Warren Evans our Chief of Police. I had known Warren, who had made a solid career for himself as the Wayne County Sheriff, and he and Charlie Beckham were good friends who had grown up together in the same Detroit neighborhood. So early on, Beckham and Saul Green, who had been Cockrel's deputy mayor and stayed on as mine, had come to me and said, "We think Warren would be perfect for the DPD."

And so Warren was the Chief on a Sunday morning less than five months into our administration, when a little seven-year-old girl named Aiyana Jones was shot and killed in a police raid on her family's Detroit home. Now at that time, Public Safety reported not directly to me but to Saul Green, and when the details finally reached me, they were troubling to say the least.

I had faith in Green as a former federal prosecutor, the U. S. Attorney in Detroit, but it turned out that Warren Evans had kept him in the dark about a deal he was working on with a TV producer. So there was a video crew shooting a Cops-type episode for this show Evans had approved, and they got the whole awful scene on tape. Evans apparently thought this TV series was somehow going to make him look good, but the story blew up and went national, and even international. When I finally got all the details, I was appalled and angry about being kept in the dark, and when Saul Green argued that we should fire Evans and promote Ralph Godbee from within the department, I agreed.

Godbee was highly respected in the police department. He had come up through the ranks, and I had gotten to know him when he worked with us and with the Obama Administration in securing additional funding for the department. And so we chose Ralph to take over.

And then within 18 months, Godbee had a major problem when news broke that he had been having an affair with a young female police officer he had promoted. And as that story got messier, he had to step down, and I was forced to name a third chief in three years to head one of the most crucial departments in city government.

My first year was the last year in office for Michigan governor Jennifer Granholm, a Democrat whose sympathies were certainly with our city. But with the state still clawing its way out from under the recent economic collapse, I knew about all she could offer us was sympathy.

Still, with the state's economy showing signs of a turnaround in 2011, I had more hope for help from the new governor, Rick Snyder. I knew Snyder and got along with him well as a fellow businessman, who was also coming into politics for the first time. So I was hopeful that the state of Michigan would lend a hand to its largest city at a time of its greatest need.

As it played out, though, most of the time I was not dealing with Snyder, but with the man he had named as his state treasurer, a former Democratic speaker of the state house, Andy Dillon. And while we started out cordially enough, I soon found I had little use for Mr. Dillon.

To begin with, I assembled all our dismal data on the city's financial state and shared it with both Dillon and a Snyder aide, Dennis Muchmore. And they came to the same conclusion that I had: We had to go bankrupt. Muchmore was a professional and a decent person who understood the calamity that we were facing. And I think where he could be supportive he was, so I don't have anything negative to say about him.

But Dillon (who, by the way, would resign from his post within two years over issues with alcohol and a messy divorce) was a very different story, and it wasn't long before I began to see through his tactics. Now I'm sure Dillon was not just acting on his own but was getting instructions from Governor Snyder, because I don't think he would have pulled a lot of the duplicitous things he was doing behind Snyder's back. Frankly, I think they had both decided early on that we could not handle our own affairs and that the state would need to come in and take over Detroit.

We were very open with all the financial info we were sharing with them. We weren't hiding anything, so they could grasp how bad things were and offer help. At first there was a lot of talk between Snyder, Dillon, and myself on whether we should move toward bankruptcy. And early on they sent us a bit of financial support to see, I think, if we could manage it properly. But what they were offering was never even close to what the city needed to cover cash-flow issues and get things back on track, so we were in a perpetual fiscal crisis. Again, the message I think they were sending was that these guys cannot manage their own city, so we'll have to do it for them.

Now there were a lot of outstanding taxes owed to the city, but we didn't have the staff or resources to collect even a fraction of those taxes. And when we went to the state for help on that score, they said either forget those debts, those taxes, or find your own people to deal with them. So we never got that kind of support either.

On property taxes that we owed the state, our processes had been broken for a long time, and so those taxes were in such arrears that we were drowning in paperwork. Again we needed people to deal with that, and while help from the state eventually came, it took a very long, drawn-out time to arrive.

As for Dillon's duplicity, he would go to certain City Council members and union leaders and tell them he wanted to be their friend, saying that the state was going to come in with a bunch of money and help the city out of its mess. And he did the same thing with some of the faith-based people, certain prominent ministers, as well. And I began to realize that what he was doing was all part of a plan to keep us fighting with each other. He'd promise them help from the state for the city that was never going to happen, telling them something very different from what he was telling me about the money we could, or could not, expect. Once again, I'm sure the idea was, the more infighting he could promote in the city, the better chance the state would have to come in and take us over.

As we began to hear more about his dealings with these groups, it became clear that he was getting many of them to play his game. My response was that this was crazy; here was a once-great city now going under, and all these people were dealing in dishonest and destructive politics. It was often a what's-in-it-for-me kind of thing.

Maybe I should have spent more time trying to connect and work with City Council folks, but with Pugh having his own agenda and

Dillon playing his games, it probably would not have made much of a difference, because Dillon was such a crafty snake.

What was his motivation? Yes, to facilitate a state take-over of the city. But as both White and outsiders, he and Snyder had to be careful about the appearance of the state just coming in and asserting its power. So in effect, from their perspective, things had to get worse for the city in order for them to come in and make them better.

Was I surprised that there were people at the state level, on the City Council, and even a few in my own administration who were in effect working against me? Maybe I was naïve, but to begin with I hadn't foreseen that happening. In both sports and in business, my teams and I had worked together against very clearly defined opponents. But in politics, after a while I was no longer surprised, because as I looked around, I saw so many people pursuing their own personal agendas.

And before long, I had to deal with more internal hassles that threatened the smooth operation of our administration. One of them involved Kirk Lewis and the Detroit Public Schools. The DPS was still in deep trouble, but of course the schools were not the responsibility of the mayor's office. They were reeling, but as much as we were concerned about them, we had no input and my hands were full trying to run the city. There was no way in the world I could have given any of my time and resources to the public schools.

So early in 2011, when they were making a decision to bring in another emergency financial manager for DPS, I found out the state was ready to name Kirk Lewis. And that's when Kirk and I ran into a problem and a serious disagreement. Because I told him that I wasn't in favor of him leaving to take that post. I wasn't in favor of him doing it, didn't think he was the right person for it, and didn't want to lose his good work for the city. And when I came out publicly with that opinion, he made it clear that he really wanted that new position and so he left the administration. That divided us for a while, but he finally did not get that position with the schools, and after a time he came back into the fold.

And then in June 2011, I was informed that a lawsuit against me and my top communication person, Karen Dumas, was about to be filed by a disgruntled former governmental affairs aide, Rochelle Collins. The woman had spewed all kinds of wild and absurd allegations, from wrongful termination (she had been fired by Karen Dumas while on sick-leave three months earlier) to abuse and intimidation of Collins by Dumas; an affair between Dumas and me; bad blood between Dumas and my chief of staff, Shannon Holmes; and collusion between myself, Governor Snyder, and others to execute a plot that would dissolve the City Council and the School Board and make me a veritable despot in the City of Detroit.

All of this crazed and baseless nonsense was about to crash over us the next day, unless the city came up with $750,000 for Rochelle Collins and her husband to make the lawsuit go away. Needless to say, we were not about to cave into such ridiculous untruths, so Detroiters were treated to several days of silly dirt and scandal, until we finally had to put an end to this awful waste of time and energy with the resignations of both Karen Dumas and Shannon Holmes.

• • •

One of our toughest and most intractable problems involved the unions. When I came into office we had 56 union contracts, and we were constantly in a state of flux trying to negotiate with all of the different unions that represented city workers. Now I understood that they didn't want to give anything up. But I had to let them know that I simply could not afford to keep things as they were. I'd tell them, "I can't afford the contract that you've got, and you have to take a cut like the rest of us."

But the union leadership was difficult to deal with, not only because they had a job to do—which I certainly understood—but also since they did not truly believe the city was in such horrendous financial shape. I think in a lot of cases, Dillon and the state had been doing their double-dealing, telling them that the state was going to come in and be helpful. So it made the negotiations protracted and sometimes ugly.

Some of my toughest moments came when I'd go into certain communities where I knew that the people were desperate for help. I had no choice but to let them know that I couldn't do what they wanted, because I just didn't have the money. Most of the decisions I needed to make were financial, and again a lot of those community people were talking to their local minister and Dillon had been was feeding them his line about the money that was supposedly coming from the state.

Everybody knew the state, not the city, was where the money was. And so in order for us to come out of this dire situation, the state would have to play a significant role. And when you had the state saying we're going to do this, we're going to do that, then why believe the mayor. In many cases, whether they were union people, or community people, they tried to enhance their relationship with the state, hoping that they would benefit from that. But it never happened.

People in the neighborhoods were concerned that crime was still at a very high level. And our police department didn't even have the vehicles they needed to do their job well. The department needed everything from desks to computers, and we were so far behind the standards in other major cities, you could barely say we were operational.

Half the EMS vehicles didn't work, so we were taking parts from an older vehicle and trying to put them on a vehicle we could take on the road. That's when I went to the business community, and when they asked about my most pressing needs, I told them about the EMS mess. Leaders devoted to Detroit, like Roger Penske, Gene Miller from Comerica Bank, and Chris Ilitch quickly put a package together that got us 19 brand-new vehicles.

Of course, at that point a lot of employees had to get training with the new equipment, and the same thing happened with the fire department with all the new equipment they needed. And again the business community really came to the aid of the administration.

Now because I wasn't getting what I needed from the state, I was spending a lot more time with the Obama Administration. I went to Washington several times on money-seeking missions, and both HUD and the Department of Transportation were hugely supportive. I met personally with the president at least four or five times. We got along well, and I think he respected me because he knew I was doing something I didn't have to do but wanted to do because of how important it was. And of course we'd always spend a little time talking hoops.

It wasn't often I could go home at night and feel we had accomplished a lot, but we were making progress. The problem was we were trying to dig out of a hole that was so damn deep. Any wins or small victories were something I felt we should celebrate. So I continued to take staffers out to dinner practically every night. I wanted to let them know how much I cared about what they were doing. And even though they weren't getting much credit for it, they still needed to know how much I appreciated their efforts.

In terms of accomplishments over the first couple of years, I'd start with General Motors. When I came into office in '09, the corporation was contemplating moving its headquarters from the Renaissance Center in downtown Detroit out to their campus in suburban Warren. Rick Wagoner was the CEO, and from all my years as a supplier, we had a great relationship. I went to Rick and said, "Please rethink that move, because GM leaving Detroit is about the worst message we could send." Rick responded favorably, and GM made the decision to stay.

Then there was the Cobo Center. It was sapping us with $20 million in maintenance costs every year, and we were about to lose a major Detroit event, the North American International Auto Show, to Chicago. To compete with their McCormick Place and hold onto the auto show, we needed to make a huge investment to refurbish Cobo, and the city just couldn't do that on its own. That's when I said we've got to make it a regional facility. The suburbs and the whole metro region had a stake in the auto show and all the other big-time events held there, and I felt they needed to contribute to its renovation and maintenance.

So I went to each of county executives in the area—for Wayne, Oakland, and Macomb counties—and made the case for all of them to pitch in and help. Now given the animosity over the decades between the mostly White suburbs and mostly Black Detroit, this was hardly a sure thing. But I had developed good relationships with all of those execs, and they all seemed to want Detroit to succeed. I said it was time for all of us to come together, because Cobo was truly a regional facility. There were as many people coming down from their areas for the auto show, the boat show, and other events, as there were Detroiters.

There were many good things happening at Cobo, I said, but we in Detroit simply couldn't afford the costs any longer. And now we had to raise big bucks to rebuild and upgrade Cobo so the region wouldn't suffer a huge defeat with the loss of the international auto show.

Bottom line, we went out and raised over $300 million to improve the Center and keep the auto show for at least the next decade.

On housing, we were able to work with HUD to tear down the Brewster-Douglass Projects, a hellhole filled with incredible crime and squalor. So we were able to get HUD to give us the money to tear down those decrepit buildings and open up that area for all kinds of redevelopment. It didn't happen right away, but it's happening now, and it's due to what we were able to do with HUD in that once-forsaken neighborhood.

We were also able to get HUD to give us money so that we could tear down a lot of those vacant homes that were a blight on so many streets in our city. So we started that process, and we were tearing down 2,500 to 3,000 homes a year and cleaning up a lot of neighborhoods.

As I mentioned, we found ways to secure funding for Public Safety—police, fire, and EMS—but we also moved to find some money to keep from closing any more of our recreation centers. A lot of centers had been closed before I came into office, and I wanted to make sure we didn't close any more, because from personal experience I knew how important it was in a community for the kids and seniors to have a place to go. And so we were able to secure some funding to do that as well.

So how much appropriate credit did we get from doing these kinds of things? I don't think much at all at the time. But I think now, looking back, a lot more people are saying that most of the good things happening currently were started during our administration.

Through all of this I didn't have much of a personal life. My family and my longtime friends in town were very supportive, but I simply didn't have much time to spend with them. What I really missed were my grandkids, a girl and three boys. I just couldn't see and spend time with them as much as I had hoped to at this point in my life.

About two years into my term I finally moved into the Manoogian after it had been completely renovated with funds from DTE and a few local foundations. Yvette and I picked out new furniture we thought would be appropriate for a residence that was both the mayor's home and the people's home. We wanted to make sure that it was done with first-class taste, so that whoever came in after me would have a place to be proud of.

Yvette still visited during the week, and I'd come home to Franklin on the weekends. On Saturday I would still play tennis with our usual foursome, including Kirk Lewis, Lem Barney, and Beckham, and we'd watch some sports on TV. But then come Monday I'd be back at it in the mayor's office.

Shortly after I moved into the mansion, I started taking a salary. Besides the $3,500 a month I had been paying for the condo, I had also been forced to give up all my board seats—with Steelcase, Cardinal Health, and Lear. So I had been making between $150,000 and $200,000 a year just from those board fees. But I had to give it all up because it might pose a conflict of interest. And at the same time, I was paying for my living expenses and using my own credit card to take my execs and staffers out to dinner just about every evening.

So I was spending more than $200,000 beyond my income as mayor, and I finally decided I should start taking the salary that came with my job. Yes, I was living in the beautifully refurbished Manoogian right on the Detroit River, but I didn't really live there. I slept there. That's all I did. In my office by 7:00 in the morning, I very seldom got home before 10:00 or 11:00 o'clock at night. So I slept there and that was the extent of it. And I was never able to enjoy the place.

• • •

One of the first bills passed by the state legislature in 2011 and signed by Governor Snyder was a new law that allowed the governor to declare a city to be incapable of handling its own fiscal problems and to appoint an emergency manager to come in and take over with powers worthy of a czar, basically controlling all important decisions. Under a previous law, the governor already held that power over school districts in financial trouble. But now he could apply it to cities. And at that point, when that law passed, I had a good idea of what was going to happen to our city.

Nobody, starting with me but including the unions and the City Council and all kinds of community groups, wanted the City of Detroit to be run by an emergency manager, if only because of what we had seen when the state had appointed emergency managers to the Detroit Public Schools. It just didn't work. So to inflict that on the city made no sense to any of us.

But later in 2011, it became clear to me that this idea of a state takeover of our city was a real threat, when the governor asked me to go to Washington, D.C., to meet with a fellow named Kevyn Orr. Snyder said Orr was a very accomplished Black lawyer from one of the top firms in the country, and he wanted to see whether Orr and I could get along. If we could, Snyder was going to hire him to come in and help us out.

Orr had graduated from both the University of Michigan and the U. of M. Law School, so he knew something about the region and its issues. I found him to be an impressive guy, both very smart and easy to get along with, and there was no doubt that we could work together. Back in Detroit, I told Snyder I had no negatives to report about Orr and that we had gotten along well. The governor said, good, but then there was no more mention of hiring Orr, or his firm, to offer help in Detroit.

Still, in the back of my mind, I thought, "Yes, this is a first step in doing what the governor really wants, a state takeover of the city."

It was obvious to me at that point what was going to happen. And so I could fight it, but I always felt it was a fight I could never win. Another mission impossible.

14

THE TAKEOVER

MY MOST IMPORTANT SPEECH AS MAYOR came about two years into my term, in mid-November of 2011. More or less for the first time I really laid out what the city was facing. The reason for the speech was that, thanks mostly to Andy Dillon, and I'm sure with the Governor's backing, there were just so many different kinds of stories and opinions floating between the City Council, the unions, and Lansing concerning the true state of the city's finances and what might happen in the future. At that point, I had all the data I needed to provide a bleak but comprehensive picture. And so I called in my key people: Kirk Lewis (who was back with me after our little dustup over the possibility of his going to the DPS), Chris Brown, Bob Warfield, and Karla Henderson, who headed our planning group. And together we crafted the speech.

The venue we chose was not the City-County Building or a major auditorium downtown, but the Northwest Activities Center, smack in the middle of the city's troubled neighborhoods. Shortly after 6:00 PM. I walked onto the floor of the basketball court, a place so familiar to me from the rec centers of my childhood so many decades earlier. The speech took about a half-hour to deliver. Here is some of what I said:

"Simply put, our city is in financial crisis, and city government is broken. That's not new. That's not opinion. That is a fact. I promised when I ran for this office that I would tell you the truth, even when it wasn't pretty or popular. The reality we're facing is simple. If we continue down the same path, we will lose the ability to control our own destiny.

"For decades, the city refused to face its fiscal reality. We cannot continue to operate that way. Without change, the city could run out of cash by April with a potential cash shortfall of $45 million by the end of the fiscal year. City government has to work within a budget. And like you, we've tightened our belts, cut our spending, and tried to do more with less. We have eliminated approximately 2,000 positions since I entered office, but with the bills continuing to pile up and core services suffering, it is clear that we have to do more.

"Residents are frustrated, and I understand why. I ride around our city and talk to people every day. I receive your letters, your calls, and your emails. You want a safe city. You want officers on the street, fire and EMS services that have the resources to respond quickly when you call during an emergency. You expect the city's streetlights to be on and keep you safe from criminals. You need a bus system you can rely on to get to work, to school, and to the doctor on time.

"Those are all reasonable expectations for city government, and they are expectations that haven't been met for far too long. I refuse to do what's been done in the past. I refuse to sugarcoat the situation or [kick] the can down the road, expecting someone else to solve our problems. I stand before you tonight to outline what we're going to address and ask your support in this effort.

"Let me make one thing perfectly clear. I don't want an emergency manager making decisions for my city. I am your mayor, and I want to continue to lead the city back. I am going to tell you what we are doing to get the buses up and running. I am going to tell you what we're doing to turn the lights on and

keep our city safe. And I'm going to ask for your help to push for the reforms, tough choices, and structural changes we need to control our own destiny.

"We have less revenue coming in and service demands higher than ever, we have to shift our fiscal priorities and fundamentally restructure how city government operates. Public safety is the most important service we provide. I will not allow police and fire to be gutted. I will not allow criminals free reign over our city. We need every officer we have out on the street fighting crime. I will not eliminate hundreds of our firefighting force. We depend on them to protect us and save lives every day."

Those last few lines got to the core of our dilemma. If cuts went too deep and imperiled areas like Public Safety, what remained of our middle class would soon leave the city, and then there would be no coming back for Detroit. So while calls for shared sacrifice helped set the tone of the speech, I also promised to deliver essential city services, advocated a new approach that would privatize certain things like mass transit, and insisted the unions do their part with across-the-board cuts of 10 percent.

Certainly, it was not a speech laden with applause lines, and in fact its 30 minutes drew no applause at all. The message was just too stark and serious for that, but my key staffers who had helped put it together were pleased with its delivery. The business community was also happy with the speech, pleased that we were able to put the facts out there and let people know the dire situation the city in fact confronted. And the day after the speech, I underscored that message by announcing the layoffs of 1,000 city employees.

But in the papers in the days after the speech there was a drumbeat of negative opinion, the gist of which was that we were late in giving Detroiters this info and that we should have been tougher in responding to the crisis. But most of those critics had little idea of the efforts of Dillon, the unions, the City Council and the ministers to spread misinformation and false hope in order to undermine what we were trying to do. "It didn't go far enough," said the Council's Gary Brown, "He says he's determined to make the drastic cuts, then he goes out and makes a speech that's only done to placate an audience." Not surprisingly, I got only sharp criticism from the unions, who argued that the cuts should come from elsewhere, from supervisors, for example. The Teamster president said, "The mayor paints us like we're no-good people. But he has layers and layers of supervisors."

And from Governor Snyder came a written statement that more or less gave his game away: "I want to avoid an emergency manager [for Detroit]. Based on the mayor's remarks and the severity of the situation he described, we anticipate he will be submitting a request for a preliminary financial review in the near future."

I held my peace for a while, but on the day before Thanksgiving, which by the way was an unpaid furlough day for all municipal employees, I let my feelings hang out a bit. At a press conference, I told reporters:

"I've always been a team player, and I've always been accessible. I think I've always been professional and I've always been a gentleman. I have not attacked anybody. All that bullshit's off the table for me right now. It's time to go to war. Council has done a lot of talking about their plan, but nobody has seen their plan."

And then I went after my two favorite Council members, Gary Brown and Charles Pugh: "You've got two leaders who do nothing but run to the press and, anything we want to do, always seem to be in opposition." And about Brown I added, "You got one guy who's getting three damn paychecks from the city. From a character standpoint, if I were in that position, there's no way that I would take three checks from the City of Detroit with the financial problems we're having."

My little outburst apparently had some effect. Because early in December in a press briefing in my office with everybody involved in our budget talks, including Council members and the unions, there was a helpful new tone. We titled the briefing: "Detroit created this mess. Detroit will solve it." And the union folks, led by United Auto Workers (UAW) president Bob King, delivered a potent message to everyone in the room, especially the Council members: Either we stand together or separately we'll get picked apart.

It was a theme that bode well for the new year. And many of us would vow to lead a charge against that newly expanded emergency-manager law that Rick Snyder was surely banking on. But in the months ahead there would be more than a little contention between all the parties assembled in my office, and I would suddenly face not one, but two life-threatening illnesses that I never saw coming.

I had always been healthy. I had the two serious eye injuries, but, while potentially disastrous, they hadn't been life threatening. Number one, I was blessed with good genes from my parents, and then, over the years, I had taken good care of myself. I was never a smoker nor an excessive drinker, didn't do drugs, ate well, and got my rest. Basically, I understood what I had to do to take care of my body, and part of that was seeing my doctor on a regular basis and having the appropriate tests.

In January of 2012, I was due for a colonoscopy, so I set it up on my schedule. Like most of us in our sixties, I had been through this minor ordeal before and thought little about it. Afterward, I was told by the doctor who did the procedure that everything looked good. He'd see me again in 10 years, he said.

So far the New Year was looking good, with a major win in our often difficult and frustrating negotiations with the city's unions. Our newly revised labor agreements generally featured the 10 percent cuts in both salary and benefits that I had been asking for and showed that the UAW and others, who had promised cooperation back in December, had meant what they said. They clearly saw that they could get a better deal now from me than would be available with an emergency manager ruling Detroit, or under the Consent Agreement that Governor Snyder had begun pushing.

The Consent Agreement posited a Financial Advisory Board made up of nine members chosen by the governor, the state treasurer, myself, and the city council, but weighted in favor of the State. That Board would have complete power to control all city budgets and to develop a comprehensive plan to move the city out of fiscal insolvency. To me it was clear that the choices made by this body would be completely unrealistic and impossible to carry out. But I also knew where the power resided in this deal, so it would be pointless to fight Dillon and Snyder on it.

Finally, on March 12, the governor officially circulated a proposal for the Consent Agreement and told us, in effect, here you go, debate and discuss the particulars all you want, but come up with something you can all live with by April 5, 2012, or I'll be forced to name an emergency manager for the city of Detroit.

Reactions were varied. Some saw this as the city's financial salvation, others thought it was just another way for the State to grab control. City Council members (who knew they would lose basically

continued to get from the state in
een for more than a decade, much
so I wondered more than ever how
an emergency manager.
f because he wanted to look like he
nt a real shot. Maybe he continued
ld look like for mostly White state
Black city of Detroit. Or maybe he
ing sentiment against the emergen-
before in 2011.
roved to be very unpopular. It was
s in the city but by many across the
aign to repeal it had placed a refer-
in November of 2012. And once the
the people didn't want that law and
short-lived.
verified and unchallenged financial
announced the appointment of his
Detroit's finances. And the following
he Republican-dominated state legis-
y-manager law. Unlike the previous
t the city, to pay the EM's hefty salary
r the public to get rid of the law. At
iting was on the wall, but I was not
quietly.
vould prove to be my final State of
ve the governor as much as possible
e many Detroiters, I too am a fighter.

all of their power under the Agreement) said the only way they'd support it was if the State showered millions on Detroit. Good luck with that, I thought. All of Dillon's dishonest promises were about to be exposed. As for my own opinion, knowing what Snyder really wanted, I simply saw it as a sham.

And a pain in the gut. No, I mean that literally. Over the past two months I'd been feeling some occasional discomfort in my gut, which I thought might be caused by all this Consent Agreement nonsense. But a couple of weeks later, on a day I was scheduled for an afternoon flight to D.C. to give a speech at my old high school, Spingarn, I got up in the morning with a nasty upset stomach. So I took some Maalox.

When that didn't help, and the pain had become acute, I called security, and they took me to Henry Ford Hospital. At first, the docs thought it was colitis, an inflammation and swelling of the intestine. But after they did an MRI and found a perforation of the large intestine, they said, "You can't leave. You're not going to D.C. You're not going anywhere, and we'll operate in the morning."

So when they cut me open the next day, they found two places that were a problem. They took out six inches off my upper intestine and four inches off my lower. And when I came to, they told me it looked like it was a problem from that colonoscopy back in January, perforations that had festered and inflamed. They said, "If you were not in such a good, healthy condition, you were going to die." The head of the hospital's surgery department told reporters: "I expect a faster than normal recovery due to Mayor Bing's spectacular physical health."

Of course, like everybody else, I had signed an agreement before the colonoscopy, absolving the doctor who performed it of any responsibility. And so there was nothing that I could do other than spend the next nine days in the hospital and, hopefully, begin to heal.

Following the City Charter's directive, I named my chief of staff, Kirk Lewis, as Deputy or Acting Mayor, and during those nine days in the hospital I lost 22 pounds. I went in at 192 and came out a week and a half later at 170. It was just rest and recuperation in the hospital. They wouldn't let me try to get any work done.

On April 2, I went home to the Manoogian with instructions to recuperate there for the next three weeks. In the meantime, Kirk Lewis had been conducting heavy-duty discussions with the city council over the Consent Agreement. And finally, the night before Snyder's deadline, he called to tell me that the Council had voted 5-4 to go with the C.A.

In the weeks and months ahead, I knew we'd be trying to do the impossible—implement an agreement I considered mostly smoke and mirrors. There was just no way we could cut the city government budget of over a billion dollars by as much as the state-controlled C.A. Board would require, no way we could cut our expenses that much. So, while it might delay the inevitable, I had no real faith in this process.

At the Mansion, Yvette and my daughters were coming every day in shifts, taking good care of me, and that went on for several more days. But one of things the doctors at Henry Ford had required of me was that I test my breathing and lung power. Every day I had to blow into this apparatus they had sent me home with to make sure I was breathing well. I'd blow into it and see if I could get this little ball to

couldn't live with. But what we
revenue sharing was, as it had b
too little and much too late. And
long it would be before we'd see

Maybe Snyder was holding o
was giving the Consent Agreeme
to be worried about what it wou
officials to take over the mostly
was concerned about the gather
cy-manager law, passed the year

Once in place, that law had
opposed, not only by most of u
state as well. An effective camp
endum on the state-wide ballot
vote was in, it turned out that
tossed it out. But our relief was

In December, despite all the
info we had provided, Snyder
own team of experts to examine
month, on January 24, 2013, th
lature passed a new emergenc
version, it required the state, no
and also made it impossible fo
that point we all knew the wr
about to roll over and go away

On February 13, in what
the City address, I tried to gi
to think about, declaring, "Lik

We can't and won't give up on our city." I pointed out: "Despite the nay-sayers' predictions, there have not been any payless paydays. No emergency manager to date. And no declaration of bankruptcy for the City of Detroit."

I praised and thanked many business and community leaders but pointedly, not Snyder. I underscored the significant decrease in state revenue sharing over the past decade and said, "Last year, we received $93 million less than in 2009, when I took office." And then I added: "It is clear that if Detroit had received its agreed-upon share of revenues from the state, our financial picture would not be as grim today."

I explained how effective we had been in "working to eliminate blight, neighborhood by neighborhood, street by street." I touted how the city had outsourced three existing departments, saving millions of dollars and gaining substantial efficiencies. But I refused to sugarcoat serious problems. With homicides at a 20-year high, I spotlighted major issues in policing the city. At the same time violence had increased, the city's police force had shrunk, with officers on street patrol back in 2000 numbering 3,000, versus only 2,000 today. I said it was imperative that we do a major restructuring of the police department to increase officers on patrols and in investigations.

Finally, on the upside, economic development was a good-news story in the city. Dan Gilbert, the owner of Quicken Loans and the Cleveland Cavaliers, had started on a skyscraper buying spree and now owned 15 downtown buildings; Chrysler's $198 million investment in its Mack Avenue Engine Plant had created hundreds of new jobs; and the Red Wings were talking about a $650 million sports and entertainment complex downtown.

None of this would matter to Snyder, of course, since I was sure he had already made up his mind about what Detroit really needed. So I was not surprised on March 1 when I received a call from state treasurer Andy Dillon, who was pleased to inform me that the governor had finally decided that we should move on from the Consent Agreement to rule by an emergency manager. And who would this person be? Who would assume essentially dictatorial powers over the fate of our city and its citizens? Again, I was not surprised it was the man I had met in D.C. over a year ago, Kevyn Orr.

How did I feel about having most of my power usurped? Well, I had carefully considered my position, and I was not leaving over this. I felt I still had a role to play. Yes, I respected Orr, but more importantly, I was certain that he was going to get the kind of help and financial support from the state that I had never received, and that would definitely benefit the city of Detroit.

And so I wasn't ready to throw up my hands and say, "I quit. You got it all now. You are the guy in charge." I had always been a team player, and now I was pretty sure that Orr and I could work together. When he arrived in town, and we had our first conversation about it, he said, "I still want and need you to do the things, day to day, that you do."

In fact, Kevyn and I had a lot of respect for each other as professionals. I knew his reputation as a bankruptcy lawyer was sterling, and a few years earlier he had won kudos for the way he had taken Chrysler through the process. He seemed to admire my athletic and business backgrounds, and he knew that I had been thrown into an impossible situation as the mayor of a bankrupt city. So we both said we were not crossing swords over this. We needed to figure out how to work together to help Detroit, and we were determined to do that.

Kevyn moved into a condo at the Book Cadillac Hotel where he'd be living for the next 18 months. On the weekends he would fly back to D.C. to spend time with his wife and two young children. On Monday, March 19, his first official day on the job, I found him in his office, next to mine in the City-County Building, when I arrived at 7:00 AM. Later that morning when we met with the press, he said he was extending a "sincere olive branch" to me and other city leaders. Pledging to check with us on plans to improve services and establish fiscal discipline, he said, "We're going to work together as best we can to do what we can for the city."

At the same time, Orr said he alone would be responsible for decisions on how to deal with our serious cash shortfall and our billions in long-term liabilities, like health care and benefits. He said, "The statute spells out some pretty clear powers," and noted that as the state's E.M., he held the authority to sell city assets, renegotiate labor contracts, and ultimately recommend a bankruptcy filing.

Generally, I felt he made a good first impression and came across as fair-minded and well-intentioned. No doubt he had a lot of very tough decisions ahead, just as I had confronted during my first three years. But when Kevyn came in, all of a sudden the state made significant money available for him to do certain things that had never been possible for us. He was immediately able to go out and hire a lot of high-priced experts and experienced firms to help get things done.

His job was to be an effective financial manager, to find the resources to deal effectively on things like debt restructuring, debt negotiating, and the whole health care and benefits package. And while he spent his time on those areas, he said he wanted me to stay in place and run city government, meaning that all the city's departments would still be overseen by me and my administration. And that would give him the time to do his thing.

So with the E.M. in place, I personally would no longer have to face those terrible financial decisions that were going to impact people so negatively, but I felt no real sense of relief, because the city was still facing crises day in and day out, and I still had to find ways to resolve them. I still had to try to run the city's government with a limited staff and a serious lack of funding. I could never take my eye off the ball. And even though Kevyn Orr was now in the office next door, my life didn't really change, other than the fact that I had to cede authority to him on anything related to the budget.

At the same time, I could still go to my other public and private sources for help, financial and otherwise. For example, shortly after Orr got started, I was able to bolster our troubled police department by forming a new task force with the United States attorney, the FBI, and others to pursue the city's most violent criminals. And then I announced that several of the city's major businesses, including all of the Big Three automakers, had agreed to donate $8 million to lease 100 new police cruisers.

In terms of public transportation, we had been able to produce cost savings by consolidating from four bus terminals down to three, and with help from the Obama folks we put several new buses into service. As for Parks and Recreation, I had never been able to give the department the funding it needed, so I had gone to my friends at the Lear Corporation and secured $5 million for upgrades at two different rec centers.

But that was all before Orr came in, and at that point it became much harder to come up with those kinds of contributions, because I think a lot of the foundations and major corporations didn't want to get on the wrong side of the governor.

In May, I announced my decision not to run again, and through the remainder of my last year I found absolutely no reason to change my mind. I knew what was coming, meaning Orr would be taking the city through bankruptcy, and I was likely to have even less power. There was speculation for a while that I was looking to run for another office, even published reports that I was considering a campaign for Wayne County Executive or running for Congress.

Did I think seriously about running for anything else? No, I'd had more than my share of politics.

My relationship with Orr continued to go well, but occasionally there was a disconnect. Our disagreements were usually about how things should be done in a particular city department and how its money should be spent. It quickly became clear that he needed to have the final say on such things. I'm sure some of that came from his talking with Snyder and with outside consultants who really didn't know Detroit. They were mostly hired guns, so they had a steep learning curve about things you had to live with for a while to comprehend. At best they were getting only a surface understanding of what was really happening in Detroit. But Orr had all that new State money, $300 or $400 million, to spend on outside consultants, and that's where he'd turn for the advice he wanted.

So even when there was federal money involved, like HUD funds for the demolition program to reduce blight in the neighborhoods, we had disagreements. I couldn't handle that the way I thought best, with a very focused approach to how we used that money. I didn't want a scattershot approach, hitting areas all over the city. That didn't make sense to me. I wanted it to be much more focused and concentrated on neighborhoods where there were still a lot of people residing, so we could make some real and lasting progress. But politically, Orr, with input from those consulting firms he had hired, wanted the scattered approach, so it would look like we were having a broad and widespread impact. And though I disagreed, we ended up doing it his way, because ultimately the power was in his pocket.

Now the public lighting on our streets was one of the big issues within city government because it impacted safety in the city. We only had 30 or 40 percent of the neighborhoods with lights working. And we couldn't afford to go out and borrow money for the lighting department because it was defunct. It was broke. So we had to pass state legislation to develop a Public Lighting Authority that was independent of city government. And then we were able to go out and borrow money for new lighting, to start getting the lights back on in the city.

But once again, I wanted to focus on more heavily populated neighborhoods, areas where we knew the need was the greatest, but Orr wanted the scattered approach across the city. That way, he thought, you could make people in certain neighborhoods believe that good things were about to happen when in fact they weren't. And once again his authority carried the day and just kept growing.

Now there were also times, when I noted how much money the state was pouring into Orr's efforts, that I felt strongly about providing more dollars to areas of special need. Like the recreation department, for example. We were being forced to talk about closing certain parks and recreation centers, and I said that was something I surely did not want to do. But he said, no, there was no money for that, and he backed me off. I knew his answer probably had something to do with the fact that he was negotiating a lot of different contracts. So this was something deeply important to me, but nonetheless beyond my control.

I was very strong on regional transportation because our own system was in awful shape, and there were regional bus lines that weren't being utilized appropriately. For example, wherever there were concentrations of people with kids going to school, I wanted to make sure that the transportation investment went into those areas. For me it was very important to help get those kids back and forth to school. But once again Orr pushed back on that. It wasn't a high priority for him.

On all these matters and issues it was almost always just Orr and myself meeting together in an office. He would meet with his people, and I would meet with mine, and then the two of us would come together and talk, with the result generally a foregone conclusion. As for the City Council members, their role and their power had been so diminished by the E.M.'s appointment, they couldn't do much of anything on their own. They were basically pushed to the side, and when they tried to deal with Orr, they were less effective than I was. They had no leverage at all.

• • •

On July 18, 2013, Kevyn Orr employed his authority as emergency manager and took the city of Detroit into Chapter 9 bankruptcy. It was the largest municipal bankruptcy filing in U.S. history, with its debt estimated at $18–$20 billion. No other such filing had come close.

Many thought it was the city's death knell. Others thought it might be Detroit's way out of deep trouble. As I had from the beginning, I knew it was inevitable, and however difficult and painful it was going to be, it was time to get it underway.

Of course, Orr would be doing all the heavy lifting. Certainly he faced enormous challenges, negotiating with creditors and making deep cuts in health care benefits and the pension fund. But what he had going for him (that I never had) was major support from Lansing. With it, he was able to get enough funding to hire a team of top professionals to come in and work with him. Clearly with Orr on the job, the state was totally committed to helping the city. The last thing Snyder wanted was for the bankruptcy filing to go badly, because that would have been a direct reflection on his decision to impose an E.M. on the city.

But some of the issues Orr was facing seemed insurmountable. A group of angry creditors were insisting the city pay them by selling off the extremely valuable collection of masterpieces held by the Detroit Institute of Arts. From a cultural standpoint, the D.I.A. was looked upon as the biggest asset we had, an institution of unique cultural and historical value. And it was something that the business community and the foundations wanted to save at all costs. So Orr and others put together a high-powered coalition that in effect bought the art and put it in a trust for the D.I.A., with the resulting $816 million being used to solve the terrible problem of having to take pension benefits away from retired city employees, in some cases reaching back more than two decades.

As we headed for the end of 2013 and the close of my time in office, Orr still had a long way to go. But I thought what he had already accomplished was pretty remarkable. I also appreciated how he handled the city's residents and employees. He could have come in with a cold-blooded focus on the bottom line. Instead I think he showed genuine concern for the people of Detroit, and that really impressed me.

· · ·

With my announcement that I would not seek a second term, a field of 15 candidates quickly assembled. The one that I, and seemingly most Detroiters, favored was Benny Napoleon, the former police chief for several years under Mayors Archer and Kilpatrick. I knew Benny well. We were friends, and since he was the obvious frontrunner, I met with him on more than one occasion to share the data and information I had accumulated in the mayor's office.

Now there had been a lot of talk that Mike Duggan wanted to run. I had also known Mike for quite a while. I knew him when he was the Wayne County Prosecutor, knew him when he headed up the Detroit Medical Center, and we had run across each other at a lot of different affairs in the city. He had a reputation as a take-charge kind of guy, and I respected him as a politician. But there was a lot of pushback in the community against Duggan for a couple of reasons. Number one, he was White. And number two, he did not live in the city.

For decades he had lived in suburban Livonia, but like me, he had established a residence in the city and had been spending a lot of time on a listening tour of Detroit. And then, ironically, for a guy who was a lawyer and advised by top political talent, Mike Duggan filed a week too soon for the mayor's race and was ruled off the primary ballot.

So it was over for him, right? No, Duggan presented himself as a write-in candidate, and unbelievably, he won the primary with 52 percent of the vote. Benny came in second, so the two of them would face off in the November election.

Duggan never called me, but if he had, I would have given him the same info I'd given Benny. Nonetheless, he knew Kevyn Orr, had gone to law school with him at Michigan, and may well have gotten all he needed on the true state of the city from Orr. In any case, I was surprised when he got 55 percent of the vote in November and was elected Detroit's first White mayor in 50 years.

Soon after the election, I called Duggan and we met. I wanted to make sure that we afforded him all the information and support we could muster. We had a number of meetings with him and his people and offered as much help and insight as possible into what was happening in the city. There was no comparison between that and what we got from Cockrel and his people when I first took the office. Back then I had come in basically empty handed.

I knew Duggan was a strong personality, so it would be tough on him to be the mayor but have the emergency manager as the guy in charge. I told him I'd had a positive relationship with Orr. I didn't like the arrangement, but it was something you just had to deal with. He would have to go through nine months of that just as I had. But Duggan never asked much about my experience with Orr. Of course, Mike is a guy who's very sure of himself, a guy who figures he's got the answers. So I don't think he would have been very receptive to any advice.

Frankly, during that transition period of a month or so, I was glad it was coming to an end for me. A lot of the leadership in the business community and with the foundations let me know they appreciated what I had done. They said it was a thankless job that I had handled with honesty and professionalism.

And until the very end I refused to stop working. I still thought I had to communicate with my staff people, who knew that a lot of their jobs were probably going to end with a new administration coming in. I felt I should really stay close to those people to let them know that they couldn't just stop working. Don't leave early, I told them. We've still got responsibilities here.

From my own vantage point, as the end approached, there was a sense of relief more than anything. I knew I had done my best to work well with Kevyn Orr, and the emergency manager's work, I thought, was moving in the right direction.

My feelings when I walked out of that office on the very last day? Our team and I had given everything we could to help our city.

15

ONE-ON-ONE

ONE DAY DURING MY LAST WEEKS IN OFFICE, a reporter asked me about my future plans. With a chuckle I told him, "First, I'm going to do something that I've never done before in my life. I'm going to take about three to four weeks off in the month of January." But once we got to those first few weeks in 2014, I learned pretty quickly that one of the things I'm really not good at is sitting around and doing nothing.

Naturally, I did spend some time looking back and thinking about my four-and-a-half years as mayor, detailing especially what I would personally consider to be wins and accomplishments. I started with this: When I came into office, Detroit was widely viewed as America's ultimate urban disaster, a deeply troubled place, broken and debt-ridden, riddled with graft and incompetence with a former mayor so corrupt that he had been sentenced to decades in prison for fleecing the city. Given all that, I thought any fair-minded person would agree that my administration had brought integrity, honesty and openness back to Detroit.

In this bankrupt city, we had set out to find ways to substantially improve areas such as public safety, mass transit, public lighting, neighborhood blight, and recreation, and we had managed some real improvements in all of those.

A $60-million, state-of-the-art Public Safety Headquarters had been opened on our watch, consolidating police, fire, Homeland Security, EMS, and IT operations. And along with all the new vehicles and equipment I've already mentioned, we added 100 officers on street patrol or in investigations and opened 14 police mini-stations. The police department had been under two federal consent decrees governing the behavior of its officers, and its compliance rate was 29 percent when I first took office. By the time I left, we had reached 92 percent.

We had changed minds at General Motors about leaving the city and fostered enough goodwill in the formerly hostile suburbs to secure their investment of more than $300 million in the Cobo Center and help us save the auto show for Detroit. We instituted policies and approaches that spurred lots of small businesses and pop-ups to open and convinced Goldman Sachs to invest in the city and help spark more economic growth.

Was all that enough for beleaguered Detroiters? Of course not. Was there more we could, and perhaps, should have accomplished? Yes, but was it a start worth every bit of the time and effort given by our dedicated staffers and city workers. I truly think so, and increasingly over the next couple of years, I would note the opinions of observers and commentators on some of the surprisingly positive things that would be happening in Detroit. In 2014, just a year after I had stepped down, a *New York Times* best-selling author would write that Detroit was "poised to be the greatest turnaround story in American history."

•   •   •

After he took office, I called Mike Duggan, and we had lunch together. I was curious to see how he was doing. But it was clear to me that the main thing he was waiting for was Orr's departure so he could finally take over. In those months after the first of the year, I followed what was happening with considerable interest. But I didn't play Monday-morning quarterback by getting in touch with those leaders I knew who were still part of city government. I didn't want to compromise anybody by calling them to say: "Why did you do this? What's the direction you're going in?" So I never played that game.

Whatever Duggan thought, I remained impressed by the emergency manager's operation. Orr and I continued to talk, and I appreciated the way he kept me in the loop and how he handled our relationship. I admired how Orr and his people dealt with some of the most difficult issues, with the huge amounts of money the city owed to major companies and concerns. He often struck surprising deals with them, but frankly I don't think he worried all that much about the plight of some of those creditors. In many cases his feeling seemed to be that they had taken advantage of the city's dire straits and its desperate need for money. They had to know those loans were high risk and probably not going to be paid back. Or if they were, then at some kind of a discount down the road. And in the meantime, they were making a lot off the insurance.

In some cases, Orr did a kind of horse-trading, making outside-the-box agreements that turned two of the most embittered creditors into investors in the city's future by ceding them major assets, such as potentially lucrative riverfront properties, on condition that they be re-developed in a timely fashion.

Ultimately, nine months later, when the bankruptcy judge accepted the city's plan, Orr had managed to cut $7 billion out of that huge $18 billion debt. It was, I thought, an extraordinary accomplishment on Orr's part. He and his team had been worth every one of those $300 million the state had contributed to their remarkable effort.

•   •   •

So what was next for me? Actually, during my last month or so in office, I had begun to formulate a plan that would keep me busy full-time for the foreseeable future. I started with the fortunate fact that I was again in good health, so I could give this next chapter in my life all the time, energy, and effort it might need.

Next I thought about the past four-and-a-half years and how I had so often traversed the city, going to every corner to better understand how people were living and the kinds of problems they were facing. And among the most prevalent issues I found were the challenges that kids confronted in our school system, African American boys in particular. In so many instances, they were not being given the kind of solid support in their lives that I had enjoyed in mine. And one of the things that stood out the most was the preponderance of single-family homes led by women. To me it seemed obvious that many of these boys, as they verged on their teens, already had little chance to succeed.

Dad wasn't there, and they had a deep need for solid and successful Black men in their lives. The school system offered little interaction with Black men, because these days most of the teachers and administrators were women. Yes, most of them were doing a wonderful job, but the way I saw it, they simply could not take the place of a man in a boy's life.

I was aware of all the sad stats about young men of color filling up the penal system. I had seen how the breakdown of families often made it more difficult for women trying to raise their boys alone. Crime was permeating our city, and it was clear that lots of young Black boys heading into manhood felt that they had few or no good options. And I soon found myself thinking that this was a situation that I wanted to do something about.

Mentoring, of course, had been an important part of my life for a long time, starting with Big Brothers Big Sisters when I first joined the Pistons, and over the years I had often connected with boys and young men. Some, like Benny White and Kirk Lewis, had ended up working with me in my business and political careers. And others, like Derrick Coleman and Jalen Rose, had gone on to sports stardom themselves. While still others had simply built good, solid lives for themselves and their families. The question I was considering now was how I could establish an organization that would formally bring together successful Black men with African American boys in need. That would certainly be a natural extension of what I had been doing most of my adult life.

My first move was to talk to Bob Warfield to gauge his interest. We'd always had a good working relationship, I admired his communication skills, and when he said, "Hell, yes, I'm interested," I knew I had the right guy to help me think through the process of setting up this project. Neither of us had a job, so we could devote most our time to putting a plan together. But in order for this thing to really succeed, we knew we needed to go out and talk to many of the people already working in this field. We wanted to gather as much data as possible, so we could devise an operation that would be as effective as possible.

To begin with, the only office we had was my car. We said we had a mobile office. So we traveled around, visiting as many of these organizations as we could, collecting information, getting lots of feedback, and then writing everything up. Online, we read about regional and national organizations and learned as much as we could about how they operated. But most of the time we'd go out and meet with people locally and maybe take them to lunch. And afterward we'd challenge each other. "What were your thoughts?" "What did you get out of that meeting?" "Here are my thoughts." And then we'd get it all down on paper.

And that's what we did for three or four months. One of our most important tasks was to formulate a mission statement that really captured what we wanted to do and why. In doing our research, there were things we learned from folks at certain organizations that we wanted to use and some that we didn't. Sometimes with an outfit like Big Brothers Big Sisters, for example, we knew we didn't want to follow a certain path and so needed to forge our own way.

Also, with certain groups we decided they employed a lot of lip service. We thought many of them were top-heavy, meaning that not enough of their money was going to support their programs. With some, 60 to 70 percent of their funding was being spent on overhead, so only 25 to 30 percent of what they raised was going into programs that actually impacted kids. Obviously, some people were making a lot of money on these programs. But that would not be our approach. I was not doing this to make money.

And then there were people who liked to talk about how many kids they were mentoring. But we quickly understood that their figures were not real or true. I knew for certain that talking personally to a kid a few times a year was not mentoring. Neither was sitting him in a lecture or a presentation. Yes, there were many charities and foundations concerned with youth issues, but some of the outfits we were talking to seemed to be in business mostly because there were so many available dollars. And my question was, were they really having an impact? I wondered if anyone had ever challenged them and asked, "Okay, so are you really mentoring all these kids you say you are? What's the impact? What's the outcome?"

So we knew what we didn't want to do, but there were good, helpful ideas out there as well. To us, the most important lesson was to not play the numbers game, because we felt the key was one-on-one mentoring. If we truly wanted to have an impact on a boy, it had to be through his relationship with a man in his life. That was how we were really going to make a difference.

And, of course, this idea was consistently reinforced by the experiences I'd had throughout my life. I knew one-on-one worked because I had those four little brothers and several other relationships with boys and young men over the past 30 or 40 years, and they were all very rewarding and successful.

But, as we continued to hear from many people, the biggest problem we would have in focusing exclusively on the African American community was that there never seemed to be enough Black males who were stepping up to give of their time and of themselves. We weren't sure if that was because they were never asked, or if they just didn't think it was all that important, or that they were so consumed by their own lives. But we were about to find out.

As for funding, fortunately through my years in business I knew a lot of the CEOs, and during my time as mayor, I had gotten to know all of the top foundation people. With those relationships, I knew all their doors would be open to me. I would be able to show them our plan, and hopefully get their solid support.

So with the financial help of many area foundations, groups, and individuals, the Bing Youth Foundation came to life and quickly began to flourish. The mentoring component, called BINGO (for Boys Inspired through Nurturing, Growth and Opportunities) pulled together schools and several different organizations, such as the Fellowship of Christian Athletes, the National Basketball Retired Players Association, and the NFL Alumni Association, all cooperating to put one Black man with one Black boy to build a solid and lasting relationship.

I knew that our foundation's approach was not the only model. But I was sure it was one that would work, because it had been designed from the ground up to have an impact on individual lives. It did not involve just writing a check or touching someone in a superficial way, with a quick handshake or an autograph. It was forging an emotional connection that can actually change lives.

Now there were some people advising me to go out and put together as much money as possible, but that was not how I wanted to go. I only wanted to raise enough money to cover my budget for our first year. So that way, after I had collected as much data as possible on how we were doing, I could go back the following year and demonstrate that we hadn't wasted their money. I could actually show them the results of their investment.

And so already in my third year—because our first two were so successful—some of our funding sources were saying, "Okay, instead of you coming back every year, we are willing to cover two years." That was the kind of trust we had already built.

Our first-year's budget was in the $300,000 range. I didn't take a paycheck then, and I still don't. We had a slim staff, starting with Bob, but also employing a small number of retirees, including people I knew from the mayor's office, who were already on Social Security and so had a pension. So my overhead costs were very low. And then I heard from two women from another mentoring organization who were unhappy with how it operated. And so they both came on board with us, wanting to have an impact and make a difference.

As for Yvette and my daughters, they knew, of course, that I was never going to be the kind of guy to stay home and do nothing. They all knew how often over the years I'd been involved with helping boys and young men. My new plans were not a big surprise.

Maybe you're wondering why we focused just on boys and not kids in general. But in my view, when you bring boys and girls together in a program for teenagers, there is so much they're going through, so many additional issues to deal with, that it's difficult at best. Besides, we saw that boys of color were dealing with so many vital, make-or-break issues—with going to school, graduating, and staying out of jail—that all the statistics were terrible, not just in Detroit, but across all of urban America.

Those sad stats say if you look at boys in the ninth grade, not more than half will graduate from high school. And now you've got youngsters with no education, no degree, and not ready for the job market. So what will they do? Most likely they'll end up involved with what they see around them. Maybe it's robbing people, selling drugs, or something else that's neither healthy nor productive. And we wanted to try to break that cycle.

Our central insight was that if we created the right kind of environment for boys and young men, widened their horizons, and gave them access in their lives to solid Black men who could serve as good role models, we could actually change kids.

We focused on three things that we felt could really have an impact. Yes, one-on-one mentoring was by far the most important. But we also found early on that a lot of our kids knew nothing more about the world around them than what they saw in their school and their neighborhood. Even in a major city like Detroit they had never been exposed to the many activities and experiences that were available beyond their own few square blocks. So we decided to expose them to a lot of different things that were available in the city and its surrounding area.

Also, while there weren't a lot of gang problems in Detroit, it was more of a neighborhood or school clique-versus-clique situation that was likely to cause conflict. These boys rarely if ever had a chance to get to know somebody from outside their own narrow slice of life. And from that came a lot the city's mindless youth violence. So our answer was to bring these kids together from different schools and different parts of the city and allow them to see how many problems and issues they all shared: a tough environment, a single-parent home, a school system that wasn't working for them, and all this pressure from people telling them everyday not to hope or dream because there was so much they could not do.

Our answer was also to show them that there were many Black males in our city who were successful in many different walks of life. It was not necessary to be a professional athlete, a rapper or an entertainer to have a good life. What was wrong with being a doctor or a lawyer or the owner of a business? So many of the boys we were looking at did not consider those things as genuine options for themselves, probably because nobody had ever encouraged them to think that way.

But what would happen if we put them together with motivated Black men who were professionally employed and had all their adult responsibilities well in hand? Many of them had come from the same environment these kids were trying to navigate. And our bet was that once the boys and their mentors started spending time together and having all these one-on-one conversations, the minds of these kids would begin to open. We felt there was a good chance that they would start thinking in new ways: "Hey, there is somebody who really cares about me," and "I'm a person who can bring value to what I do." Yes, all of those little things that most of us simply take for granted.

So where did we find the boys for our new program? I went to Jack Martin, who was my CFO with the city and was now the emergency manager for the Detroit Public Schools. I told him I thought I understood some of the problems in the schools, and I wanted to help. I explained my ideas and approach and asked if he would help us find the right kids for our program. Specifically, what I needed from Jack was for him to identify two middle schools and two high schools whose principals would work with us to find the kind of kids we were looking for.

I would meet with the principals, outline our program, and ask them to pick the kids. But I would explain that I did not want any A or B students. My thought was that they would probably be okay without our help. But those kids from homes without a father or a positive male presence, who were C or D students, who were on the cusp of dropping out and not giving a damn, who felt perhaps that nobody loved or respected them—those were the kids I wanted, because those were the ones I thought we could save.

And so they gave us entry to four schools, and we were able to select 10 kids from each. So now we had our first 40 boys from a single-parent home, struggling in school, having motivation and other kinds of problems, not bad kids really, but ones who clearly needed help. Where did those criteria come from? In part from all the data that we had been out there collecting in those first few months, but also from a gut feeling on my part that these were the kinds of kids who would benefit most from what we were offering. So that was our focus, and now all of a sudden we had 40 boys in need without any mentors.

So where did I find the Black male mentors I needed? In the beginning, I approached certain people I knew and let them know what I was going to do and that I needed them to be a mentor. Would they be interested in that? Several people said, "Yes, I think you're doing something important."

But I needed a lot more men, so I started going to the business community: Blue Cross Blue Shield, the UAW, the Black McDonald's owners, and many others. I approached those folks and described our program. I told them that I not only needed some funding but also wanted to get in front of their Black men and challenge them to join us in this all-important work.

I spoke to all these groups, and it was time consuming but necessary. Starting from scratch, there was no other way. A lot of these business people knew of me but didn't know me. So they needed to see me up close and decide for themselves if I really, deeply, cared about this. I had to let them know what was really in my heart, because I was asking them to make an emotional investment and a serious commitment of time and dedication.

For my presentation, I'd usually remind myself of the reason that I started this initiative in the first place. And that is, that the plight of young men of color has reached a crisis level. Our young Black men are at a significantly higher risk for negative educational and health outcomes. Violence, obesity, disconnectedness, poor school attendance, and high dropout rates often lead to unimaginable conditions and disrepair for Black youth in our city. Compounding these day-to-day struggles is the challenge of combating negative perceptions of young men of color in America. Much needs to be done immediately to change this trajectory and perception. To not do so is to rob the city and its citizens of the untapped potential of thousands of young men.

The Bing Youth Institute (BYI), through its mentoring initiative BINGO (Boys Inspired through Nurturing, Growth & Opportunities), seeks to reverse these trends by connecting young men of color with impassioned, relatable, professional, and successful Black males. Through the creation of deep, meaningful mentoring relationships, BINGO prepares our young men to become viable and productive citizens, challenging the negative images associated with men of color. Our program transforms the minds of young men and enables them to see that they are capable of greater achievements.

In short, the mission of BINGO is to create a meaningful mentoring experience that will help to unleash the unlimited potential of urban young men.

I had to work hard and fast for a couple of months to secure those 40 mentors for our 40 mentees and put us in a position to launch. Generally, I found the men I was trying to recruit very receptive. Many of them clearly understood the need from their own lives. In a lot of cases, they had come up in the same kind of environment. And here they were successful male adults, and nobody had been asking them to get involved.

I underscored my conviction that becoming engaged with our program and being a part of our success would be a genuinely rewarding experience, not just for the boys who would be their mentees, but for themselves as well. When our mentors joined us, they signed up to be with a boy for a minimum of one year, because a big negative in our boys' lives was the constant turnover. A guy might promise, "I'm going to be with you," and then he'd disappear. So we asked for a minimum of one year. Fortunately, once we were under way and that connection was made, our mentors soon felt just how important it was to both of them.

One day each week, mentor and mentee met for an hour at the boy's school. Why the school? Because that was the one place we knew for sure that the kid was supposed to be. So we would call the school from our office that morning to make sure that the boy was there. If the mentor arrived and found no mentee, that would be a big waste of time and a turnoff. So we set up a lot of the communication and coordination between our office and the coordinator at school.

And when school was out for the summer, the boy and his mentor would continue getting together. Usually by then their relationship had become pretty stable, and in a lot of cases, the mentor would introduce the boy to the mentor's family, and maybe take the boy and his own kids on some kind of outing, to dinner or a movie or a picnic.

So how did that first year go with those first 40 boys? We monitored everything very closely and set up methods of getting detailed feedback from both mentees and mentors. What was working and what was not? How could we improve certain outcomes or do something more effectively? Any time we needed to tweak a program, we did it with constant input from both the mentors and the mentees. In many cases, the principals or the school coordinators would give us their views on how the boys were doing.

And then we began to see our boys starting to think in more positive ways about themselves and their lives, and their academics started to improve. So all of those positive things that we had thought were going to happen were happening now. And it was deeply gratifying to say the least.

With the meetings at school an imperative, many of our mentors needed to take time off from work. So we had gone to their CEOs and presidents and asked if those mentors could have that time off, and the answer was yes, and it won't negatively impact their careers. So that was a very important commitment the corporations were making as well.

We are currently in our sixth year, and frankly, I think we've made a tremendous difference in the lives of both the boys and the men they've connected with. We had 18 young men in our first graduating class, our senior class. As I've noted, Detroit's normal high school graduation rate is no more than 50 percent. And in our senior class, 18 graduated out of 18, and 14 of those are now in college. For the other four we have found good jobs.

In 2018, we asked the respected firm of Formative Evaluation Research Associates (FERA) to undertake a detailed study of our program. And after a lot of focus groups, surveys, and analysis, they reported results that made us proud of our work so far and enthusiastic about our future. In broad strokes here were their findings:

> "Mentees have grown and changed through the BINGO program in the following ways:
>   "Increased exposure to new experiences and places
>   "Improved self-awareness and responsibility
>   "Increased ability to trust and communicate
>   "Developed new networks and relationships
>   "Made improvements related to school
>   "Improved outlook on their future"

And about the mentor experience, FERA offered some surprising findings. Often the mentor was getting as much out of his involvement as was his mentee. As a part of a valued community program, the mentor felt he had become a better employee and was more admired by the folks in his workplace. He often said he had also become a better father and a better husband. And so the rewards were substantial indeed.

• • •

I know that by putting each of 150 boys in Detroit together with a solid mentor we are making a real difference in their lives. But because the need is so great, I'm often asked how we can reach more kids. That's a question I spend much of my time these days thinking about and exploring with others. To me, the key to having a real impact is our one-on-one approach, mentor and mentee. So, I remind myself not to get caught up in a numbers game, because if we're not smart about our approach, we could grow ourselves out of control and into failure.

The challenge is to foster growth that brings not only more youngsters but more mentors as well. Obviously, one good way to do that is to use our very successful program as a model, to replicate its foundation and vital elements with a wider scope. To that end, we have been involved in numerous meetings and conversations with organizations, foundations, and well-placed individuals to extend our program.

In the process, we have found strong interest in communities throughout the state of Michigan with substantial populations of young African American boys, including cities like Saginaw, Flint, Pontiac, and Benton Harbor.

And thinking more broadly, we have been in discussions with NBA officials, including commissioner Adam Silver, about finding ways to develop a version of our program in each of the 30 NBA cities. The response from the League office has been encouraging, with the possibility of both financial and marketing support. One promising approach would be to involve the NBA team in each city, as well as its retired players chapter, with a current or retired player serving as the face of the program and a key fundraiser.

Additionally, friends of mine, often with illustrious histories in other professional sports, have encouraged me to approach the National Football League and Major League Baseball with the idea of getting them involved as well. Our initial efforts in those directions have been promising indeed.

In short, many people in a position to help, both individuals and groups, clearly see the need and are impressed with our approach to meeting it. The future of our mentoring program is very bright. As always, we are attacking the rim and moving forward with optimism and hope.

ACKNOWLEDGMENTS

I AM GRATEFUL TO MY WIFE AND LIFE PARTNER, YVETTE, who has stood by my side through it all.

A special thank you to Robert Warfield, my friend and chief operating officer of Bing Youth Institute, and book writer Tom LoCicero for their encouragement and valuable contributions to making this book a reality. And to all those who have poured their hearts, energy, wisdom, time, and knowledge into my life.